THE JOY OF RELI

All religions describe spiritual experience as pleasant and the goal of the religious pursuit as profoundly joyful. But many religions also condemn sensory pleasures and the desire for objects of pleasure. In this book, Ariel Glucklich resolves this apparent contradiction by showing how religious practices that instill self-control and discipline transform one type of pleasure into the pleasures of mastery and play. Using historical data and psychological analysis, he details how the rituals, mystical practices, moral teachings, and sacred texts of the world's religions act as psychological instruments that induce well-being. Glucklich also shows that in promoting joy and pleasure, religion also strengthens social bonds and enhances an individual's pursuit of meaning.

ARIEL GLUCKLICH is Professor of Theology and Religious Studies at Georgetown University. A scholar of Hinduism, he has also published in the field of religious psychology. His book *Sacred Pain* won the American Academy of Religion Award for Excellence in 2002.

THE JOY OF RELIGION

Exploring the Nature of Pleasure in Spiritual Life

ARIEL GLUCKLICH

Georgetown University

CAMBRIDGE
UNIVERSITY PRESS

CAMBRIDGE
UNIVERSITY PRESS

University Printing House, Cambridge CB2 8BS, United Kingdom

One Liberty Plaza, 20th Floor, New York, NY 10006, USA

477 Williamstown Road, Port Melbourne, VIC 3207, Australia

314–321, 3rd Floor, Plot 3, Splendor Forum, Jasola District Centre,
New Delhi – 110025, India

79 Anson Road, #06–04/06, Singapore 079906

Cambridge University Press is part of the University of Cambridge.

It furthers the University's mission by disseminating knowledge in the pursuit of
education, learning, and research at the highest international levels of excellence.

www.cambridge.org
Information on this title: http://www.cambridge.org/9781108486422
DOI: 10.1017/9781108674256

© Cambridge University Press 2020

First published 2020

Printed in the United Kingdom by TJ International Ltd. Padstow Cornwall

A catalogue record for this publication is available from the British Library.

Library of Congress Cataloging-in-Publication Data
NAMES: Glucklich, Ariel, author.
TITLE: The joy of religion : exploring the nature of pleasure in spiritual life / Ariel Glucklich,
Georgetown University, Washington DC.
DESCRIPTION: New York, New York : Cambridge University Press, 2020. |
Includes bibliographical references and index.
IDENTIFIERS: LCCN 2019037007 (print) | LCCN 2019037008 (ebook) |
ISBN 9781108486422 (hardback) | ISBN 9781108460163 (paperback) |
ISBN 9781108674256 (epub)
SUBJECTS: LCSH: Pleasure–Religious aspects. | Spiritual life–Christianity. | Experience (Religion)
CLASSIFICATION: LCC BL65.H36 G58 2020 (print) | LCC BL65.H36 (ebook) |
DDC 204/.2–dc23
LC record available at https://lccn.loc.gov/2019037007
LC ebook record available at https://lccn.loc.gov/2019037008

ISBN 978-1-108-48642-2 Hardback
ISBN 978-1-108-46016-3 Paperback

Contents

Acknowledgments

I wish to acknowledge the help and encouragement I have received from Mark McWilliams, Alex Sens, Robert C. Fuller, Paul Heck, and participants in the workshop he organized in 2018 titled "Sensation and Devotion: The Study of Affect(ion) and Emotion in Religious Experience," Wayne Proudfoot, Dan Alexander, Scott Powers, Adam Cohen, Yulia Chentsova Dutton, Eric Brandt, and Jennifer Hansen Glucklich. I am grateful to Georgetown University for the material support during the leave to finish this project and to Beatrice Rehl and the editorial staff at Cambridge University Press.

Introduction
Religion, Pleasure, and Evolution

Pleasure is a pervasive and familiar feeling we all know. It can be a response to good food, seeing a loved one, accomplishing a difficult task, or receiving praise. Informally, pleasure is often distinguished from positive emotions such as love and joy, although such feelings are often pleasurable. Negative emotions like anger or hatred can also cause pleasure, as we all know – especially the righteous anger we feel toward those who wronged us. Hence, we commonly think that emotions and pleasure are distinct phenomena. Psychologists who work in the fields of emotion and affect reject this commonsensical view. Some experts prefer the language of "affective process" or "psychological construction," in which emotion is one element in a framework that includes what we call pleasure or positive affect.[1]

While the subject of emotion and religion has received significant attention by scholars, the affective-hedonic dimension of the religious life has been relatively neglected.[2] This is surprising considering the astounding wealth of attention lavished on the subject of pleasure within religious documents and performances around the world and throughout history.

In many cases, pleasure has been regarded as an obstacle to the spiritual life. Early Buddhist texts such as the *Majjhima Nikaya* were committed to controlling pleasure in its variety of forms. For example, the teachings of Buddha on the First Jhana (meditative state) are severe: "Udayin, the

---

[1] G. L. Close and A. Ortony, "Appraisal Theories: How Cognition Shapes Affect into Emotion," in eds., Michael Lewis, Jeannette M. Haviland-Jones, and Lisa F. Barrett, *Handbook of Emotion*, 3rd edn. (New York: Guilford Press, 2008), 628–642; James A. Russell, Emotion, Core Affect and Psychological Construction," *Cognition and Emotion* 23, no. 7 (2009): 1259–1283.
[2] As this manuscript is finalized, a new book has just come out: Frans Jespers, Karin van Nieuwkerk, and Paul van der Velde, eds., *Enjoying Religion: Pleasure and Fun in Established and New Religious Movements* (Lanham, MD: Lexington Books, 2018). However, this remains a rare title indeed.

pleasure and joy that arises dependent on these five cords of sensual pleasure are called, sensual pleasure – a filthy pleasure, a coarse pleasure, an ignoble pleasure. I say of this kind of pleasure that it should not be pursued."[3] Meanwhile, at the other end of the ancient world, at about the same time, the book of Ecclesiastes advised something else: "Enjoy life with your wife, whom you love, all the days of this meaningless life that God has given you under the sun." (9:9) Proverbs 5:19 was even more detailed about that (young) wife: "May her breasts satisfy you always, may you ever be intoxicated with her love." Of course, the Hebrew Bible praised much more than marital sex. Second Samuel, Chapter 6, described David bringing the Ark of the Covenant to Jerusalem with ecstatic dance, shouting, and trumpets blaring in what was clearly a pleasurable celebration.

Sometimes, pleasure is used in a negative and positive manner in the very same source. For example, Martin Luther declared the following concerning the hypocrisy of some Christians: "But the holy cross which Christ lays upon all his followers and which cannot be reconciled with sensual pleasure they have perverted in a masterly manner; they have encased it in silver." But earlier in that text, Luther also wrote: "Behold, such a heart delights in God's law and keeps it with pleasure. Such people love God and righteousness, they hate and fear naught but unrighteousness."[4] In both cases, pleasure is a response to some objective fact – sensory stimulation in one case and the law in the other. It's the objective fact, not the subjective affect, that is either condemned or praised. One sees the same pattern in other religious figures. For example, St. Francis of Assisi proclaimed: "Blessed is that religious who feels no pleasure or joy save in most holy conversation and the works of the Lord, and who by these means leads men to the love of God in joy and gladness. And woe to that religious who takes delight in idle and vain words and by this means provokes men to laughter."[5]

Religious documents and secondary descriptions by anthropologists and other observers record religious rituals that promote pleasures in a variety of ways. There are weddings, feasts and carnivals, inaugurations and coronations, annual celebrations such as New Year, agricultural and

[3] Keren Arbel, *Early Buddhist Meditation: The Four Jhanas as the Actualization of Insight* (Oxon: Routledge, 2016), 55.
[4] Martin Luther, *The Complete Sermons of Martin Luther, Volume 1* (DelmarvaPublications.com, 2014), 400, 93.
[5] St. Francis of Assisi, *The Writings of St. Francis of Assisi* (New York: Magisterium Press, 2015), 18.

fertility celebrations, and many others. McKim Marriott famously
described the Hindu spring festival of Holi in a remote village, in the late
1950s, as a wild bacchanalian affair. And even today, in urban centers, the
colorful and riotous Holi sends people into wild displays of pleasure.[6]
However, the object of such celebrations is never pleasure itself: it can be
Krishna, agricultural fertility, beginnings of Lent, escape from evildoers, as
in the Jewish festivals of Purim or Passover, and many others. But
pleasures – in song, dance, food and drink, sensuality, family gatherings –
are essential for the fulfilling and meaningful celebration of the religious
occasion.

This material resolves itself into a few models based on the nature of
pleasure discourse or description. At the most "shallow" level – that is,
subject to the informants' conscious awareness – the pleasures divide
according to their observed causes: sex, food, family, reading scripture,
story telling, travel, and many others. This is a folk-theoretical level of
classification, which is far too specific, and a more abstract one must be
recruited in order to deepen the analysis. The many folk-theoretical
pleasures usually take shape with the help of theological, cosmological,
mythical, moral, or other types of discourse. Hence, one can divide the
pleasures into those of the body or the mind, those of the natural world,
those of God, a holy event, and so forth. This method of categorization is a
significant reduction compared to the first and takes us to more theoretical
domains within the conscious awareness of religious actors. However,
further classifications of pleasure move into realms that often transcend
the level of religious awareness: socially integrative pleasures, socially
disruptive pleasures, motivational pleasures, pleasures that contribute to
the achievement of valued goals, those that prevent such achievements,
and so forth. On an even deeper level of analysis, the pleasures can be
divided according to biopsychological criteria – that is, according to
the neurochemicals involved, the neurophysiology of pleasure, and the
evolutionary and adaptive factors. Religious actors are not conscious of
these "deepest" dimensions of their pleasure experiences and values – but
this book argues that there must be a link between all the levels.

To give an example of how such a linkage may work: at the evolutionary
level, pleasure can be divided according to its behavioral-adaptive function
into novelty, mastery, and play. Novelty usually manifests in those models
that religious actors call sensual (related to food or sex), and mastery can

[6] On Holi, see Chapter 8.

manifest in those models that religious actors praise as virtuous, such as enjoying a difficult pilgrimage or memorizing scripture. This link can then be elaborated according to whether it is excoriated as socially disruptive or praised as socially integrative, and a pattern emerges in which some types of religious groups, such as sects and monasteries, promote austere but satisfying mastery – for example, long vigils – while other broad denominational groups celebrate novelty – a hearty family meal – and downplay the rigors of extreme self-control. One could then pursue a theory in which the positive motivation of mastery pleasure demonstrates the way that self-control, indeed moral virtue, links distinct types of social organization with complex evolutionary factors such as enforcing codes of conduct. This is a rough example, naturally, and will be worked out in detail within this book.

In other words, in order to explain the way that religious actors attribute their affect to some valued or condemned fact in the world, or transcendent reality, we must establish a connection between their conscious awareness and language and deeper psychological factors. This is a complicated task due to the sharp division in religious scholarship between cultural constructions and scientific explanation. For example, do distinct religious cultures understand pleasure itself, or positive affect, in their own unique ways, or is there a universal way of talking about pleasure? And, assuming that pleasure is a universal psychological and even biological phenomenon shared with many species of animals, how has it emerged as such an important factor in the diverse religious cultures of humans everywhere? Can the religious modes of articulating pleasure – assuming we accept the patterns outlined earlier – be linked to the fact that pleasure is a biological and psychological fact?

Pleasure, Biology, and Religion

The pervasiveness of pleasure in religious literature and in religious practice raises a far more general question than the ones of I have touched upon up to now. This book's working theoretical assumption is that pleasure, understood from a functional point of view, is the product of behavioral adaptation. The feeling of pleasure we experience is the result of ancient evolutionary adaptations that have led to survival, reproduction, and prosperity. And the pervasiveness of pleasure discourse in the religious life indicates that there must be some connection between our embodied nature and the social and cultural role of religion in human history. This fact makes it necessary to situate the project of this book in the wider context of discussions on the evolutionary function of religion in human culture, as well as the influence of biological psychology on religion and religious scholarship. The present work does not offer a new theory of religious evolution but pursues a specific cultural and psychological analysis of the views that currently guide scholarship on this subject. The questions for consideration are the following: What does the prevalence of pleasure in religious discourse and performance tell us about the interface between biological, psychological, and cultural factors in the history of religion? And how do we explain the sharp divide between excoriated and celebrated pleasures associated with religion?

The theories that currently dominate the subject often trace back to a dilemma or conflict that Darwin had already observed, which was connected with the evolutionary interest of groups versus that of the individual within the group. On the level of groups, evolutionary selection benefited those groups that had advantages over other groups with which they conflicted or competed: those groups with the highest level of internal cooperation and with large numbers of "courageous, sympathetic and faithful members" enjoyed a great advantage over the others.[7] However, within the group itself, there is no reason to think that altruistic individuals would have a significant advantage over selfish ones and would reproduce more successfully. This is the problem of multi-level selection: the genes for altruism and self-sacrifice would be favored at the group level but not so at the individual level where genes for selfishness are more beneficial. The question then is as follows: How would success at the level of the group be achieved – how would a sufficient number of altruistic individuals be obtained to promote the success of the group? According to Darwin, there were a number of likely factors: "social instincts" – that is, a need for social affiliation, reciprocity among individuals who know one another and finally, the desire for praise, and the avoidance of blame. In other words, the reputation one acquires within the group as a cooperator was critical to one's success in reproducing.[8] As a result of competitive pressures at the group level, certain moral sentiments would evolve such that honor, loyalty, generosity, and cooperation would emerge as highly prized values, and those who possessed them, or demonstrated them, would make for an attractive mate.

---

[7] *The Descent of Man*, Chapter 5, quoted in Jonathan Haidt, *The Righteous Mind: Why Good People Are Divided by Politics and Religion* (New York: Vintage, 2012), 225.

[8] Martin A. Nowak, *Super-Cooperators: Evolution, Altruism and Human Behavior, or Why We Need Each Other to Succeed* (New York: Free Press, 2011), 55. According to Nowak, a positive reputation is associated with the same reward circuitry in the brain as money – it is highly gratifying.

However, with praise–blame and the display of generosity as a factor that mediates the group and the individual fitness, the problem of cheating or free riding remains. The emergence of religion can provide one solution to this problem. According to theorists such as Pascal Boyer and Scott Atran, religion – specifically, the identification of some supernatural agency – emerged as a by-product of the evolving human brain's capacity to anticipate and react to unseen causes and intentions in the world around us.[9] In a way, gods are the extensions of minds, and the ability to read minds – and share "intentions" in Jonathan Haidt's term – is a key to regulating social behavior. The Darwinian dilemma is further indirectly explored by Ara Norenzayan and colleagues, and a resolution in connection with the function of religion is offered based on four theoretical approaches: development of cognitive mechanisms, evolved social instincts, cultural learning mechanisms, and intergroup competition.[10] Under the heading of cultural learning of a religious nature, which enhances prosocial behavior, are content- and context-based mechanisms along with credibility-enhancing ones. What may be missing, and the contribution that the present book is making, are motivational mechanisms or, more specifically, patterns of hedonic training.

In the domain of motivation, the cognitive-evolutionary approaches have generated two ways of thinking about the relationship between religion and prosocial behavior in human evolution: surveillance policing on the one hand and nurturing-motivational on the other. For example, Will Gervais has summarized research that shows empirically that people react in a similar manner to "both reminders of gods and cues of social surveillance."[11] And both of these lead to increased prosocial behavior – that is, avoiding cheating. Such notions of the divine as law enforcer are associated with both a sort of invasive reading of internal motivation and the punishment of selfishness.[12] But there is

[9] Pascal Boyer, *Religion Explained: The Evolutionary Origins of Religious Though* (New York: Basic Books, 2007); Scott Atran. *In God We Trust: The Evolutionary Landscape of Religion* (New York: Oxford University Press, 2004); Todd Tremlin, *Minds and Gods: The Cognitive Foundations of Religion* (New York: Oxford University Press), 2006.

[10] Ara Notenzayan, Azim F. Shariff, Will M. Gervais et al., "The Cultural Evolution of Prosocial Religions," *Behavioral and Brain Sciences* 39, no. 1 (2016): 1–65. These researchers are exploring a related question: the rise of prosocial religions – not precisely the conflict between individual and group fitness.

[11] Will M. Gervais, "Perceiving Minds and Gods: How Mind Perception Enables, Constrains, and Is Triggered by Belief in Gods," *Perspectives on Psychological Science* 8, no. 4 (2013): 380–394.

[12] Ara Norenzayan, *Big Gods: How Religion Transformed Cooperation and Conflict* (Princeton, NJ: Princeton University Press, 2013), 6.

another side to the human–divine interaction within evolutionary theorizing. For example, Lee Kirkpatrick offers a highly organized attachment theory of religious psychology within the broader evolutionary framework. His theory situates human religiosity within the concern for comfort and protection rather than observation and punishment – and the theory does so without the Freudian infantilizing of attachment theory.[13] Robert C. Fuller takes this idea further in *The Body of Faith*. Quoting William James, he writes: "We reconstitute the world in ways that are likely to satisfy what James called 'the social affections, all the various forms of play, the thrilling intimations of art, the delights of philosophic contemplation, the rest of religious emotion, the joy of moral self-approbation, [and] the charm of fancy and wit.'"[14]

Broadly speaking, this second approach is highly motivational and shows the evolving human brain not only as a tool of practical utility but far beyond: the source of meaning and complicated satisfactions.[15] Indeed, Nicolas Baumard and Pascal Boyer have argued that there are limits to the surveillance theory and that the emergence of the so-called moral religions was related to economic conditions that enhanced human pursuit for meaning, well-being, aesthetics, and similar higher forms of enjoyments.[16] This is the framework in which I choose to study the role that pleasure plays in religious history and experience when religion is conceived as a product of organic and cultural evolution. I will argue that religion functions as a way of reducing selfishness when it monitors and censures certain kinds of pleasure. But religion also enhances social existence when it celebrates other kinds of pleasure – indeed, making those pleasures possible in the most effective manner. For instance, when James writes about "delights of philosophic contemplation," he is referring to a pleasure that is entirely distinct from the enjoyment of chocolate, and such a pleasure needs to be cultivated – it is already a product of

[13] Lee A. Kirkpatrick, *Attachment, Evolution, and the Psychology of Religion* (New York: Guilford Press, 2005), 19.
[14] Robert C. Fuller, *The Body of Faith: A Biological History of Religion in America* (Chicago: University of Chicago Press, 2013), 9.
[15] In the Norenzayan et al. discussion – citing Baumard – worldly pleasures are said to be denied on behalf of "spiritual goals." The present argument is that such pleasures are regulated and transformed into mastery and play pleasures. "The Cultural Evolution," 20.
[16] Nicolas Baumard and Pascal Boyer, "Explaining Moral Religions," *Trends in Cognitive Science* 17, no. 6 (2013): 272–280.

social existence. And religion makes such a pleasure possible in a variety of ways, as we shall see.[17]

What this book seeks to achieve in examining the religious uses of pleasure is the joining of a close cultural study of religious phenomena such as values, doctrines, experiences, and actions, with psychological-evolutionary theories in a manner that is non-reductive. Pleasure is an ideal area of examination because, like pain, it is both an explicit topic of religious discourse – a complicated cultural product – and an empirical fact of human and animal psychology.[18] For example, rituals are probably historically related to ancient games, and games – structured forms of play – are both culturally and biologically connected with less structured play behavior. A fundamental feature of play (and games) is fun – or the distinct pleasures of bodily manipulations, pretend, mastery of rules, and so forth. These facts are universal features of known cultures throughout history and, as archeological evidence shows, prehistory. The pleasure of games and rituals, thus, are key to understanding the function of religion in the evolution of culture, including cognitive, emotional, and social dimensions.[19]

Two goals are thus accomplished here: Evolutionary theory – grossly simplified, to be sure – is recruited to explain an apparent paradox in religious attitude toward pleasure, both celebratory and excoriating. At the same time, this book does not reduce specific religious phenomena, such as the pleasurable celebration of a New Year ritual, to biology or evolutionary psychology. The religious experience of any given individual, as we shall see in Chapter 8, is far too subtle and complex. It is only the pleasure dimension of religious experience, including thought and action, that allows me to explore the link between the scientific theory and religion.

However, as we have already noted, pleasure is not an easy phenomenon to understand and can be a source of serious methodological errors, especially with regard to religion and religious experience. That is, while it is easy to discuss pleasurable displays and pleasure discourse, the heart of pleasure remains ineffable. Psychologists call this "hedonic tone" or "hedonic gloss" – the very goodness of the feeling: Is this the same feeling

[17] Yosef Garfinkel, "Dancing with Masks in the Proto-Historic Near East" in *Ritual, Play and Belief, in Evolutionary and Early Human Societies*, eds., Colin Renfrew, Iain Morley, and Michael Boyd (Cambridge, UK: Cambridge University Press, 2018), 143–169.
[18] Paul Bloom, *How Pleasure Works: The New Science of Why We Like What We Like* (New York: W.W. Norton & Company, 2010), 5.
[19] Colin Renfrew, "Introduction: Play as the Precursor of Ritual in Early Human Societies," in *Ritual, Play*, eds., C. Renfrew et al., 9–22.

exactly when we eat ice cream and solve a word puzzle? Does the external "cause" of the pleasure change the nature of the hedonic tone, or is the gloss the same even when we are aware of distinct causes such as ice cream and achievement? This is a critical question because we see pleasure both celebrated and excoriated in religious texts, and it is important to decide whether the pleasure feel itself is condemned or only its perceived causes. I believe that in order to properly understand the way that evolutionary motivational psychology functions in religious thought and practice this question must be addressed. I will therefore discuss the ineffability of hedonic tone in some detail in the next chapter. However, it is essential to begin by explaining in a bit more detail what I mean by the three behavioral-adaptive types of pleasure.

Behavioral-Adaptive Classification

If one accepts the cognitive implications of evolutionary theory as situating pleasure in a prosocial motivational context, it is necessary to introduce a classification of pleasure that is also located in evolutionary theory. In this case, the relevant subfield is behavioral adaptation – that is, approach–avoid behavior that leads to beneficial adaptive consequences.[20]

Novelty-replenishment pleasures are those derived from responding to novel situations such as stressors and returning to some sort of homeostasis. They are relatively simple biological – neurologically hardwired – pleasures and roughly correspond with the affects that religious ethical systems tend to curtail – that is, enjoyments that individuals find irresistible, including sex, food, gambling, or watching violent sports. Augustine, perhaps most famously, described these as highly addictive and, in another age and location, even the Dalai Lama considered them as obstacles to happiness.[21] Such pleasures tend to be thrilling, sometimes surprising, peaky or quick to fade, and followed by a desire for a new stimulation. They represent the hedonic treadmill, a term used today to describe addiction to novelty pleasure worn down by habituation.

Mastery pleasure, in contrast – which is longer lasting, controlled, and accompanied by a feeling of empowerment – is the satisfaction one gets from mastering the organism's response to the first set of pleasures; these are highly social and prized in religious ethics. Examples include learning

---

[20] See Chapter 2.
[21] Saint Augustine, *Confessions*, 10.31.43–44. Dalai Lama and Howard C. Cutler, *The Art of Happiness: A Handbook for Living* (New York: Riverhead, 1998), 13.

to control emotions and desires; mastering the body in ritual or meditation; acquiring difficult skills like learning a difficult language, memorizing
scripture, and liturgy; becoming altruistic; controlling dietary and sleep
habits; and so forth.[22] Children who grow up to become well-adjusted
adults will have learned self-control, emotional regulation, and other forms
of hedonic training as keys to their future well-being. Mastery pleasure is
not just accomplishing these socially oriented tasks but learning to obtain
satisfaction from the achievement.

Finally, play pleasures are untethered to immediate need but also free
from the constraints of the cultural agendas that underlie mastery pleasure.
According to Jaak Panksepp and his colleagues, play corresponds to the
arousal of the SEEKING system that marshals energy toward approach
behavior, but in the absence of any object.[23] Play is an immense subject in
the fields of religious studies. Robert Bellah discusses play in detail in his
thesis on the role of religion in human evolution: "Play is not universal; it
is especially well developed among mammals and birds . . . Play is largely,
but not exclusively, an activity of the young. It is commonest in species
that continue child care for a long time so that the young of the species are
not directly involved in the quest for survival: they are fed and protected
and have the energy for just having a good time." Finally, play includes
"sheer joy" that is seldom seen in other things.[24] K. R. Jamison describes
play in terms of "a feeling of free or unimpeded movements; activities
involving fun or amusement and characterized by a swift, exuberant,
irregular or capricious motions . . . or darting to and fro, a joyous gamboling and frolicking about."[25] Although play is a biological fact, for many
species, it extends to culture; that is, cultures create contexts in which play
is utilized for a variety of possible purposes. According to Huizinga, "In
play there is 'at play' which transcends the immediate needs of life and

[22] Psychologists today have studied the effect of what they call religious self-regulation on the
promotion wellbeing. See, for example, Michael E. McCullough and Brian L. B. Willoughby,
"Religion, Self-Control, and Self-Regulation: Associations, Explanations, and Implications,"
Psychological Bulletin 135, no. 1 (2009): 69–93.

[23] Antonio Alcaro and Jaak Panksepp, "The SEEKING Mind: Primal Neuro-Affective Substrates for
Appetitive Incentive States and Their Pathological Dynamics in Addiction and Depression,"
Neuroscience and Behavioral Reviews 35, no. 9 (2011): 1805–1820.
    Panksepp and Moskal, "Dopamine," 68.

[24] Robert N. Bellah, *Religion in Human Evolution: From the Paleolithic to the Axial Age* (Cambridge,
MA: Harvard University Press, 2011), xxi–xxii.

[25] Kay Redfield Jamison, *Exuberance: The Passion for Life* (New York: Vintage Books, 2005), 42. We
shall see later that the picture is more complicated – the chess player does not exhibit much of what
this passage describes.

imparts meaning to action."[26] Contemporary cultural studies of play and games are not as clear-cut as Huizinga would have it, as we shall see in later chapters. Moreover, play pleasure is not simply the pleasure one derives from play or from games. From the perspective of just pleasure, play mediates between episodic and dispositional pleasure and from the perspective of adaptation play mediates between novelty and mastery and generates a high level of arousal. While there may be a biological function for such a pleasure, it is not related to the response to either some immediate environmental stressor or to some extrinsic social demand or agenda. In fact, the joy comes from more than the activity itself – it is the pleasure of the seeking system running itself, like the warming of a car engine in the morning, before being put into gear.

In the religious life, these are often associated with mystical states of consciousness and, more commonly, with certain aspects of rituals such as games, dances, or songs.[27] This type of pleasure, as opposed to the behavior, has not been studied as extensively as the other two, though Mihaly Csikszentmihalyi's *Flow* spends a considerable amount of time on it as a sort of process in which intrinsic interest diminishes the distance between an active agent and an objective world.[28] The concept of flow in this sense resembles the Zen monk in Eugen Herrigel's *Zen in the Art of Archery* who explains to the author how to release the bowstring, like "snow sliding off the leaf of a bamboo as it bends down."[29] It is spontaneous, unwilled by the archer, a perfect flow. In its purest form, play pleasure is joyful, and it can come in many areas of life ranging from art, sports, and even science, as Richard Feynman shows in *The Pleasure of Finding Things Out*. All of these require mastery but move beyond it, beyond the need for a goal or a method, for overcoming novelty-replenishment pleasure.

[26] Johan Huizinga, *Homo Ludens: The Play-Element in Culture* (Boston: Beacon Press, 1971), 1. Colin Renfrew, "Introduction: Play as the Precursor of Ritual in Early Human Societies," in *Ritual, Play*, eds., Renfrew et al., 9–22. As we shall see in the next chapter, play figures prominently in the psychology of D. W. Winnicott (*Playing and Reality*, London: Tavistock, 1971) and in the virtue ethics of Alasdair MacIntyre (*Dependent Rational Animals: Why Human Beings Need the Virtues* (Peru, Il: Carus, 2001).

[27] The role of play in religious and anthropological scholarship is prominent and will be discussed in Chapter 5, dealing with mysticism, and elsewhere throughout this book. Works under consideration will include H. G. Gadamer, *Truth and Method*; R. Schechner, *The Future of Ritual*; A. Droogers, *Playful Religion*; D. Handelman and D. Shulman, *God Inside Out*; H. Cox, *The Feast of Fools*; D. Miller, *Gods and Games*; and others.

[28] Mihaly Csikszentmihalyi, *Flow: The Psychology of Happiness* (New York: Harper Collins, 2008). See especially Chapter 3.

[29] Eugen Herrigel, *Zen in the Art of Archery* (New York: Vintage, 1999), 49.

A Musical Analogy

If pleasure is not a simple enjoyable bodily response to external stimuli, a more nuanced theorizing becomes necessary for both the description of the phenomenon of pleasure and for the theory that explains its place in religion. This will be the overall task of this book, and I briefly illustrate this with an instructive example derived from another domain: musical pleasure.

The diverse and rich repertoire of musical offerings produces pleasure that from an evolutionary and neurological perspective is limited to fairly circumscribed features of the adaptation/survival process. Music acts on networks associated with memory, expectation, and fulfillment, and it produces a hedonic tone, which adds a powerful emotional component to the more "discursive" and cultural dimension of the overall event.[30] This is a place where evolutionary biology and culture unite to produce a highly complex experience. The same is true for religion where evolutionary adaptive factors trigger the hedonic tone in a subtle manner beneath the discursive elements.

In music, we commonly attribute our pleasure to a variety of factors such as melody, harmony, rhythm, instrumentation, lyrics (where present), and so forth. These are all qualities of the music itself. There is no true awareness of the precise way that specific features of music actually cause pleasure as a brain event. However, psychologists can explain how specific brain systems are activated by specific qualities of sound such as tempo or pitch in such a way that the ancient neurological circuits used for reward that had been essential for survival in evolutionary times are stimulated to produce the pleasure. For example, as Robert J. Zattore and Valorie N. Salimpoore write: "Pleasure in music arises from interactions between cortical loops that enable predictions and expectancies to emerge from sound patterns and subcortical systems responsible for reward and valuation."[31]

Notice that some elements of music are easy to enjoy, even by infants, while others represent an acquired taste. Few toddlers can spontaneously enjoy a Bach oratorio, and few Americans spontaneously enjoy the "Raga

[30] Robert J. Zatorre and Valorie N. Salimpoore, "From Perception to Pleasure: Music and Its Neural Substrate," *Proceedings of the National Academy of Sciences* 110, Supplement 2 (2013): 225–241; Nils Wallin, *Biomusicology: Neurophysiological, Neuropsychological and Evolutionary Perspectives on the Origins and Purpose of Music* (York: Pendragon Press, 1991); N Wallin, B. Merker, and S. Brown, *The Origins of Music* (Cambridge, MA: MIT Press, 2000).
[31] Zatorre and Salimpoore, "From Perception," 225.

Bilakhani Todi." Music enjoyment often requires learning, which implies repeated listening, openness to musical comprehension, and perhaps even acquired cultural sensitivity. In a word, a certain level of mastery must be developed if a simpler type of musical enjoyment is to give way to sophisticated and complex appreciation.

I argue that while religious phenomena do not necessarily activate the same cortical loops, at the very least, it is reasonable to assume that in the case of religion, as in music, the subject who experiences pleasure is rarely aware of the physical and even psychological causes underlying the good feeling. But more importantly, it is worth inquiring, what are the qualities of religion – those possibly equivalent to music's temporal and sonic qualities – and what are its evolutionary reward features like the anticipation–tension–fulfillment of music that reward successful adaptive choices by means of pleasure in religious contexts? Additionally, which elements of a religious experience require training and education in order to enhance the quality and duration of the pleasure?

In order to identify the basic adaptive reward features in the cases of religious pleasure, it will be necessary to begin by providing a wide-ranging description of several instances of religious pleasures. A number of patterns will emerge as the basis for a classification that can then be linked to the behavioral-adaptive process that causes pleasure in the brain of religious actors. A thesis will gradually become clear, thanks to the collection of pleasure data that relates the affective feeling to aspects of behavioral adaptation. Behavioral adaptation ranges from Jean Piaget's assimilation and accommodation process in the life of the child to the evolutionary theory that deals with human encounter and coping with novel stressors in contexts of environmental and social survival.[32] With this in mind, the thesis looks roughly like this, where the classification of pleasure I have introduced into the behavioral-adaptive categories of novelty, mastery, and play begins to be applied to religious phenomena:

> Sensory, addictive, socially dysfunctional and disintegrative pleasures, which are usually excoriated in religious discourse, are the "novelty" pleasure in the language of behavioral adaptation. Difficult, socially integrative pleasures that depend on complex learning and are acquired with effort are "mastery" pleasure. These are generally the pleasures that religious groups promote. Free-flowing, imaginative and even fantastic, ego-transcending

[32] Jean Piaget, *The Construction of Reality in the Child* (Oxon: Routledge and Kegan Paul, 2002), 350–360; Jay Schulkin, *Adaptation and Well-Being: Social Allostasis* (New York: Cambridge University Press, 2011), Chapter 7.

pleasures are "play" pleasures. These are the most complex of the three and go to the heart of religious experience.

This analysis resembles the comments on music in the following manner:

The three broad types of pleasure listed earlier – novelty, mastery, play – are commonly accompanied by attribution and evaluative conceptualization that misidentifies the basis for the hedonic tone. For example, the pleasures of alcohol, often condemned in religious texts, could sometimes be attributed to the transgressive nature of the behavior generated by drunkenness. Similarly, the pleasures of Ramadan fasting are attributed to the feelings of conforming to God's will. The two imprecise attributions become associated with the judgment that the two pleasures, the hedonic tone of both, are distinct. And, consequently, one pleasure is said to be sinful while the other is holy. However, evolutionary psychology indicates that the brain event that accounts for the hedonic tone is neither transgression or conformity to God's will but nonconscious factors that can be explained in terms of the adaptive mechanisms we have inherited from ancestors who predated the notion of transgression and the idea of God. One factor is associated with environmental adaptation while the other with social adaptation, and that distinction accounts for the difference in hedonic tone. While religious writers are interested in transgression and divine approval and see these as the causes of conflicting pleasures, evolutionary psychology is interested in the ways that religious groups have developed techniques for transforming novelty pleasures into mastery pleasures and utilizing both in the context of play pleasure. The reason for this is the viability of the group itself, and, thus, the role of religion as a cultural mechanism for promoting group-oriented motivation by means of mastery pleasure becomes clear. Such evolutionary theorizing, abstract at this point, will become clarified and developed in great detail in the body of this book.

Plan of the Book

The argument driving this book is complex. In simplest terms, I argue that the pervasiveness of pleasure and pleasure discourse in world religions can be partially explained in psychological-evolutionary terms. However, the ambivalence of religious sources on the subject of pleasure requires a more refined approach than merely stating that pleasure is a social motivator utilized to promote religious goals. Consequently, the argument needs to be developed gradually and several difficulties dealt with. For example, the first chapter begins with the examination of pleasure and, in particular, the difficulty in describing pleasure by those experiencing it. Unlike pain, which is described using more than seventy embodied metaphors – throbbing, burning, cutting, shooting, gnawing, and others – the feel of pleasure rarely receives such descriptive terms. This has impeded our understanding of pleasure and the so-called hedonic tone, which remains ineffable and leads to confusion in the classification of pleasures. The chapter introduces the behavioral-adaptive classification that will guide the book as a whole – novelty replenishment, mastery, and play – and begins to describe their role in religion. The second chapter focuses on the second pleasure, mastery, and explains its nature as a biopsychological adaptive phenomenon. The chapter also analyzes the way such a pleasure is learned, especially in religious contexts and certainly by children in religious cultures. The next few chapters are historical as well as analytical. The third chapter discusses the way that mastery pleasure emerged in ancient Greece and India – and Israel, to a lesser extent. Utilizing the social and cultural parameters of the Axial Age theory, the chapter explains the significance of the emergence of mastery pleasure as a cultural factor. The fourth chapter continues this discussion with an examination of Philo of Alexandria's literary use of mastery pleasure as a religious and ethical motivator. That same chapter then moves to a discussion of play pleasure – the most complex of the three pleasures – with reference first to Plotinus and then C. S. Lewis and William Finnegan, who was a surfer. The fifth chapter pauses from the historical trajectory of the discussion and examines the role of pleasure in magical belief and magical thinking. This chapter stands out a bit in relation to the others, but it does explore in some detail the psychological implication of hedonic psychology in relation to one aspect of religious experience – that is, magic. The sixth chapter returns to historical analysis, coupled with social and cultural theorizing. The chapter builds upon the famous church-sect theory and examines the hedonic implications of this theory, arguing that the promotion of mastery pleasure is correlated with the exclusivity of such relatively small religious groups as the Qumran sect, the Pashupata and Aghori groups in India and the Anabaptist Bruderhoff groups. The seventh chapter explores the role of pleasure in religious narratives and rituals basing the discussion on material from Hinduism and Judaism but using the phenomenology of Paul Ricoeur as a guide for the discussion. The final chapter is an intimate look at religious experience during a Shabbat morning service in a conservative synagogue in Virginia. The chapter de-exoticizes the concept of religious experience while describing the subtlety and complexity of something as ordinary as enjoying such routine service.

The book closes by tying up the threads to demonstrate that while pleasure is a complex psychological and biological phenomenon, religions have utilized pleasure in elaborate ways for a variety of purposes. While the most obvious purposes include motivation toward social engagement and prosocial behavior, the more interesting purposes are subtle. They include the development of skills to enjoy counterfactual realities and to find meaning and fulfillment in a life that is characterized by internal conflict and contradictions.

CHAPTER I

The Variety and Mystery of Religious Pleasure

In common speech, pleasure is associated with the enjoyable feel of such experiences as eating tasty foods, engaging in sex, visiting with family members, swimming in the sea while on vacation, and so forth. People generally nod in surprised agreement when they hear that completing a painful marathon is also pleasurable, and so is the work of solving a difficult crossword puzzle or suffering the burn of hot chili. Personally, I love the feel of the chili burn as much as I hate the itch of a mosquito bite – both of them roughly similar in level of sensory irritation. The common features of the definitions given by Merriam-Webster and the Oxford English dictionaries is the positive quality of a special feeling and the nature of that feeling as the product of some external cause. The dictionaries define the feeling as a "state of gratification," and a "source of delight or joy." It is often caused by "sensual gratification" in response to some event: "The touch of his fingers gave her such pleasure"; "I paint for the sheer pleasure of it." Similarly, one can say, "It is a special pleasure for me to be here with you today."

Given these general observations – pleasure will be analyzed in greater detail in a following chapter – it is no surprise that we link pleasure to pleasant actions, objects, and events, and in the process, we tend to ignore our internal contribution to the feeling of pleasure – which philosophers call "disposition." This contribution can include judgments, values, and emotions. It is this common and informal view of pleasure that generates the judgment that painful, irritating, and immensely difficult situations cannot cause pleasure; or that, if they do, as religious literature amply illustrates, this is deserving of a thorough (and perhaps counterintuitive) explanation.

Note that the dictionaries link "pleasure" with terms such as gratification and joy, which are usually understood as feelings and judgments and as distinct from simple hedonic experience. But is pleasure itself a feeling or emotion or something else? What is the precise relationship between an emotion like joy and positive affect – that is, pleasure? Is joy a kind of pleasure? If so, can we say that a pleasure gives us pleasure? In fact, at times anger can also give us pleasure, but no one would identify pleasure with anger in the same way that the dictionaries identify pleasure with joy. Clearly, greater precision is required. According to James A. Russell and others, the categorical distinction between joy and pleasure, feeling versus affect, is imprecise and based on informal linguistic usage that ought to be discarded.[1] A broader framework, called "core affect" situates both emotion and pleasure on a scale within a "psychological construct." Phenomenological writers like Merleau-Ponty, Paul Ricoeur and Emmanuel Levinas, and others considered this relationship in detail, as we shall see later in the book. Taken informally – and incorrectly – as entirely distinct psychological phenomena within religious literature, joy and pleasure assume the identity of morally opposed values. The present book will gradually bring the two terms into the one psychological framework, thus providing a more precise explanation for why pleasure is often censured while joy is always praised in religious discourse.

Furthermore, the pleasure or positive affect terminology from other languages such as Latin, Spanish, Sanskrit and Hebrew in religious contexts are quite imprecise. For example, when Teresa of Avila speaks of "consolations" (*gustos*) and "joys" (*contentos*), both of which she finds enjoyable, can we understand these as forms of pleasure? Are they pleasure-giving emotions or judgments, or are they the pleasure itself, like the Greek term *hedonon* in *James* 4:1 where such "pleasures" are said to cause fights and quarrels? Clearly, such questions go to the heart of religious experience and discourse and require that we investigate when and in what manner religion both inspires and censures pleasure.

As noted, due to serious conceptual issues with emotion as an imprecise commonsensical designation, James A. Russell prefers a broader framework, which he calls "core affect": This is a "pre-conceptual primitive process, a neurophysiological state, accessible to consciousness as a simple non-reflective feeling: feeling good or bad, feeling lethargic or energized."[2] Within this framework, the distinction between what we call pleasure

[1] James A. Russell, "Emotion, Core Affect, and Psychological Construction," *Cognition and Emotion* 23, no. 7 (2009): 1259–1283. See also G. L. Clore and A. Ortony, "Appraisal Theories," 630. For related ancient Greek discussions of joy as a form of pleasure, see Kathy L. Gaca, *The Making of Fornication: Eros, Ethics, and Political Reform in Greek Philosophy and Early Christianity* (Berkeley: University of California Press, 2003), 34–35.

[2] Russell, "Emotion," 1264. It strikes me that this core affect corresponds to what some phenomenologist writers (Paul Ricoeur, Emmanuel Levinas) regard as the basic affectivity of non-intentional consciousness. See, for example, Paul Ricoeur, *Fallible Man* (New York: Fordham University Press, 1986), 84.

(hedonic feeling) and emotions – including joy – is false. Psychologists can construct a more precise taxonomy of terms pertaining to good feelings in which the hedonic/emotional boundaries are redrawn. At the very minimum, for example, "Pleasure and arousal combine to form the single feeling of ecstasy."[3]

Inasmuch as religious documents in English, usually translations from other languages, use words such as joy, ecstasy, rapture, and similar ones, I will use the semantic range of such words as overlapping with the hedonic feeling in a strong family resemblance. The notion that those events we commonly call emotion are distinct from and merely modified by positive or negative affect will be rejected. The overarching term "pleasure," used throughout this book, should thus be read as a shortcut for the more nuanced picture.

To give a mere taste of the distribution of the subject at hand, a number of prominent discursive references to pleasure are offered from diverse religious sources: biblical (Hebrew and New Testament), Christian, Jewish, Islamic, Hindu, Buddhist, and others. The literary genres are scriptural, theological, philosophical, poetic, biographical, and anthropological accounts of rituals with implicit and explicit testimonies of participants. The material is divided into two primary types: negative and positive evaluation of pleasure. The reader is invited to peruse the cases quickly or study them in detail. The theoretical conclusions that serve the thesis of this book will follow the descriptive material in a later section.

Negative Evaluation of Pleasure

- Proverbs 19:10 – "It is not appropriate for a fool to have pleasure (*ta'anug*) much less for a slave ruling over ministers."
- Ecclesiastes 21:17 – "A man who loves pleasure (*simha*) will be poor, who loves wine and oil will not become rich."
- Isaiah 5:11 – "Oh those who rise early for pursuing alcohol who stayed late at the feast, wine set them afire."
- Psalms 5:5 – "For you are not a God who delights (*hafets*) in evil."[4]
- Luke 8:14 – "The seed which fell among the thorns, these are the ones who have heard, and they go on their way they are choked with worries

---

[3] Russell, "Emotion," 1264. See also Rainer Reisenzein, "Pleasure-Arousal and the Intensity of Emotions," *Journal of Personality and Social Psychobiology* 67, no. 3 (1994): 525–539.

[4] *Hafets* is a verb that literally means desires. Hebrew and Sanskrit diacritical markings are added when in quoted text, where used, or primary text but are omitted in my own narrative.

and riches and pleasures (*hedonon*) of this life, and bring no fruit to maturity."

• James 4:1 – "What causes fights and quarrels among you? Don't they come from your desires [pleasures – *hedonon*] within you?"

• James 4:3 – "When you ask, you do not receive, because you ask with wrong motives, that you may spend what you get on your pleasures (*hedonon*)."

• *Summa Theologiae* 41.1 – "But temptation which comes from the flesh cannot be without sin, because such a temptation is caused by pleasure (*delectatio*) and concupiscence."[5]

• *Bhagavad Gita* 18.36-39 – "Threefold too is pleasure ... [that pleasure – *sukha*] which at first seems like ambrosia, arising when the senses meet the objects of sense, but in time transmutes itself into what seems to be poison – that pleasure, so it is said, is in Passion's (*rajas*) way."

• Jiva Gosvami – "In this matter, there are some who think that the object of *dharma* is wealth, that wealth is meant for enjoyment, that enjoyment is meant for sensual pleasure, and that sensual pleasure again leads to the cycle of *dharma* and so on. This is truly a misconception."[6]

• *Bhagavata Purana* 1.2.9-10 – "Transcendent dharma is not meant for amassing wealth ... the objects of enjoyment should not be used for sensual indulgence (*kāma*), but only for maintaining life." (Bryant)

• *Bhagavata Purana* 11.8.1 – "The glorious *brahmana* said: O king, as the senses give pleasure (*sukha*) in heaven, so also they cause suffering (*duhkha*) in hell. Therefore, one who discerns this should not wish (for sensual satisfaction)."

• *Fundamental Wisdom of the Middle Way* 17.5 (commentary) – "In general, morally good actions are done for the sake of the pleasure for others; morally bad actions sacrifice others' good for one's own pleasure."[7]

• *Lotus Sutra* 3 – On the parable of the rich man who tries to save his sons from the burning house: "[B]ut my sons are inside the burning

[5] Thomas Aquinas, *Summa Theologiae*, Question 41, Article 1, "Reply to Objection 3," in www .newadvent.org/summa/4041.htm (accessed September 24, 2018). Aquinas did not regard all pleasure as sinful – Joy was a pleasure of the soul in his psychology. See *Summa Theologica: First Part of the Second Part* (Ontario, Canada: Devoted Publishing, 2018), 138.
[6] Edwin F. Bryant, ed., *Krishna: A Sourcebook* (New York: Oxford University Press, 2007), 405.
[7] Jay Garfield, trans., *Wisdom of the Middle Way: Nagarjuna's Mulamadhyamikakarika* (New York Oxford University Press, 1995), 233.

house enjoying themselves and playing games, unaware, unknowing, without alarm or fear."

- *Majjhima Nikaya* – The second of the Four Noble Truths: "Craving (*tanha*) in its three aspects: craving for sensual pleasures (*kāma*); craving for being, that is, for continued existence; and craving for non-being, that is, for personal annihilation."[8]
- *Mahadukkhakkhanda Sutta* – "And what, monk, is the gratification in the case of sensual pleasures? Monks, there are these five cords of sensual pleasure . . . Forms cognizable by the eye that are wished for, desired . . . sounds cognizable by the ear" and so forth.[9]

In conclusion, as we evaluate the nature of those negative religious statements about pleasure, the following features of pleasure stand out: pleasure causes addiction; it binds the subject to objects of desire; it is a product of the senses, a distorter of reality that causes error; it is an obstacle to valued goals, a destroyer of moral purity, and a pathway to hell. These assessments cover a wide range of philosophical topics, such as ontology, epistemology, ethics, and axiology. Despite the breadth of human concerns surrounding the condemnation of pleasure in religious literature, not a single word has yet been identified with which the hedonic tone, the actual feel of the pleasure, itself can be expressed. There is nothing that parallels the religious descriptions of pain as the feeling of penetrating arrows or being torn asunder by a storm (Book of Job). Why is that? Why do religious masterpieces remain mum on the feel of pleasure? Can we expect that the positive evaluations of pleasure, in the following section, will, in fact, feature such descriptions?

Positive Evaluation of Pleasure

- Ecclesiastes 2:24 – "Is it not good for a man that he eat and drink and show himself enjoyment in his toil? This too I have seen that it is from the hand of God." [10]
- Ecclesiastes 3:13 – "And also, every man who eats and drinks and enjoys (*roeh tov*) what is good in all his toil, it is a gift of God."

---

[8] Bhikkhu Nanamoli and Bhikkhu Bodhi, *The Middle Length Discourses of the Buddha: A Translation of Majjhima Nikaya* (Somerville, MA: Wisdom Publications, 2015), 29.

[9] Bhikkhu Bodhi, *In the Buddha's Own Words: An Anthology of Discourses from the Pali Canon* (Somerville, MA: Wisdom Publications, 2005), 194.

[10] For a very substantial and uplifting new collection of pleasures in religious life around the world, see Frans Jespers, Karin van Nieuwkerk, and Paul van der Velde eds., *Enjoying Religion: Pleasure and Fun in Established and New Religious Movements* (Lanham, MD: Lexington Books, 2018).

- Ecclesiastes 3:22 – "And I saw that there is nothing better than that man rejoice (*sameah*) in his deeds."
- Song of Songs 7:6–7 – "Thy head upon three is like Carmel, and the hair of thy head like purple; the king is held captive in the tresses thereof. How fair and how pleasant art thou, O love, for delights!" (Jewish virtual library).
- Song of Songs 7:7 – "How beautiful my love and how pleasant, in pleasures (*ta'anugim*)."
- *Taittiriya Upanishad* 2.4.1 – "Before they reach it, words turn back, together with the mind; One who knows that bliss (*ānanda*) of *brahman*, he is never afraid."[11]
- *Mundaka Upanishad* 2.2.7 – "By perceiving him (*brahman*) the wise see what becomes visible as the immortal in the form of bliss (*ānanda*)."
- Nammalvar in "Weaving Garlands," – "When you make love and embrace my full breasts, a tidal wave of pleasure, unchecked by our union rises to the firmament, and soars beyond making my wits drown in the flood. And it then recedes like a dream."[12]
- Jagad Guru (Chris Butler), "Yoga Wisdom" – On surfing a wave: "Then the wave you are riding is your entire life. This is actually what a person is searching for – pleasure in unity with the Supreme Person."[13]
- *Lotus Sutra* 3 – Shariputra reporting his joy on hearing the voice of the Law (from the Buddha): "My body and mind are at ease and I have gained a wonderful feeling of peace and security."
- Qur'an Surah 101: 6–7 – "Then, he whose balance (of good deeds) will be (found) heavy, will be in a life of good pleasure and satisfaction."
- Qur'an Surah 7: 19 – After Allah admonishes and expels Iblis: "O Adam! Dwell thou and thy wife in the Garden, and enjoy (its good things) as ye wish: but approach not this tree, or ye run into harm and transgression."
- Teresa of Avila, *Interior Castle* – "So I think, daughters, that the happiness we should pray for is to enjoy the complete security of the

---

[11] For discussions of *ananda* as a positive type of pleasure, see J. A. B. van Buitenen, "Ānanda, Or All Desires Fulfilled," *History of Religions* 19, no. 1 (1979): 27–36; Patrick Olivelle, "Orgasmic Rapture and Divine Ecstasy: The Semantic History of Ānanda," *Journal of Indian Philosophy* 25, no. 2 (1997): 153–180.

[12] Vasudha Narayanan, "Tamil Nadu: The Poetry of the Alvars" in ed., Bryant, *Krishna*, 194.

[13] Chris Butler, "Riding Transcendental Waves; Surfing and Meditation," www.freebsd.nfo.sk/hinduism/meditacia.htm (accessed September 14, 2018).

blessed; for what pleasure can anyone have when beset by these fears if his only pleasure consists in pleasing God?"[14]

- Teresa of Avila, *Interior Castle* – "Worldly joys have their source in our own nature and end in God whereas spiritual consolations have their source in God, but we experience them in a natural way and enjoy them as much as we enjoy those I have already mentioned."[15]

- Julian of Norwich, *Revelations* – "And not only we shall receive the same bliss that souls afore have had in heaven, but also we shall receive a new [bliss], which plenteously shall be flowing out of God into us and shall fulfill us."[16]

- Julian of Norwich, *Revelations* – "And in these three words: It is a joy, a bliss, an endless satisfying to me, were shewed three heavens, or thus: For the joy, I understood the pleasure of the Father; and for the bliss, the worship of the son; and for the endless satisfying, the Holy Ghost."[17]

- Nicholas of Cusa, *The Vision of God* – "For such harmony would draw to itself our soul's reason, because it is all reason, just as infinite light would attract all light; thus freed from the sensible, the soul would not without rapture hear this supremely concordant harmony with the ear of the intellect. Here we could derive great pleasure from contemplating not only the immortality of our intellectual and rational spirit ... but also the eternal joy into which the blessed are taken when they are freed from the things of the world."[18]

- St. Perpetua –"The day of victory dawned, and they marched from the prison to the amphitheatre, joyously, as if going to heaven, their faces radiant."[19]

While textual and literary expressions of pleasure are explicit, religious and anthropological writings offer a great deal of descriptive ritual material in which pleasure is implied by what the author is showing us. For example:

---

[14] Teresa of Avila, *Interior Castle* (First Start Publishing eBook, 2012), 42.   [15] Ibid., 63.
[16] Julian of Norwich, *Revelations of Divine Love* (s.l.: Skyros Publishing 2015), 183.   [17] Ibid., 49.
[18] H. Lawrence Bond, trans., *Nicholas of Cusa: Selected Spiritual Writings* (New York: Paulist Press, 1997), 129.
[19] Thomas J. Hefferman, *The Passion of Perpetua and Felicity* (New York: Oxford University Press, 2012), 133.

- McKim Marriott, "Holi: The Feast of Love" – "Joyful celebrants ran from door to door, handing bits of the new crops to working residents of all quarters."[20]
- "A festival of love? I asked by neighbors again in the morning. Yes! All greet each other with affection and feeling. Lord Krishna taught us the way of love, and so we celebrate Holi in this manner."[21]

Another example of ritual-celebratory pleasures is the South American "Day of the Dead":

- Regina M. Marchi, *Day of the Dead* – "Jeane Milne observes: In the Andean countries it is customary to bring food and people feast, dance and make merry in the cemeteries until dawn of the third [November 3]." (18) "This is about an attitude change and looking at life a little differently. Life is short and death is long. Let's enjoy it while we're here."[22] (87)

Most ritual pleasures are shown in context and reported by the observer rather than those experiencing the pleasure. This is certainly true for ancient material – Indian, Greek, Roman, Hebrew, and certainly older material such as Assurbanipal's celebration after defeating Elam.[23] The Inca Inti Raymi marked the southern winter solstice (June 21), and it was celebrated with "libations, sacrifices, songs, and dances." Such celebrations, when initiations and passage were also marked – for example, in the southern summer solstice of December 21 – also showed the pleasures of mastery and courage, by means of contests, fasting, and flagellation.[24] But even contemporary ethnographic literature tends to focus on actions such as eating, drinking, dancing, or singing rather than pinpointing subjective descriptions of affect. The best exceptions are contemporary accounts in memoires, journals and blogs of ritual participants, such as the following account of pilgrimage:

- E. Valentine Daniel, *Fluid Signs* – "The mountain track involves as well the crossing of two rivers and two or three streams. The icy-cold

---

[20] McKim Marriott, "Holi: The Feast of Love," in *Krishna: Myths, Rites and Attitudes*, ed., Milton B. Singer (Chicago: University of Chicago Press, 1966), 202.
[21] Ibid., 205.
[22] Regina M. Marchi, *Day of the Dead: The Migration and Transformation of a Cultural Phenomenon* (New Brunswick, NJ: Rutgers University Press, 2009), 18, 87.
[23] Anthony Spalinger and Jeremey Armstrong eds., *Rituals of Triumph in the Mediterranean World* (Leiden, the Netherlands: E. J. Brill, 2014).
[24] Yves Bonnfoy, *American, African and Old European Mythologies* (Chicago: University of Chicago Press, 1993), 85.

water flowing over sore and blistered feet gives pleasure – this being the only physically pleasurable experience of the entire pilgrimage."[25]

Analysis of Pleasure Cases

The brief survey of pleasure accounts from around the world and varied historical periods has ignored the local cultural dimension of the pleasure discourse in each individual case. Even a single example – for instance, the erotic pleasure of Song of Songs – varies dramatically in its passage from its expression in the court of King Solomon to the mystical commentary of early church fathers. Still, the collection of cases shows the prevalence of relatively few and impoverished patterns of expression relating to the actual "texture" of an experience that is central to human existence. Only Nammalvar in these cases actually describes pleasure as a tidal wave that rises, crests, and recedes – a description that beautifully corresponds to the dynamic feel of the hedonic tone. This is a sense-based metaphor that articulates the way pleasure seems to behave in relation to the body. It is the hedonic equivalent of the nociceptive shooting pain in the tooth. The other two conceivable metaphorical dimensions that can define pleasure, the emotional and the evaluative – that is, pleasure felt as satisfying or pleasure judged to be addictive – are far better represented in this material. This compares poorly with pain in religious literature, where the sensory metaphors (burning, throbbing, shooting, gnawing, etc.) are precise and rich.[26]

Indeed, the salient dimension linking all the varied examples of pleasure discourse is the assumption that pleasure is some sort of reaction or response to a "cause" – that is, some "trigger" that acts on the body, mind, or soul of the subject where the effect is experienced as pleasure. That cause ranges from objects in the world, such as "sensory objects," to

---

[25] E. Valentine Daniel, *Fluid Signs: Being a Person the Tamil Way* (Berkeley: University of California Press, 1984), 256.

[26] Ariel Glucklich, *Sacred Pain: Hurting the Body for the Sake of the Soul* (New York: Oxford University Press, 2001), ch. 1. The relative poverty of pleasure terms is not a religious phenomenon, nor is its attribution to external causes. Great literary works suffer from the same poverty. Thomas Mann, *Death in Venice*, trans., Stanley Appelbaum (New York: Dover Publications, 1995), 34; Patrick Susskind, *Perfume: The Story of a Murderer*, trans., John E. Woods (New York: Vintage International, 2001), 18, 19. The cultural-ethical implications of pleasure's ineffability cannot be fully explained in this space, but see Sidney W. Mintz, *Sweetness and Power: The Place of Sugar in Modern History* (New York: Penguin, 1986); Marshal Sahlins, "The Sadness of Sweetness: The Native Anthropology of Western Cosmology," *Current Anthropology* 37, no. 3 (1996): 395–428. The most striking consequence is the moral split between pleasure and righteousness.

thoughts and emotions present in the mind of the subject and, in religious contexts, some mysterious inner reality, such as *ātman* or self, or mysterious outside reality – God. The evaluation of the pleasure as positive or negative depends on the normative judgment relating to the assumed cause of the pleasure; the pleasure is rarely morally neutral.

The pleasure discourse usually appears in the context of a theoretical discursive construction that is cosmological, psychological, or ethical: celebratory, rewarding, inhibitory, addictive, constraining, damning. Depending on the apparent cause, the pleasure can be read as sensory, mental, spiritual, or social as the broad domains in which it takes place. The terms used to designate that pleasure in various languages – *hedone*, *kama*, *sukha*, *ananda*, *simha*, *oneg*, *felicitas*, *delectatio* – pertain to the discursive dimension of pleasure. That is, these terms are descriptors loaded with evaluative connotations. Hence, *sukha* is almost always good, and so is *simha*. After all, when is "joy" bad? For example, for some in 1955, the pleasure of listening to a choral mass was good, and the pleasure of listening to Elvis was sinful.[27] Meanwhile, as noted, the sensory-metaphorical dimension of pleasure expression – which one may have described, for example, as throbbing, explosive, hot, flowing, saturating, expanding, or peaking pleasure – remains largely ineffable.[28]

Religious theorists, even the most sophisticated among them, did not possess the scientific data to identify the true causes of pleasure in the same way that evolutionary psychologists and brain scientists today can. This leaves us with two parallel tracks for the analysis of the entire field of religious pleasure: the attributional track where religious literature accounts for the value of pleasure based on the assessment of informally perceived causes – both good and bad – and the biological track, consisting of psychological theories that serve as our means of understanding pleasure. Naturally, it is important to ask whether the two tracks converge, and

---

[27] James A. Cosby, *Devil's Music, Holy Rollers and Hillbillies: How America Gave Birth to Rock and Roll* (Jefferson, NC: McFarland and Company, 2016). The "sin" was attributed both to the ecstatic dancing and to the African American origins.

[28] Some researchers, like Feldman (*Pleasure and the Good Life: Concerning the Nature, Varieties, and Plausibility of Hedonism*, New York,: Oxford University Press, 2004) argue that pleasure does not actually have a "feel," and so no terms could be attached to it. It is possible, according to this theory, that pleasure is a sort of attitude toward attractors and that the *attitude* (but not the hedonic tone) can be described. Elinor Mason, "The Nature of Pleasure: A Critique of Feldman," *Utilitas* 19, no. 3 (2007): 379–387. However, Kenneth Mah – a student of Ronald Melzack at McGill University – collected several terms for (orgasmic) pleasure: shuddering, quivering, building, shooting, exploding, hot, throbbing, spreading, flooding, and others. See Glucklich, *Sacred Pain*, 46.

we must determine if this convergence provides a useful theory of religious pleasure.

If the true causes of pleasure, as noted in the Introduction, are the mechanisms of behavioral adaptation and the activation of neural circuits that evolved to reward adaptive decisions, do these also account for the way that diverse and unrelated religious traditions evaluate pleasure and pleasurable experiences or the way that modern individuals engage in religious activities?[29] Is the link between behavioral adaptation and religious ideology subtle enough so that we shall not be accused of careless reductionism? The answer, worked out throughout the book, is a cautious "yes."

The negative evaluations of pleasure in the aforementioned cases indicate that pleasure is taken to be an obstacle to socially prized goals. Pleasure is a cause of addiction and social dysfunction; pleasure is also a distorter of the ability to perceive reality and plan rational and constructive courses of action. As such, excoriated pleasures are socially and personally disintegrative. They are selfish and short sighted; they lead to mental and spiritual states that undermine one's capacity to function and prosper in social and spiritual contexts. Is it then the case that positively evaluated pleasures do the opposite? Is it a fact that some pleasures are socially and personally integrative and affirm the long-range values of societies and individuals? How could behavioral adaptation – a natural process and the scientific explanation for the causes of pleasure – have produced two diametrically opposed types of positive affect? But that is precisely the case, as mastery pleasure shows. Indeed, mastery is a splendid example of a learned skill, a contributor to social fitness, and, yet, a product of broadly conceived evolutionary processes.

The Mystery of Religious Pleasure

We must now look in greater detail at a small number of religious pleasure cases. This examination illustrates the puzzle that pleasure discourse poses for understanding religious experience – especially the experience that appears to be saturated with profoundly hedonic feel. Pleasure has played a prominent role in mysticism and mystical theology. Bernard McGinn, who has produced leading studies of western mysticism, has identified an internal affective state, which he called "affective intentionality" in the

---

[29] Recall from the Introduction that there is a conflict between the selfish interests of the individual and the group survival in competition with other groups. The simultaneous success of both requires a complicated solution.

reported mystical experiences in relation to the ultimate object – that is, God.[30] It appears that the only way to articulate this extraordinary affect is by means of a translation from the realm of inner experience ("the soul") to bodily-sensory experience, an exercise begun in the West by Origen and then developed by Gregory of Nyssa in his commentary on Song of Songs.

For Origen, the source of the analogy by means of which the mystic translates the supreme pleasure of the soul is biblical. The Song of Songs provides ample examples: "May he kiss me with the kisses of the mouth" (Song 1.1); "Let me see your form, let me hear your voice" (Song 2.14), or "The curves of your hips are like jewels" (Song 7.1). These are sensory expressions that open up spiritual possibilities because, for Origen, the words of the Bible are divine logos. McGinn notes: "The erotic descriptions of the Song of Songs need to be translated into the language of internal sensation, where the soul comes to feel and to know God the Word."[31]

Gregory of Nyssa in his homilies on Song of Songs continues and develops this tradition where there is an analogy between the activities of the soul and those of the bodily senses, but the relationship remains strictly metaphorical: a matter of quality rather than quantity. The analogy extends to the relationship between pleasure and desire, as McGinn notes: "Every enjoyment of God is also at one and the same time the kindling of a more intense and unfulfilled desire" – in a sense, a sort of addiction, just as a pleasurable object causes us a desire for more.[32] However, the translation from sensory to spiritual affect is not direct or simple. Rather, what is at work is a complex form of synesthesia, McGinn argues, "that is, descriptions within which different or opposing sense perceptions are combined, exchanged, or fused with one another to present a message that is both cognitional and affective."

For example, Song of Songs 2.5 states: "Strengthen me with perfumes, surround me with apples, for I am wounded with love" raises the question of what it means to be wounded with love. Origen provides the answer, demonstrating McGinn's point about synesthetic interpretations:

> If there is anyone who has been pierced with the loving spear of his knowledge so that he yearns and longs for him [God] by day and night, can speak of nothing but him, can hear nothing but him, can think of nothing else, and cannot desire nor long nor hope for anything same him, that soul truly says, "I have been wounded by charity.[33]

---

[30] Bernard McGinn, "The Language of Inner Experience," *Spiritus: A Journal of Christian Spirituality* 1, no. 2 (2001): 156–171.
[31] Ibid., 158.   [32] Ibid., 157.   [33] Quoted in McGinn, "The Language," 159

The description shows longing at the same time that it implies strong affect (the cause of the longing), both of them dominated by the pain – the wound – of separation. Clearly, this pained longing has become a powerful trope for the affective relationship between the mystic and God, with the immense joy of union in the backdrop. This description has been valid for other mystics in other historical periods in the Christian tradition. To give one example, Meister Eckhart, the fourteenth-century German mystic, wrote the following:

> We are blessed with a power in the soul, which touches neither time nor flesh, flowing from the spirit, remaining in the spirit, altogether spiritual. In this power, God is ever verdant and flowing in all the joy and all the glory that He is in Himself. There is such heartfelt delight, such inconceivably deep joy, as none can fully tell of, for in His power the eternal Father is ever begetting His eternal Son without pause.[34]

All of this raises an interesting and important question: Why is it so difficult to express the inner "affective intentionality" of religious experience in its own terms? Why does the mystical theologian require tropes taken from the sensory realm? Is it because the experience of the soul in its relationship to God is transcendent due to its unique Object, or is it because the special affect itself – the pleasure – defies words? After all, when the mystic, or the biblical source of mystical tropes, wishes to express negative affect pertaining to his hurting body, no such difficulty stands in the way. The authors of the book of Job are able to have him say, "hizei shadai 'imadi" ("the arrows of God have pierced me"). Subsequently, the mystic Teresa of Avila is also able to talk in spiritual terms about the "wound of love" and the pain that it causes in the same tropes as the authors of Job, "as though it were a sharp point in the substance of the spirit, in the heart of the pierced soul," and the observer understands that certain injuries, certain types of pain – even those dealing with the divine – feel like being pierced with an arrow, or stabbed with a knife.[35] The pain metaphors describe the affect itself, the sensory feel of the pain, a concrete and vivid metaphor that succeeds in describing the affect. For Teresa, the experience is paradoxical – that is, a blissful stab. Of the two (bliss and stab), only the quality of the piercing is accessible through language. In contrast, the pleasure tropes are different: Song of Songs gives

---

[34] M. O'Conner Walshe, *Meister Eckhart: Tractates and Sermons*, vol. 1 (London: Watkins, 1978), 74. See also Teresa of Avila, *Interior*, 6. 2.9–12; 6.4.14.

[35] Thomas Dubay, *Fire Within: St. Teresa of Avila, St. John of the Cross, and the Gospel – on Prayer* (San Francisco: Ignatius Press, 1989), 47.

us triggers or causes of pleasure – such as hips, jewels, and apples – not the description of the pleasure feel – that is, the hedonic tone or gloss. And clearly, the soul requires no such worldly triggers or causes as apples and hips in its encounter with the divine. Hence, these pleasures are presumed to be of a different order.

The need to translate the mystic's "affective intentionality" into biblical eroticism derives from its inexpressibility, and, at the same time, it is the nature of that mystical affect that it cannot be caused by objects such as hips and apples because the realm of the mystic transcends sensory and embodied experience. However, there is a more basic issue here, and of this one the mystical theologian may not be aware: the move between affective metaphysical experience and ordinary sensory pleasure must fail because even ordinary ("sensory") pleasure – the one ostensibly caused by hips and apples – defies words. The Bible may speak of the pleasure of the breast or the hip or the pleasure of an apple, and some readers may know what that means and how it feels, but neither the poet of Song of Songs nor the reader can describe those pleasures. The pleasure itself remains ineffable. Hence, one may legitimately ask, is sexual pleasure the same as eating pleasure – that is, do the two situations produce the same hedonic tone? What would a description of the pleasure itself look like? There is a profound psychological difference between the trigger of a pleasure and the feeling of the pleasure, and until the poet describes the pleasure (hedonic tone) itself – for example, as Nammalvar's cresting wave – we are left with mere hints and suggestions. The issue, to repeat, is that ordinary pleasure, in the Bible or anywhere else, and sublime "affective intentionality" share the quality of ineffability; and while the mystical theologians tell us that an act of translation must relate the two radically different types of pleasure, in fact, they are very similar as inexpressible phenomena. The only true difference, apparently, is that mundane pleasure appears to be caused by some trigger while the sublime pleasure does not appear to be caused in such a way – the feel itself is a mystery in both cases.[36]

This raises a number of interesting questions: If both the mystical affective intentionality with its transcendental object and ordinary pleasurable affect defy articulation, is pleasure essential to the mystical or religious experience? Can there be no intimacy with the divine if a significant positive affect is not generated by some method? Or is pleasure a mere epiphenomenon that attends, or a reward that follows, some other feature

---

[36] This topic will be discussed in the phenomenology of intentional and non-intentional pleasure (by Paul Ricoeur and Edmund Husserl) in a later chapter.

of the mystical path or more general religious life? Finally, how significant is the difference between the ordinary pleasure that is described in terms of triggers (hips and apples) and the pleasure that is described in terms of an uncaused and generalized state of consciousness that is separate from empirical triggers?

All of these questions are addressed in this book in a systematic manner. However, it may be futile to broach this topic only by means of Christian examples. If we assume the position of many contemporary scholars, including McGinn, that the traditional context in which the mystic or religious individual operates shapes the religious experience itself, everything I have discussed up to now may be an accident of Christianity's debt to the Hebrew Bible.[37] We would then be hard pressed to generalize based on this data and emerge with a viable theory on the relationship between religious experience and the psychological phenomenon of pleasure. How would these questions be articulated if we were to look at another tradition? A brief look at Sri Caitanya and devotional Vaishnavism may provide an interesting answer to this.

The Gaudiya Vaishnava devotional tradition that originated with the Bengali-born Caitanya (1486–1533) is very familiar to scholars of Hinduism. However, historians of Christian mysticism rarely touch on this tradition with some of its important texts, such as Krishnadasa Kaviraja's *Caitanya Caritamrita*.[38] Comparative studies of mystical traditions usually focus on Vedanta and, more specifically, Shankara's Advaita Vedanta. But the devotional tradition that focuses on Krishna as the supreme God makes for a more suitable comparison in the present context, due to its strong emphasis on a personal God and the devotee's powerful affect – much like McGinn's "affective intentionality" in the mystical theology of Gregory of Nyssa and the others.[39]

At the core of this tradition is the narrative of Krishna's childhood as told in the *Bhagavata Purana* (Book 10) and *Harivamsa*. The young Krishna grew up in Vrindavana as a playful and flirtatious boy spending time with the *gopis* or shepherd girls. Around this delightful narrative, a

[37] This now-familiar position is associated with the collaboration of several scholars that began to appear with the publication of Steven T. Katz edited volumes (*Mysticism and Philosophical Analysis*, *Mysticism and Language*, etc.).
[38] Edward C. Dimock, Jr., trans., *Caitanya Caritāmṛta of Kṛṣṇadāsa Kavirāja: A Translation and Commentary*, Harvard Oriental Series (Cambridge, MA: Harvard University Press, 1999).
[39] Advaita Vedanta, beginning with its earliest texts (Upanishads), also identifies high level of achievement in practice with supreme pleasure (*ananda*), but this requires an entirely distinct mode of analysis.

variety of artistic works – poetic, musical, theatrical – emerged, not unlike the Song of Songs. The Vaishnava theologians reflected on the simultaneous difference and non-difference between the geographical/historical Vrindavana and the heavenly or mystical one. More abstractly, they reflected on the difference/non-difference of earthly and heavenly affects – that is, emotions and pleasure – in the realm of devotion to Krishna.

One key to the devotee's (*bhaka*) relationship with Krishna is a very powerful affective state, a highly pleasurable love. In some ways, this love is like earthly love, or at least not different. In other ways, it is entirely different. The Vaishnava theologians use the language of artistic or poetic theory, extending it beyond art to describe the feeling and its relationship to ordinary feeling. The term they use comes directly from poetics – *rasa*.[40] *Rasa*, or aesthetic pleasure, is a technical concept that applies to the unique appreciation that a true connoisseur can derive from an excellent work of art. That type of enjoyment differs radically from simple pleasures, which are caused by sensory and other types of experience. The famous example illustrating this is the theatrical staging of the abduction of Sita by the demon Ravana in the *Ramayana*. The scene is heart wrenching, and yet the refined viewer still derives pleasure from it.[41] The aesthetic enjoyment is non-particular: it is free of the circumstances of life including sensory and emotional events. This idea may have already started in the ancient Upanishads (Taittiriya 2.7) where *atman* – the self – is described as *rasa*. Meanwhile, Sita's own pain, and even the pain the audience feels in sympathy with her, is particular and does not act as the cause of the enjoyment depicted as *rasa*.[42]

The devotee's feeling toward God is of that type: "The man of sensibility, the *sahṛdaya*, the man who alone can truly appreciate the fine points of poetry and arts, becomes the *bhakta*, who alone can taste the ultimate experience of joy which the worship of Kṛṣṇa brings."[43] Hence, the divine bliss is generalized or non-specific, like *rasa*. That is, it is uncaused or disconnected from mundane experience. This pleasure is not even "caused" by Krishna; it is not the pleasure of Krishna – otherwise the devotee would have to be no less than God himself. However, that universal and undifferentiated joy of loving Krishna is not merely

[40] David L. Haberman, "A Selection from the *Bhaktirasāmṛitasindhu* of Rūpa Gosvāmin: The Foundational Emotions (*sthayi-bhavas*)" in *Krishna: A Sourcebook*, ed., Edwin F. Bryant (New York: Oxford University Press, 2007), 410.

[41] In a later chapter, I shall call this "Stabat Mater pleasure." See *Augustine: the Confessions*, trans., Philip Burton (New York: Alfred A. Knopf 2001), 3.2.3.

[42] Dimock, *Caitanya*, 123.   [43] Ibid., 122.

analogous to poetic *rasa* – it is one and the same, only many times more powerful. And *rasa* itself is not analogous with ordinary pleasure – it is both the same and different. It is the same in terms of hedonic tone, but it is also unlike the empirical pleasure that is tethered to specific causes.

All of this leaves us with a situation that resembles the case of Origen and Gregory of Nyssa. Pleasure remains ineffable both in its ordinary and divine forms: we are merely told that the two are both somehow the same and yet different. They are the same in possessing hedonic tone and different in that while one is tied to specific empirical causes, the other is independent of such causes, is general, and far more intense. In both cases, the pleasure itself remains inexpressible.

One may be justified in wondering whether it is just an amazing coincidence that mystical theologians East and West distinguish between the unity and autonomy of divine affect and the plurality and contingency of worldly affect and that hedonic theorists, psychologists, draw a distinction between the unity of hedonic tone and the multiplicity of apparent hedonic causes. In the case of multiple pleasures, the distinction between types of pleasure is the linguistic practice of referring to pleasure in terms of its causes, such as eating pleasure or swimming pleasure. Meanwhile, the hedonic tone, the subjective feel or gloss of the pleasure, remains singular. Indeed, one seldom speaks of hedonic tones. Tied to this question, we may also wonder whether this apparent similarity between the one and the many pleasures in religion and in psychology may have something to do with the fact that both the divine affect and the hedonic tone defy verbal communication.

Up to now, the discussion was limited to what is generally regarded as mystical theology. That seems to limit the scope to uniquely elevated psychological states said to be inexpressible due to mystical epistemology. A more commonplace example taken from the pleasure of the Shabbat meal may remove this concern and sharpen distinction between pleasure and pleasures, or the role of pleasure in religious experience. The example is a Talmudic story (Tractate Shabbat 119a):

> Rabbi Joshua ben Hananiah once received an invitation from Hadrian, the Roman emperor, who asked him about the secrets for preparing the Shabbat meal. Hadrian assumed the meal had to be remarkably tasty because it clearly gave the Jews such exquisite pleasure on Friday night. Rabbi Joshua taught the emperor's chefs how to make the best foods with the choicest ingredients and spices, but the emperor, despite enjoying the meal, could not discern anything unusual about the pleasure he received from the food. He summoned Rabbi Joshua again, and the two of them

interrogated the chefs. Surely, the emperor insisted, there was some special spice, some rare and secret ingredient or cooking procedure that gave the Sabbath diners their bliss. The rabbi responded that indeed something special did exist, but it was not in the food – it was the love of the Sabbath.[44]

This example nicely demonstrates that the unity of pleasure is not just a mystical phenomenon; the independence of uncaused pleasure from the ostensible cause – here, food – is not mystical at all but a matter of a certain attitude that can be called dispositional. Finally, this book will demonstrate that the dispositional attitude that defines enjoyment can be found across a spectrum of traditions. So, a "perennial philosopher" might argue, there appears to be some as yet unproven universal quality in religious experience that defies a locally constructed cultural understanding of religious experience. This is a possibility that needs to be addressed in the course of this book.

The two mystical cases – East and West – and even the Shabbat example, raise profound difficulties for understanding the relationship between pleasure and religious experience. We have seen earlier in the chapter that the many instances of religious condemnation of pleasure come from sources where pleasures are regarded as an obstacle to religious and social goals – proximity to God, purification of sins, obedience to authority, and others. And yet, in the cases of Origen and Sri Caitanya, we see pleasure, indeed bliss, at the very core of religious experience. The most elevated religious attainments are blissful – that is, extremely pleasurable.

The logical question is, why are pleasures of the body and senses so roundly condemned when the highest levels of religious experience is profoundly hedonic, so affectively positive? The short answer is that, as we have seen in the case of mystical theology, "worldly" pleasures are identified with – or, more precisely, attributed to – their ostensible causes, such as food, sex, gambling, and so forth. In the ordinary discourse related to excoriated pleasures, there is no reference to a single universal hedonic state and a plurality of causes that bring it about. Instead, there are many pleasures: sexual pleasure, eating pleasure, and the rest. In evolutionary terms, the multiple pleasures can be obstacles to group fitness as inducements to cheating and antisocial behavior. But what does religious discourse say about them? How should one regard this state of affairs from the

44 Ellen Handler Spitz, "Reflections on Psychoanalysis and Aesthetic Pleasure: Looking and Longing," in *Pleasure beyond the Pleasure Principle*, eds., Robert A. Glick and Stanley Bone (New Haven, CT: Yale University Press, 1990), 221–238.

perspective of the religious historian, and how does it affect our under-standing of religious experience? Do these causes represent some evil, some absence of virtue, or some metaphysical block that stands in the way of an experience of God and divine forgiveness?

In order to answer these questions, we need to take a stand on what "religious experience" means in a general sense. The entirety of Chapter 8 will deal with this topic. However, in brief terms, for now, the two main approaches to the analysis of religious experience are first, a "sui generis" phenomenon, which is distinct, unique, and universal, possessing essen-tialist characteristics like pure consciousness.[45] The second approach is the culturally constructed view, or what Ann Taves calls the "ascriptive" understanding of religious experience. On this view, the religious experi-ence is shaped and constituted by cultural conceptions, and it is not a universal or singular phenomenon.[46]

In the case of religious pleasure, if one assumes the sui generis or essentialist view of religious experience, then the religious excoriation of the many pleasures that are attributed to worldly causes is due to the valuation of some distinctly religious state of mind, which ought to be intentionally cut off from cognitions, feelings, and sensory experiences. Hence, on this theory, the hedonic tone of that elevated state of religious consciousness shares only superficial resemblance with the pleasure caused by food, sex, thoughts, memories, or social contacts. Such a theory greets the evidence of Origen, Gaudiya Vaishnavism, and the Shabbat meal as splendid affirmations of the perennial consciousness, which happens to be saturated with positive affect. However, on the negative side, we learn little about the nature of this affect by studying the psychology of ordinary pleasure, or pleasures, which limits our ability to understand the psych-ology of mystical joy. For all we know, it's all a rhetorical flourish. Furthermore, we fail to understand why it is that a successful achievement of unity with the divine actually resembles the affective properties of worldly pleasure – that is to say, its ineffability.

In contrast, according to the ascriptive view of religious experience promoted by scholars like Wayne Proudfoot and Ann Taves, there is no

---

[45] Rudolf Otto, *The Idea of the Holy: An Inquiry into the Non-Rational Factor in the Idea of the Divine and Its Relation to the Rational* (London: Oxford University Press, 1958); Robert Forman, *The Problem of Pure Consciousness: Mysticism and Philosophy* (New York: Oxford University Press, 1990).

[46] Anne Taves, "Ascription, Attribution, and Cognition in the Study of Experiences Deemed Religious," *Religion* 38, no. 2 (2008): 125–140; Steven Katz, *Mysticism and Religious Traditions* (New York: Oxford University Press, 1983).

such thing as a universal state of pure consciousness, affective or otherwise.[47] The sublime experience reported by diverse mystics must be
analyzed by reference to determinative cultural factors. For example, the
euphoria of a Gregory of Nyssa is an interpretive attitude that can be
traced to distinct biblical passages. It is not a culture-free form of universal
joy. This makes it necessary to resolve the perceived conflict between:
(1) the mystic's actual claim for the distinctiveness of mystical pleasure and
the more ordinary pleasures, (2) the fact that in apparently unrelated
mystical traditions, spiritual achievement is described as steeped with
highly satisfying affect, and (3) the fact that in virtually every religious
tradition, some pleasures are excoriated while others are promoted. What is
the selection process in religious discourse whereby one pleasure is distinguished from another, and how does such an ambiguous psychological
phenomenon as pleasure become elevated – if, indeed, it is – to a near
universal feature of mystical and other religious affective states? (4) Finally,
if the culturally constructed understanding of religious experience posits
that it is a complex psychological and ideological instantiation of deep-
seated cultural values, then an experience saturated with views of theodicy
and an experience saturated with celebrative views – even within the same
cultural milieu – would be significantly distinct. And, indeed, this is
usually the case. However, if both experiences, the moral and the celebrative, also contain a highly hedonic dimension – when theodicy and
thanksgiving represent opposing views of pleasure – one must then focus
on and explain pleasure as the outstanding shared feature of the two
ostensibly opposed religious ideas.

Because I am subscribing to the ascriptive theory of religious experience,
it is incumbent that I deal with these questions and that I show that the
way these questions are formulated is based on a number of incorrect
assumptions about the nature of pleasure. For example, I must show that
the linking of pleasure to its apparent causes is mistaken from a scientific-
psychological point of view. This link is due to a commonsensical but
imprecise observation of states of consciousness that leads to a false
attribution where the wrong causes are identified as responsible for the
pleasure we feel when engaged in certain behaviors such as eating or
swimming. We therefore think, informally, that dining pleasure and water
pleasure (or reading pleasure, etc.) are distinct pleasures. This attribution
error is extremely common – indeed, universal. This requires a very brief

---

[47] Wayne Proudfoot's *Religious Experience* (Berkeley: University of California Press, 1985) is generally
regarded as the seminal contemporary text on the social constructivist theory of religious experience.

excursion into the philosophy of pleasure. The purpose is simply to clarify the basic philosophical assumptions regarding pleasure so the exploration of the role of pleasure in religious life can proceed with some measure of precision.

Pleasure Theory

Pleasure has produced an immense corpus of philosophical writings since the Greeks took it up. The three dominant views in this large field, greatly oversimplified here, have been termed by Leonard D. Katz as "the simple picture of pleasure" and, following Bennett Helm, "felt evaluations."[48] The first, associated with the British empiricists of the nineteenth century, takes pleasure as "simple uniform feature of momentary conscious experience that is obviously good in itself and is consequently attractive to whoever experiences it." This view overlaps significantly with what philosophers have considered as the episodic view of pleasure. The second view involves judgments or considerations that "impress themselves on our feelings by virtue of larger patterns of evaluations." This position, originating with Greek philosophers, significantly overlaps with the dispositional view of pleasure. In a third perspective, philosophers like Gilbert Ryle, who discover no intentional content about their inner mental life that can be reported as pleasurable, deny that pleasure is any episode of conscious experience at all. It is rather, as Fred Feldman puts it, a "propositional attitude," a plan of action lacking any essential feel.[49]

The philosophical interest in pleasure, in contrast with the psychological, generally aims at resolving moral questions dealing with the good. These normative aspects of hedonic psychology are clearly relevant for understanding religious attitudes toward pleasure, but there are more fundamental questions relating to the anthropology of religion and pleasure. For example, psychological studies substantiate the philosophical link between pleasure and motivation but also demonstrate the neurological

---

[48] Leonard D. Katz, "Pleasure," *Stanford Encyclopedia of Philosophy* 1.1 https://plato.stanford.edu/ (accessed May 8, 2016). Bennett W. Helm, "Felt Evaluations: A Theory of Pleasure and Pain," *American Philosophical Quarterly* 39, no. 1 (2002): 13–30. The distinction and relationship between the two types of pleasure theory are discussed by Murat Aydede, "An Analysis of Pleasure Vis-à-Vis Pain" *Philosophy and Phenomenological Research* 61, no. 3 (2000): 537–570, especially 541.

[49] Gilbert Ryle, *Dilemmas: The Tarner Lectures* (Cambridge, UK: Cambridge University Press, 1954), ch. 4 ("Pleasure"), 54–67. Fred Feldman, "Hedonism," in *Encyclopedia of Ethics*, 2nd edn., 3 Vols., eds., Lawrence C. Becker and Charlotte B. Becker (New York: Routledge, 2001), vol. II, 662–669. See also Fred Feldman, *Pleasure and the Good Life* (Oxford: Oxford University Press, 2004), 79: Is the pleasure of warm and dry on a cold day the same as the pleasure of cold and wet on a hot day?

distinction between pleasure and desire.[50] It will become evident later that
the desire–pleasure link also played a significant role in the discovery of
dispositional pleasure during the mid-centuries of the first millennium
BCE – that is, as an internal affective-evaluative state of mind rather than a
momentary response to intrinsically pleasurable stimuli.[51] This discovery
had a significant influence on the religious traditions that developed with
the aid of Greek thought – that is, Judaism, Christianity, and Islam – and,
similarly, those traditions that evolved from Indian thought – Hinduism
and Buddhism. The affective dimension of religious experience – not just
religious ethics – cannot be understood without exploring the subject of
pleasure and the distinction between modes of conceiving pleasure. The
dispositional view of pleasure, I believe, is most useful for understanding
the ways that religions have promoted well-being, while the episodic view
helps us understand religious excoriation of pleasure. Unfortunately, Feldman's "felt evaluations" theory, related to the dispositional view, would
only work for humans of a certain age, possessing the capacity to evaluate
inner states or affects.[52] But a preponderance of evidence suggests that
animals and newborn infants are also capable of experiencing pleasure,
though they appear to lack the Greek philosopher's judgment associated
with the dispositional view. It is clear, then, that the dispositional theory
must be refined, saved from its cognitive implications, by looking to some
biologically instantiated mechanism that accounts for the "evaluative"
function of positive affect. Such a standard must account not only for
natural pleasures such as food and sex – the ones that have been termed
"novelty" in the Introduction to this book but also for the most complex
and "cultural" pleasures such as reading scripture, enjoying a long and
difficult pilgrimage, and, to be sure, enjoying the sadness of Mary in the
Stabat Mater. All of these would be considered "mastery pleasure" in the
threefold scheme offered in the Introduction. A functionalist-evolutionary
theory of pleasure meets these requirements. The natural standard of
evaluation, demanded by the dispositional approach to pleasure, is thus

[50] Kent C. Berridge, "Pleasure of the Brain," *Brain and Cognition* 52, no. 1 (2003): 106–128.

[51] Katz, "Pleasure," 2.1; See also Jacques Lacan's comments on Empedocles of Agrigentum (b. 495
BCE) in *Ecrits: A Selection*, trans., Bruce Fink (New York: W.W. Norton & Co., 2002), 100.
Clearly, the transition from pleasures to pleasure (the discovery of dispositional pleasure) needs to
be systematically elaborated.

[52] See J. C. B. Gosling and C. C. W. Taylor, *The Greeks on Pleasure* (Oxford: Clarendon Press,
1982), 196.

the product of behavioral adaptation.[53] Hence, we close the circle and arrive again at the three behavioral-adaptive pleasures discussed in the Introduction. This, then, is the place where evolutionary biology and religious history join tracks: the mastery and play pleasures of the evolutionary theory will be found to serve complex and fascinating functions in the religious life of humans everywhere, while novelty pleasures are most often (though not always!) censured. In other words, we shall see that religious discourse reflects the tension between socially adaptive and socially maladaptive choices, where some pleasures are enhanced while others are controlled. The contrast demonstrates, implicitly, the motivational versus the punitive cognitive approaches to group fitness. At the loftiest levels of theological and ethical reflection, this contrast is still present, as we can see in the tension between so-called punitive theodicy (Augustinian) and the eschatological theodicy (Irenaean), which is redemptive.[54] Affect is situated at the very core of theological speculations – that is, questions of sin, suffering, redemption, and the search for meaning – but this affect is a spectrum at the negative end of which is the seduction of pleasure while at the other end is the promise of joy. Even theologians understand that the two are related and that the control of the former serves the attainment of the latter.[55]

---

[53] The literature on pleasure and adaptation is very substantial and dominated by so-called approach and avoidance theories. An authoritative overview is Andrew J. Elliot, ed., *Handbook of Approach and Avoidance Motivation* (New York: Psychology Press, 2008). See also appraisal theory as an evolutionary approach that supplements adaptation: P. C. Ellsworth, "Appraisals, Emotions, and Adaptation," in *Evolution and the social mind*, eds., J. P. Forgas, M. G. Haselton, and W. von Hippel (New York Psychology Press, 2007), 71–88.

[54] John Hick, *Evil and the God of Love* (New York: Palgrave Macmillan, 2010), 236–237.

[55] Hick, *Evil*, 258.

CHAPTER 2

The Nature and Cultivation of
Complex Pleasure

The subject of pleasure belongs in a variety of scientific fields ranging from neurobiology to evolutionary psychology. Perhaps the most appropriate – that is, prolific – focused subfield is behavioral adaptation and within that, the theories of approach and avoidance, along with motivation. Andrew J. Elliot defines approach and avoidance (AA) motivation in the following way: "Approach motivation may be defined as the energization of behavior by, or the direction of behavior toward, positive stimuli (objects, events, possibilities) whereas avoidance motivation may be defined as the energization of behavior by, or the direction of away from negative stimuli."[1] The capacity to act in such a manner is predicated on some discrimination of positive or negative valence that guides the appropriate action if successful adaptation is to take place.[2]

However, at the most basic level, this discrimination is not conscious. In fact, organisms at all levels of complexity, including amoeba, possess AA mechanisms that guide adaptive action, even if only toward a light source. At somewhat higher levels of complexity, organisms are hardwired to make immediate AA responses – that is, that evoke appetitive reactions such as food getting, shelter, mating, or avoidance of threats to these.[3] This basic design is true for humans, too – even below the level of conscious awareness or control. For instance, the salivary reflex and the startle response (blinking) are autonomous of conscious intention and very rapid. The former is an approach thriving response while the latter is an avoidance survival response.

---

[1] Andrew J. Elliot, ed. *Handbook of Approach and Avoidance Motivation* (New York: Psychology Press, 2008), 8.
[2] Mark Chen and John A. Bargh, "Consequences of Automatic Evaluation: Immediate Behavioral Predispositions to Approach or Avoid the Stimulus," *Personality and Social Psychology Bulletin* 25, no. 2 (1999): 215–224.
[3] Elliot, "Introduction and Overview," in *Handbook of Approach and Avoidance,* ed. Elliot, 6.

However, predicting human behavior as an adaptive response to objects, events, or possibilities is far more difficult than in lower organisms because the AA system involves higher cortical processes than mere reflexes. Hence, humans operate on several levels of approach and avoidance and possess flexible and creative regulatory repertoires, including delay of gratification, attention control, impulse control, goal setting, and other conscious abilities.[4]

Putting this in terms of pleasure – positive affect or "positive experienced state" – humans may actually curtail contact with approach stimuli. For example, one may reject a helping of ice cream or cake in order to maintain one's figure, which may be more satisfying and the satisfaction longer lasting. Adaptation in humans thus involves a more complex evaluation of valence, such as preference for a trim figure and health as opposed to momentary sweetness, and a more complex design of behavior than merely approach the sweet and pleasurable object or event. In other words, human adaptation requires learning, and it forces us to rethink the meaning of pleasure beyond the basic concept. At that simpler biological level, pleasure as adaptive response is a subcortical reward system or systems that is essential for survival. It allows animals to "make choices" among courses of action by rewarding the appropriate appetitive action. It is even critical for animal learning.[5]

For instance, the approach action-guide system in many animals "mediates a certain kind of emotional-behavioral presence that includes vigorous investigative sniffing, exploration, foraging, and in hunting species, predatory urges."[6] Panksepp and Moskal call this a SEEKING system. It is constituted by elaborate neurophysiological and neurochemical substrates that interact with higher cognitive mechanisms to generate positively valenced "expectancies and hopes" about the world.[7] In other words, the approach system can be activated by these internal processes in complex organisms – which can manifest in play, exploration, or predatory meanderings. In humans, the internally generated activation of approach

[4] Andrew J. Elliot and Todd M. Thras, "Approach-Avoidance in Personality: Approach-Avoidance Temperaments and Goals," *Journal of Personality and Social Psychology* 82, no. 5 (2002): 804–818.
[5] Michel Cabanac, "Pleasure: The Common Currency," *Journal of Theoretical Biology* 155, no. 2 (1992): 173–200.
[6] Jaak Panksepp and Joseph Moskal, "Dopamine and SEEKING: Subcortical 'Reward' Systems and Appetitive Urges," in *Handbook of Approach and Avoidance*, ed. Elliot, 68; Antonio Alcaro and Jaak Panksepp, "The SEEKING Mind: Primal Neuro-Affective Substrates for Appetitive Incentive States and Their Pathological Dynamics in Addiction and Depression," *Neuroscience and Behavioral Reviews* 35, no. 9 (2011): 1805–1820.
[7] Panksepp and Moskal, "Dopamine," 68.

can manifest in games, desire, exhilaration, or tension of anticipation that makes various cultural forms such as music, art, and film pleasurable.[8]

The SEEKING system can be recruited in a variety of hedonic cultural contexts, including those that are used to curtail the basic approach response – for example, to sweet, salty, and fatty substances by promoting long-term behavioral choices toward goals that fight appetitive eagerness. The rewards of pilates and yoga – attractive outfits, hip studios, happy music, and social bonding – are examples of arousing the SEEKING system to control approach behavior. But, as we shall see shortly, promoting long-term goals also involves a number of suppressive or self-regulatory systems. Sophisticated and learned human adaptation relies on the suppressive and the arousing systems in tandem.

As Elliot notes, the actual adaptive behavior in humans often involves overriding the initial behavioral predisposition of the AA mechanism. Furthermore, a positive outcome is not just approaching the "good"; it is also avoiding the "bad."[9] This can require higher-level evaluations based on experience, learning, and analysis. In adult humans, these are socially acquired skills at the root of which is the fact that "people (and other primates) are tenaciously motivated to form and maintain strong and stable social bonds."[10] The basic approach–avoid system promotes positive social outcomes such as closeness, intimacy, approval and helps avoid negative social outcomes such as rejection, loneliness, and ostracism. Both approach and avoidance, understood in this way, are sources of pleasure, manifested as positive social outcomes.[11] The social context for the AA mechanism is critical for understanding self-regulation, which is the mechanism, broadly conceived, for hedonic control away from the simple appetitive pleasures toward long-term and more complex gratification.

It should be reasonably clear by now that the AA mechanism operates at a variety of levels ranging from the simple behaviorist stimulus response to the elevated sociocultural system involving learned conscious choices.

[8] Kent C. Berridge, "Pleasure, Pain, Desire, and Dread: Hidden Core Processes of Emotion," in *Well-Being: The Foundations of Hedonic Psychology*, eds. Daniel Kahneman, E. Diener, and N. Schwarz (New York: Russell Sage Foundation, 1999), 525–557.

[9] Elliot, "Introduction and Overview," 7.

[10] Shelly L. Gable and Elliot T. Berkman, "Making Connections and Avoiding Loneliness: Approach and Avoidance Social Motives and Goals," in *Handbook of Approach and Avoidance*, ed. Elliot, 4; this will be discussed in the next chapter in reference to Merlin Donald's theory of mimesis.

[11] E. Tory Higgins, "Beyond Pleasure and Pain," *American Psychologist* 52, no. 12 (1997): 1280. Kenneth Rubin, Robert Coplan, Nathan Fox, and Susan Calkins, "Emotionality, Emotion Regulation, and Preschoolers' Social Adaptation," *Development and Psychopathology* 7, no. 1 (1995): 49–62.

Still, at every level, one may speak of "goals, sub-goals, programs, strategies, tactics and behaviors" that can serve a higher level.[12] To say that the end and means of human social adaptations differs from that of the monarch butterfly is not to deny some structural homology in the relationship within the adaptive hierarchy – the relationship between the goal and the tactics that serve that goal. For instance, in both cases, there is a difference between regulation that consists of promotion and regulation that consists of prevention or suppression.[13] And in both cases, the hedonic product of regulation is a relationship – a ratio, so to speak – between the goal and the perceived current state, even when the subject (the monarch butterfly) possesses limited conscious awareness.[14]

To summarize the discussion of adaptation and refresh its link to pleasure, adaptation has been described as a complex AA mechanism that enables the survival and flourishing of organisms in natural and social environments. Adaptation allows us to think of pleasure in three basic ways: pleasure is the outcome of approaching flourishing-inducing situations and avoiding threatening or destructive situations. The approach/avoid neurological and psychological system can be suppressed or regulated toward long-term goals, which results in what I have called mastery pleasure. But the same system can be activated or aroused – even without the presence of actual objects – and this results in what I have called play pleasure. All three pleasures are "natural," but mastery and play are recruited for a variety of social and cultural purposes.[15] Both figure prominently in the religious life of humans in a wide variety of ways. In the following section, I will discuss the manipulation of self-regulation to promote mastery pleasure. A section on play pleasure will follow. I will then show how mastery and play are utilized in the developmental process of children and the way schooling promotes, via hedonic regulation, highly valued cultural goals.

---

[12] Abigail A. Scholer and E. Tory Higgins, "Distinguishing Levels of Approach and Avoidance: An Analysis Using Regulatory Focus Theory," in *Handbook of Approach and Avoidance*, ed. Elliot, 490.

[13] Higgins, "Beyond," 1280.

[14] C. S. Carver and M. S. Scheier, "Principles of Self-Regulation: Action and Emotion," in *Handbook of Motivation and Cognition: Foundations of Social Behavior*, vol. 2, eds. E. T. Higgins and R. M. Sorrentino (New York: Guilford Press, 1990), 3–52.

[15] This is true for novelty as well, which is highly exploitable in consumerist capitalism, and the hedonic treadmill is a major driver of economic growth. Lindsey Patterson and Robert Biswas-Diener, "Consuming Happiness," in *The Good Life in a Technological Age*, eds. Philip Brey, Adam Briggle, and Edmund Spense (New York: Routledge, 2012), 147–156. In religion, see Vincent J. Miller, *Consuming Religion: Christian Faith and Practice in Consumer America* (New York: Bloomsbury Academic, 2005).

Self-Regulation

Adaptive systems in nature and in human societies need to self-regulate. Some regulate as the function of hardwired mechanisms with behavioral inflexibility. What adapts is the "wiring," and behavior is a mere instantiation of that. More complex systems, certainly humans, are able to self-regulate and display a great deal of behavioral freedom.[16] The cybernetic design of such systems consists of three key dimensions: standard, monitoring, and strength. The standard is the goal – that is, the ideal or desirable state envisioned by the subject that possesses conscious awareness. Monitoring is the ability to observe the actual state of the system at the present time and compare it to the standard or desired state. As noted earlier, this comparison yields a ratio that defines affect, ranging from simple pleasure such as the warmth and sweetness of a cup of tea to complex life evaluations as in career satisfaction. Strength is the motivational dimension that allows the subject to recruit resources for changing the current state according to the perceived standard. According to Panksepp and Moskal, the SEEKING system arousal acts to increase strength. Brandon Schmeichel and Roy Baumeister describe strength as, among other features, one internal state overriding another.[17]

The feelings that accompany the human self-regulating system "arise as a consequence of a feedback process" – that is, "checking on how well the first process (the behavior loop) is doing at reducing its discrepancies."[18] The feeling of pleasure is the reduction in the discrepancy between standard and the present state or, more broadly, "a behavioral system [is] making rapid progress in doing what it is organized to do."[19] The feeling of pleasure, understood from this adaptive perspective, informs the subject on how well it is doing in the natural and social environments relative to the standard. One may monitor and regulate affect itself in order to change one's position in the world: "Individuals take action either to maintain or to change (enhance or suppress) the intensity of affect, or to prolong or

---

[16] On this behavior freedom as "executive function," see Russell A. Barkley, "The Executive Functions and Self-Regulation: An Evolutionary Neuropsychological Perspective," *Neuropsychology Review* 11, no. 1 (2001): 1–29.

[17] Panksepp and Moskal, "Dopamine," 68; Brandon J. Schemichel and Roy F. Baumeister, "Self-Regulatory Strength," in *Handbook of Self-Regulation: Research, Theory and Applications*, eds. Roy F. Baumeister and Kathleen D. Vohs (New York: Guilford Press, 2004), 84–98.

[18] Charles S. Carver, "Self-Regulation of Action and Affect," in *Handbook of Self-Regulation*, eds. Baumeister and Vohs, 16–17.

[19] Ibid., 17.

shorten the affective episode."[20] Affect here refers to the hedonic tone experienced as pleasure. While the observation appears to promote a strong psychological hedonism, it is important to remember that the affect is a function of a *relationship* between present state and a goal or standard. One cannot regulate subjective hedonic tone without taking into account the social nature of powerful goals such as approval, acceptance, attachment, companionship, and, on a more elevated level, honor, justice, salvation, and so forth. In other words, the hedonic action guide contains, by definition, strong cognitive and even ideological elements.[21]

Psychologists approach this topic as "emotion-related regulation," which is defined as "the process of initiating, avoiding, inhibiting, maintaining, or manipulating the occurrence, form, intensity, or duration of internal feeling states, emotion-related physiological processes, goals, and/ or behavioral concomitants of emotion, generally in the service of accomplishing one's goals."[22] Researchers have shown that the goal itself – often a social construct – need not be conceptualized in hedonic terms at all, and hence, the experience of pleasure may seem paradoxical.[23] In the service of justice (or revenge) or sympathy with a victim, subjects may actually enjoy anger, even rage, or deep sadness.[24] This fact accounts for Augustine's observations concerning the enjoyment of theatrical audiences and conforms to our intuitive perception that we actually feel good being angry when someone has wronged us.[25] We can call this paradox the "Stabat Mater" effect – the sublime joy of negative emotions.[26]

The overall social consequences of these hedonic/adaptive features are extremely positive. They are related to internalized social compliance, development of conscience, prosocial behavior, empathetic responses to

---

[20] Randy J. Larsen and Zvjezdana Priznic, "Affect Regulation," in *Handbook of Self-Regulation,* eds. Baumeister and Vohs, 40.

[21] This links the comments of Darwin quoted in the Introduction to this book to cognitive evolutionary theory. See David C. Geary, *The Origin of Mind: Evolution of Brain, Cognition and General Intelligence* (Washington, DC: American Psychological Association, 2005), ch. 6.

[22] Nancy Eisenberg, Cynthia L. Smith, Adrienne Sadovsky, and Tracy L. Spinard, "Effortful Control: Relations with Emotion Regulation, Adjustment, and Socialization in Childhood," in *Handbook of Self-Regulation,* eds. Baumeister and Vohs, 260.

[23] This is doubly the case because the pleasure itself is ineffable – as seen in Chapter 1.

[24] Larsen and Priznic, "Affect Regulation," 42.

[25] St. Augustine, *The Confessions,* trans., Philip Burton (New York: Alfred Knopf, 2001), 3.2.3: "In both joy and grief there was pleasure."

[26] The pleasure of all negative emotions is not identical, not in theory. See, for example, Martin Nowak, *Supercooperators: Altruism, Evolution and Why We Need Each Other to Succeed* (New York: Schuster, 2011), 66, on the pleasure of policing others. See also John Morreal, "Enjoying Negative Emotions in Fiction," *Philosophy and Literature* 9, no. 1 (1985): 95–103.

others, social competence, and others.[27] This is another way of saying that mastery pleasure, the pleasure promoted by self-regulation in pursuit of valued goals, carries profound social benefits. It will be promoted by societies as a sort of virtue, or attendant on virtue, and will constitute an important aspect of child rearing and education.

However, before proceeding to the topic of teaching self-regulation – specifically delay of gratification – it is important to briefly touch on the cognitive dimensions of self-regulation. The importance of the goal ("standard") and monitoring in self-regulation derives from the capacity to conceptualize both the target and the subject (agent) in coherent ways. Furthermore, it would be difficult for a young person to recruit motivation toward a specific goal such as justice if she cannot properly evaluate the force, meaning, and function of the goal in one's life or for one's social world. In other words, the *salience* of a goal is critical for recruiting motivation – and that is a cognitive skill.[28] Motivation, as we have seen, is also the suppression of one subsystem in favor of another, which often requires attentional control.

The "standard" component of self-regulation in humans is not hard-wired. It is an idea and functions in the subject as a "mental representation of utility."[29] The representation is complex, involving both rewards and threats and a calculation of their relative weight, with an assessment of their value relative to present state.[30] The standard of comparison that emerges must be mapped onto the current self-image along with the present affective level. This is a complex act of self-representation. An infantile or narcissistic subject who cannot form a realistic view of the self in relationship to the world – and, thus, formulate realistic goals – will not be capable of properly carrying out adaptive hedonic self-regulation.[31] All of this figures in the way that children undergo socialization – that is, learn to modulate their hedonic experiences toward longer-lasting and stable positive affects.

[27] Eisenberg et al., "Effortful Control," 264.
[28] Walter Mischel and Ozlem Ayduk, "Willpower in a Cognitive-Affective Processing System: The Dynamics of Delay of Gratification," in *Handbook of Self-Regulation,* eds. Baumeister and Vohs, 111.
[29] James J. Gross, Maya Tamir, and Chi-Yue Chiu, "Business or Pleasure? Utilitarian versus Hedonic Considerations in Emotion Regulation," *Emotion* 7, no. 3 (2007): 546.
[30] Daniel Kahneman, "Objective Happiness," in *Well-Being,* eds. Kahneman et al. (New York: Russell Sage Foundations, 1999), 3–25.
[31] Roy Schafer, "Taking/Including Pleasure in the Experienced Self," *Psychoanalytic Psychology* 23, no. 4 (2006): 610.

Hedonic Education

In the developing world of children, adaptation can be thought of as the learning of social intelligence, the acquisition of coping skills, and – ultimately – the capacity to become well adjusted and happy.[32] One of the key tools in such a program, and a subject of intensive psychological investigation, is the child's ability to delay gratification. How do children learn to put off immediate pleasures in order to experience a greater pleasure in the future, and how does the successful acquisition of such a skill become a full range of gratifying experiences?[33]

Experimental psychologists have set up a number of scenarios to test children's capacity to defer gratification: the gift-wrapper experiment, the one-or-two-marshmallows experiment, and others. Lisa McCabe and her colleagues describe the following scenario involving Jacob, who is four years old, and Janelle, also four, along with a developmental psychologist called Maria. Maria tells Jacob, who is alone with her in the room, that she has a gift for him but that she needs to wrap it up so it will be a surprise. His job is to look in the opposite direction until told it is ok to turn. She crinkles the wrapping paper, and Jacob immediately turns to look, and does so repeatedly, although Maria reminds him that he promised not to. Finally, Maria hands him the present. Then it's Janelle's turn, and while Maria makes wrapping noises, the girl occupies herself with her sneaker laces and does not look back.

A week later, the same experiment repeats, but this time with four children (including Jacob and Janelle) in the room at the same time. Three of them cannot resist the temptation to look, and Janelle tries to remind them of the rules. But then, under the influence of the others, she, too, succumbs and looks.[34]

This sort of experiment, testing the delay of gratification skills, has been repeated in a number of variations. The original was Walter Mischel's

---

[32] Piaget, *The Construction*, 350–360.

[33] The literature on education, hedonics, and children's development is immense and old. See, for example, Arthur A. Krentz, "Play and Education in Plato's Republic" at www.bu.edu/wcp/Papers/Educ/EducKren.htm (accessed February 15, 2017). The leading researchers include Walter Mischel, Yuichi Shoda, Monica Rodriguez, Ozlem Adyuk, and others. The topic's relevance to child rearing has produced many less technical publications, such as Robert J. Sternberg, *Why Smart People Can Be So Stupid* (New Haven, CT: Yale University Press, 2002).

[34] Lisa McCabe, Marisol Cunnington, and Jeanne Brooks-Gunn, "The Development of Self-Regulation in Young Children: Individual Characteristics and Environmental Contexts," in *Handbook of Self-Regulation*, eds. Baumeister and Vohs, 340–341.

marshmallow version.[35] Mischel has been a leading student of children's capacity to delay gratification, and in the 1960s, he designed the experiment that has become the model of such studies. Children were left alone in a room with easy access to a single marshmallow, right in front of them. The researcher explained to the child that he needed to leave the room for an unspecified short time, and when he returned, the child would receive two marshmallows. The dependent variable for testing was how long the child held out before eating the one marshmallow, but this has also led to a plethora of other research tasks: What is the factor or factors that accounts for the ability to delay gratification? Can children be trained to increase the duration of the wait? How do such skills implicate the development of the child later in life? What are the broader cultural – that is, educational, political, economic and religious – implications of the psychological facts observed?[36]

The studies generated by Mischel's work have focused on a variety of dimensions. For example, it is possible that Janelle's socioeconomic, ethnic, family, or even medical background accounts for her greater capacity to delay gratification. However, these are likely significant only inasmuch as they influence a number of more salient *cognitive* skills that play a major role in the experimental situation. This has been the major assumption behind the psychological theories offered, and this will be the exclusive focus of the discussion offered here: the ability to reject immediate pleasure in favor of a greater pleasure in the future results from the development of a number of cognitive skills, which are subject to training and strengthening. Only later will this chapter focus on the social factors that interact with these cognitive capacities.

To oversimplify and generalize from the many theories that have emerged, attention control appears to be the primary cognitive tool that accounts for the ability to delay gratification. Walter Mischel and his colleagues have discovered and reported in numerous publications that delayed gratification had little to do with rewards, behaviorist conditioning, Freud's psychoanalytical theories of a reality principle overcoming a "pleasure principle" via renunciation, and so forth. The key, rather, is the capacity to tear attention away from the tempting object and keep that

[35] Walter Mischel, *The Marshmallow Test: Why Self-Control Is the Engine of Success* (New York: Little, Brown and Company, 2014).

[36] W. Mischel and E. B. Ebbesen, "Attention in Delay of Gratification," *Journal of Personality and Social Psychology* 16, no. 2 (1970): 329–337; Joanne Murray, Anna Theakston, and Anna Wells, "Can the Attention Training Technique Turn One Marshmallow into Two? Improving Children's Ability to Delay Gratification," *Behavior Research and Therapy* 77, no. 1 (2016): 34–39.

attention focused elsewhere – in a word, successful distraction.[37] McCabe and her colleagues found the same thing – Janelle playing with her shoelaces – and considered delay of gratification in young subjects as an "active engagement with a substitute object."[38]

This skill in self-distracting consists of various subsidiary capacities such as emotional distancing from seductive object, sustaining attention by means of entertainment, and maintaining focus in some fantasy or game. For example, Mischel has noted that children are able to distinguish between the "hot" and "cold" properties of the desired object and focus on the cold. In the case of pretzel sticks, to give one example, the hot, arousing properties are saltiness and crunchiness, while the cold property is the similarity of pretzel sticks to legs. A proper focus on the cold property suppresses the desire for the object. In a related but distinct direction, Eli Saltz and his colleagues have demonstrated that pretend and fantasy are effective at developing inner resources in children; they "facilitate the control of impulsive behavior" and lead to more successful delay of gratification.[39] The authors of these studies point back to Piaget (1951) and Vygotsky (1967) on the cognitive benefits of play and fantasy. In fact, according to Vygotsky (1930–1935; 1978), "sociodramatic" or pretend play helps self-regulation because "the social interactions involved lead children to internalize social norms and behaviors."[40] We shall see how important this can be in learning to enjoy complex experiences.

We have seen earlier that play represents the arousal of the SEEKING system. The capacity to direct this activation in the direction of a counterfactual, or fantasy-oriented, goal and sustain this attention is the great cultural value of games, plays, art, and so forth. The key in developmental hedonic psychology is not only that children can learn to wait; they may actually learn to enjoy the wait itself. Some of the games include skill-building elements, such as short delays ("peekaboo"), suspense ("tag"), tension and release ("hide and go seek"), or – in more elaborate fantasy contexts – the numerous ploys of culture, such as the telling of jokes, stories, and fairy tales. The use of fairy tales in child development is familiar and will be discussed shortly for the purpose of highlighting the hedonic implications. Katrina Cooper has a blog (Katrina Cooper's

[37] Mischel, *The Marshmallow*, 37.   [38] McCabe et al., "The Development," 343.
[39] E. Saltz and J. Brodie, "Pretend-Play Training in Childhood: A Review and Critique," *Contributions to Human Development* 6, no. 1 (1982): 97–113; E. Saltz, D. Dixon, and J. Johnson, "Training Disadvantaged Preschoolers on Various Fantasy Activities: Effects on Cognitive Functioning and Impulse Control," *Child Development* 48, no. 2 (1977): 367–380.
[40] Quoted in McCabe et al. "The Development," 349.

Psychology of Fairy Tales Blog) in which she explores the various psychological functions of fairy tales.[41] She cites Saltz's study and states:
"Research examining preschoolers who acted out fairy tales found that
these children developed greater capacities for delayed gratification than
those who simply listened to a story, discussed a story, or engaged in a non
fairy-tale related task."

The psychological skills I have been discussing are basic to human
adaptation – especially social adaptation – and to flourishing. Any healthy
culture depends on these and must cultivate them creatively and effectively. Religion plays a key role in this process. In fact, religion can be
regarded as the cultural Everest of hedonic training. However, along with
attending to the religious use of play and mastery pleasure, it is necessary to
examine hedonic training in a more elaborate manner as an intermediate
step. I call this process "enjoying complicated pleasure," but in the present
context, I will focus exclusively on fairy tales and on food-taste acquisition.
This will follow the discussion of religious-hedonic training.

Learning Religious Pleasure in Childhood

One of the best places to observe and study the way religious instruction
and moral development combine with a variety of hedonic techniques is
Sunday School, or in the case of Judaism, Hebrew School. Although these
are the institutions where early religious knowledge and values are trans-
mitted, the fact that the pupils are young children demands a close
attention to a systematic consideration of hedonic psychology. All three
forms of pleasure – novelty, mastery, and play are extensively utilized in
the service of early religious education. In the process pleasure itself
becomes elevated.

An excellent theoretical overview of the philosophy and psychology that
undergird these themes can be found in Barbara L. Rossoff's essay "Practical Application of Child Development Theory in our Classrooms: Overview of Developmental Theories and Moral Development."[42] Referring to
preschool children learning Hebrew, Rossoff writes that because these
children "learn well when their tactile and other senses are engaged, an
enjoyable way to help them learn Hebrew letters is to have them form the

---

[41] http//psychologyoffairytales.wordpress.com (accessed July 22, 2016).
[42] Barbara L. Rossoff, "Practical Application of Child Development Theory in Our Classrooms:
Overview of Developmental Theories and Moral Development," in *The Jewish Educational
Leader's Handbook,* ed. Robert E. Tornberg (Denver, CO: A.R.E. Publishing, 1998), 223–236.

letters with their bodies, hands and legs."[43] Thus, to give a couple of examples, the letter *vav* (a straight vertical line) only requires one child standing with hands against her body while the letter *shin* (one horizontal and three vertical lines) needs four children, and they need to find a way to form the shape with their body in space. For instance, they may lie down on the floor or mat, but if they tried to do this standing, the result would be uproarious. Such activities require cooperation, attention to others, following instructions and imagination. They are playful and fun.

Where the subject, still in Hebrew School, is history, the teachers still do not abandon enjoyable methods. Biblical stories are often used, and they provide both enjoyment and religious/moral instruction. Maxine Segal Handelman, in *Jewish Every Day: The Complete Handbook for Early Childhood Teachers*, is methodical in relation to this point: "Be creative in your telling ... Study the story at hand, hone your storytelling skills, and give a dramatic telling."[44] Dramatic implies both method of presentation and sequence. If the story begins placidly, leads to a crisis and resolves at the end with a dramatic denouement, reversing the sequence of events in the narration removes the drama and diminishes the pleasure of listening. Handelman adds: "Ask the children questions as you tell the story, to get them to interact and think" (80).[45] The use of props such as hand puppets, theatrical stage, kerchiefs and so forth are highly encouraged for these young ages.

An example of the way such techniques might apply to a specific text can already be seen in the 1918 book by Eva Landman, *A Kindergarten Manual for Jewish Religious Schools*, in regard to several biblical stories.[46] For instance, the story of Joseph's interpretation of Pharaoh's dreams (Genesis 41) about the fat and thin cows is a staple of Jewish culture. The biblical narrative is quite complex and traditional Jewish commentaries have picked out a fairly substantial number of themes to discuss. The Hebrew School version – as Landman presents it – begins in the manner a fairy tale: "Once up a time ..." The tale skips most of the biblical details (the seduction attempt, the imprisonment, the narrative that brought Joseph to Egypt, etc.) and focuses on the dream, the interpretation and the moral lesson for the children: "The aim of the lesson is to convey to the

[43] Rossoff, "Practical Application," 228.
[44] Maxine Segal Handelman, *Jewish Every Day: The Complete Handbook for Early Childhood Teachers* (Denver, CO: A.R.E. Publishing, 2000), 80.
[45] Handelman, *Jewish Every Day*, 80.
[46] Eva Landman, *A Kindergarten Manual for Jewish Religious Schools* (Cincinnati, OH: The Union of American Hebrew Congregations, 1918).

children's mind the idea that people must work in order to realize and enjoy the blessings of nature, and work itself is a blessing."[47] The story communicates this by demonstrating Pharaoh's need to plan ahead and work hard now in order the overcome the crisis that the future will bring. The lesson in Hebrew School is not passive either. The children will make or bring pictures showing the blessings of nature and share these in a circle. They will create and participate in activities such as playing farmer, who must operate according the lesson that had been learned. That is, he must work hard in order to enjoy future blessings.

Psychologists (Freudian or other) theorize on the attraction and effectiveness of the story/fairy tale in a variety of ways.[48] The story entertains the young children because it teaches in an enjoyable manner that one must not be lazy and must recognize the dangers of the world outside the id-dominated personality. This is as true for a biblical story as it is for, say, "The Three Little Pigs," with its lesson about industry and planning ahead.[49] The enjoyment comes from subserving fantasy to knowledge, or as Marina Warner puts it, allowing the "dreaming" to represent the "practical dimension" of life to the child's vivid imagination. In other words, this story, like all fables, helps the child grow out of her infantile stage of life and into the next one, which requires a bit of realism along with some restraint.[50]

The role playing includes biblical characters (King David, Queen Esther) and involves bodily movement, fantasy and imagination, creativity, cooperation, playing with others, following instructions – in short, the same skills utilized in learning Hebrew letters. The moral lesson – that is, invest now for future enjoyment – is not disembodied knowledge but a pleasure to discover.

There are global benefits to this sort of religious/moral education that transcend the Hebrew or Sunday School environment. In fact, the United Kingdom government has commissioned and implemented a vast multi-year educational program that combines religious and moral instruction with hedonic pedagogical approaches. This is the "Revised Scheme of Work for Religious Education" that systematically and comprehensively

[47] Landman, *A Kindergarten*, 39.
[48] Bruno Bettelheim, *The Uses of Enchantment: The Meaning and Importance of Fairy Tales* (New York: Vintage Books, 2010). For Freudean writers like Bettelheim, the key was overcoming the enchantment of the pleasure principle.
[49] Bettelheim, *The Uses*, 42–44.
[50] Marina Warner, *From the Beast to the Blonde: On Fairy Tales and Their Tellers* (New York: Farrar, Straus and Giroux, 1995), 23.

approaches religious education for children in elementary schools.[51] The "scheme" covers Christianity, Judaism, Hinduism, Buddhism, Islam, and Sikhism (see the following diagram).

Religious Education – Long Term Planning Model							
	AUTUMN			**SPRING**		**SUMMER**	
FOUNDATION TWO	I'm Special My Feelings	Christmas (A special Baby) 1C		Jesus A Special Person in a Special Book	Easter (New Life)	Helping	
YEAR ONE	Gifts – Harvest of Hands	Preparing for a Celebration / Here Comes Christmas 1B 1C 2C		New Beginnings	Easter – Surprise!	Our Planet	
YEAR TWO	Hinduism → Divali → Festivals of Light Including Christmas 1E 3B 4A			Special Places → Christianity → Easter: Alive! 1F 2D 2B		Me and Families and Friends 1A 1B	
YEAR THREE	Responsibility	Care and Concern → Christmas 5D		Sikhism 3A	Easter	Special People: Moses and Abraham 3E	
YEAR FOUR	The Bible 3D 5C	Angels (5B)	The Shepherd's Story 4B	Buddhism	Easter: Peter	Journeys 4B	Special Places 6E
YEAR FIVE	Islam 5A 5B 6B 6D	Christmas in Art		Christianity → Easter 4C		Precious 6C	The Natural World
YEAR SIX	Christian Faith in Action 3E 5D 6A	Promises	Prophecy / Magi 4B	Judaism (2A) 6C	Easter in Art	Making choices / Memories	Living in a Global Community

The program combines knowledge of the traditions – at a level appropriate for the children's ages – with moral and emotional development. The emphasis in educational methods resembles the techniques discussed in connection with Hebrew School: play, storytelling, fantasy, bodily movement, cooperation and sharing, laughter. A checklist for a successful "learning journey" is also provided in the document:

Checklist for a Successful, Powerful Learning Journey

Excite opportunities (engaging in the learning that is about to take place, predicting, anticipating, raising learning questions, raising positive expectations);

Has an end product with clearly shared outcomes and success criteria;

Encourage learners to connect new learning to what they already know, understand and can do.

Provide learners with the opportunity to formulate and ask their own questions.

Ensures that teacher engage in skillful questioning.

Has meaning, is relevant to the learners, is authentic and applicable.

Enhanced through visits or visitors, drama, role play.

---

[51] www.wirral.gov.uk (accessed October 18, 2018).

Is challenging and involves tasks which include thinking skills, problem
    solving, collaborations, creativity.
Is multi sensory.
Is chunked into achievable steps.
Celebrates learning.
Provides time for reflection.

Several publications have emerged dealing with the religions covered in
this governmental program. Similarly, professional assessments have also
been published analyzing the effectiveness of the program's approach.
Jonathan Scourfield and his colleagues have observed that "the children
in our study expressed particular delight at the prospect of being with these
teachers whom they considered fun."[52]

An Example of Complex Pleasures – Food

While religious education for children directly links hedonic training with
cultural values, a less direct but more revealing educational program
demonstrates the link between hedonics, discipline and well-being –
including health. Teaching children to eat well beyond the salty, sweet
and fatty of evolutionary pleasure is not religious education, but a brief
review will reveal the similarities. Deferment of immediate gratification,
self-restraint, courage, proper praise, and hero modeling are instrumental
here too, and the results include the ability to appreciate complicated
(mastery) pleasure along with better-adjusted and healthier children. This
area of hedonic training belongs in a book on religion and pleasure as an
exercise in demonstrating the mechanics of cultural training for complex
pleasures – a topic that naturally extends beyond, but illuminates, religious
practices.[53]

In the domain of food training, a distinction must first be made:
many children are averse to trying new foods and foods that appear
strange, perhaps scary. This could include fruits and vegetables with
unexceptional – perhaps even somewhat pleasant flavors. This is the
first category to be considered. However, there are foods and drinks
that are difficult to enjoy due to their striking flavors, which may at first
burn the palate (chili, radish) or taste bitter (espresso, beer) or rancid

[52] Jonathan Scourfield, Sophie Gilliat-Ray, Asma Khan, and Sameh Otri, *Muslim Childhood: Religious Nurture in a European Context* (Oxford: Oxford University Press, 2013), 108.
[53] David C. Kraemer, *Jewish Eating and Identity through the Ages* (New York: Taylor & Francis, 2007); Hayim Halevy Donin, *To Be a Jew* (New York: Basic Books, 2001).

(some cheeses). In other words, the child needs to overcome an actual aversion to pain.

A vast body of literature exists that is designed to help parents teach their kids enjoy healthy foods. Many of us who belong to an earlier generation are familiar mostly with punishment – and the occasional reward: "You stay at that table until you eat your liver!" Or, "Eat that beet salad and you can have ice cream!" These may force or induce the child to eat, but they do not train her to enjoy liver or beet salad – on the contrary; these will become trouble food for life, and ice cream becomes the object of emotional eating. Today's parents have a wide array of aid books and one of the best is Karen Le Billon's *French Kids Eat Everything*.[54] The author discovered that French children eat healthier and more diverse foods than American children and enjoy them thoroughly. Her book is rich with tips and advice – much of it based on psychological research. A brief list of some of her tips includes the following:[55]

- "If your kids don't like something, encourage them to believe that eventually they will."
- "Research shows that it will take them up to a dozen or more tastes before they consent to eat something new. This is normal: don't rush to make assumptions."
- "Older children who like to eat well have a magical influence on my children. Invite them for dinner."
- "Eating is more than an essential physical act. It should also be a shared social event, in which children experience a sense of pleasure, discovery and well-being."
- "No TV, radio, phones, or other electronic devices: mealtime is family time."
- "Encourage children to focus on food as a source of sensory pleasure ... Teach children to use words to describe food."
- "Try 'logical consequences' rather than punishments ... framing dessert as a reward ... may encourage children to devalue or even dislike vegetables."
- A child's refusal to eat should not be met with anger or drama but a calm indifference. To avoid hunger the meal should include one healthy item that the child already enjoys.

[54] Karen Le Billon, *French Kids Eat Everything* (New York: Little, Brown Book Group, 2012); See also Donin, *To Be*, 101.
[55] Le Billon, *French Kids*, 215–224.

- "Don't offer new foods unless you are in a sufficiently relaxed mood, and sufficiently attentive and available, to make the experience pleasant for both you and your child."

Le Bilion's suggestions are consistent with other popular sources. For instance, a recent issue of *Parade* magazine suggests making peeled carrots easily available and making sure potato chips are nowhere to be found. This sounds like weight-loss advice for adults, but the technique basically works. If your kids do not get a hold of chips at school, they probably will learn to enjoy the crunchiness of carrots. But *French Kids* offers dozens of additional suggestions and thorough explanations, in addition to personal and anecdotal examples, for the effectiveness of this approach. It is important to note that the goal is not only healthy children but happy individuals who appreciate a great source of pleasure. The author understands that the successful path to that goal must be enjoyable, just as religious educators understand that teaching religious and moral lessons must be enjoyable. Both Le Billon and the religious educator also understand that the enjoyment of the educational process demands of the child increasing self-restraint and deferment of immediate gratification, attentiveness to and cooperation with others, learning from worthy models, courage, imagination, and so forth.[56]

The matter of painful foods and drinks is somewhat different and has received interesting attention from academic psychologists like Paul Rozin. Some of the mechanisms whereby children learn to enjoy such foods – even without the active participation of parents, are outlined next. They range from the familiar to truly esoteric-sounding processes: The familiar and perhaps most common is taste masking. We call this the Starbucks or the Salad Bar Syndrome. How do you get kids to enjoy a bitter drink like coffee or to eat vegetable salad? You add milk and oversweeten the drink, and you drown the vegetables in ranch dressing. A first-time visitor to an American restaurant would have to conclude that Americans detest lettuce, cucumbers, and tomatoes and that plain coffee is something that only detectives on television drink, while making a sour face. Others are more technical:

- Benign masochism or play: This is a daunting technical term for a method uncovered by food psychologists.[57] You could call it

---

[56] Melitta Weiss Adamson, *Food in Medieval Times* (Westport, CT: Greenwood Press, 2004), 194.

[57] Paul Rozin, "Preadaptation and the Puzzles and Properties of Pleasure," in *Well-Being*, eds. D. Kahneman et al., 109–133; Paul Rozin and Deborah Schiller, "The Nature and Acquisition of a Preference for Chili Pepper by Humans," *Motivation and Emotion* 4, no. 1 (1980): 77–101.

"pretending is fun," and it works even for painful behaviors like eating hot chili. It works like this: Think for a moment about riders on a scary roller coaster or an audience at a horror movie (probably the same people). What causes their thrill? It is precisely the various sensations of falling, losing control, extreme speed, perhaps even struggling with nausea. Toss these same people out of an airplane without a parachute or put them in a runaway train, and these very same feelings would be truly horrifying. But knowing that they are safe, these paying customers enjoy the thrill. In terms we have used earlier, fantasy must be consciously distinguished from reality. According to several psychologists of food, especially Paul Rozin, the same principle accounts for the way children (young teenagers) come to enjoy spicy goods, and it may apply to frightening foods such as sushi or crab as well. A child learns to enjoy the burn of the chili because it is a safe pain, and experiencing it demonstrates mastery over childish fear. Benign masochism demonstrates a cognitive, attentional, and emotional mastery, through the use of reason or due to social motives, over emotions such as fear.

- Opponent process: This term sounds even worse than the previous one; not surprisingly, the two are related. The behaviorist R. L. Solomon discovered this mechanism in 1980, and what he described is a perfect illustration of the possibilities hidden within biological adaptation.[58] Unlike benign masochism, in which thinking tells the chili eater that it is safe to feel the burning sensation, opponent process describes the way the eater enjoys not the painful or frightening features of the food but the way the body responds to it — or any other source of threatening stimulation. Think of a dog in the bed of a pickup truck as it rounds a corner. The g-force seems to push against the dog, and he has to shift his weight. The first force is process (a), and the response is process (b), the opponent process. As we respond to new stimulations such as thirst, noise, sour taste, the body generates various responses aimed at restoring the body's original balance. A sour apple or hot chili makes your mouth salivate in order to cool down. Solomon suggested that we can train ourselves to enjoy the response (b) and even magnify

---

[58] R. L. Solomon, "The Opponent-Process Theory of Acquired Motivation: The Costs of Pleasure and the Benefits of Pain," *American Psychologist* 35, no. 8 (1980): 691–712; see also Daniel Berlyne, *Aesthetics and Psychology* (New York: Appleton-Century-Crofts, 1971). See also G. Beauchamp and Owen Maller, "The Development of Flavor Preference in Humans: A Review," in *The Chemical Senses and Nutrition*, eds., Morley R. Kare and Owen Maller (New York: Academic Press, 1977), 292–315.

it. With spicy food, the pleasure comes not from the burn but from magnifying the body's response to the burn –namely, the cooling-down process. Usually, the cooling effect is achieved with a cold beer or a soda that makes the spicy chili more enjoyable.[59]

To give a different example: Skiing gives distinct types of pleasure. One is the extended falling, which feels good because the body's response to falling is adrenaline, heavy breathing, and rapid pulse – the "rush." The opponent process is the mastery over the skills that keep the body upright and under control in response to gravity and speed. These considerations are extremely important in understanding H. G. Gadamer's discussion of play, which will be utilized extensively throughout this book.

A Note on Pleasure and Religion

This chapter has summarized some of the science that accounts for pleasure as an adaptive phenomenon. It has also covered some of the psychological studies that explain the relationship between the three (adaptive) types of pleasure – novelty replenishment, mastery, and play – and their role in hedonic training. In other words, we have seen how the simple biopsychological urge to approach or avoid certain objects or situations can be complicated by either the suppression of such urges at some times or their arousal at other times and how both suppression and arousal can be learned, controlled, and productive of long-lasting satisfaction.

On a certain commonsensical level, it is easy to see how "religion" can benefit by and contribute to such skills. Psychologists such as Earl D. Bland, A. L. Geyer, and R. F. Baumeister have made this connection explicitly, where "religion" is understood as overlapping with Aristotelian virtue and also as a comprehensive social arrangement regulating human behavior toward socio-theological ends.[60] Bland makes the following observation about the work of Geyer and Baumeister: "They specifically

---

[59] I suspect that this is what Roland Barthes had in mind (implicitly) with his "dialectics of desire," namely the contrast. See *The Pleasure of the Text*, trans., R. Miller (New York: Farrar, Strauss, Giroux, 1975). For a discussion, see Frederic Jameson, *Formations of Pleasure* (London: Routledge and Keagan Paul, 1983), 86–87.

[60] Earl D. Bland, "An Appraisal of Psychological & Religious Perspectives of Self-Control," *Journal of Religion and Health* 47, no. 1 (2008): 4–16; A. L. Geyer and R. F. Baumeister, "Religion, Morality, and Self-Control: Values, Virtues and Vices," in *Handbook of Psychology and Religion,* eds. R. F. Paloutzian and C. L. Park (New York: Guilford Press, 2005), 412–432. I should emphasize that the pleasure terminology discussed in my own work: novelty-replenishment, mastery and play is not utilized in an explicit way in this literature.

identify religion's tendency to set definite standards of right and wrong as a way for people to identify acceptable guidelines for behavior. Religion also provides the motivation for adhering to the standards."[61] According to Bland, religion does so by managing inappropriate desires, self-monitoring, regulating affect, and so forth.

This is important, though familiar, material.[62] But there are serious problems with this formulation, as noted already in the previous chapter. For example, "regulation of affect" can mean the inducement of guilt and with it, a scholarly emphasis on the pleasure-suppressive dimensions of religion, where pleasure is understood in a one-dimensional manner, which I have called novelty replenishment. The data cited in the previous chapter has shown that religious cultures, including literature, ritual practice, personal discourse, and so forth is thoroughly saturated with positive affect: pleasure, joy, ecstasy, satisfaction, bliss, happiness, and others. Hence, emphasizing guilt and pleasure suppression in scholarly analysis represents the continuation of a specific type of ideological discourse that is insufficiently self-aware of its assumptions and that perpetuates a western myth of the affective binary that we have seen in S. Mintz and M. Sahlins.[63] In contrast, I am arguing that religious affective regulation is not pleasure suppression but the prolonging, deepening, and complicating of pleasure for specific and highly adaptive purposes.

Furthermore, there is another, more difficult problem in the linking of virtue ethics – "affect regulation" in these studies – and religion, at least in the way that psychologists have presented the matter. Students of religion in the wake of Jonathan Z. Smith's work,– and that of Wayne Proudfoot, Russell McCutcheon, Ann Taves and others – fully understand how difficult it is to define, describe, and circumscribe religious experience.[64] Is there any one type of thought, feeling, or experience that can be defined as necessarily religious outside of the historical-cultural tradition that assigns to it such a valuation? Is "religion" a conventional and constructed assessment of nothing particularly universal, other than being conventional? Or is there some experiential dimension – however subtle and

---

[61] Bland, "An Appraisal," 7.   [62] See Ara Norenzayan et al., "The Cultural Evolution," 1.
[63] See Chapter 1, footnote 22.
[64] Jonathan Z. Smith, *Map Is Not Territory: Studies in the History of Religions* (Chicago: University of Chicago Press, 1978); Russell T. McCutcheon, "Introduction," in *Religious Experience: A Reader*, eds. Craig Martin and Russell T. McCutcheon (Sheffield: Equinox, 2012); Ann Taves, *Fits, Trances and Visions: Experiencing Religion and Explaining Experience from Wesley to James* (Princeton, NJ: Princeton University Press, 1999).

elusive – that must accompany – that is, phenomenally paint – such a cultural evaluations before we can call them "religious?"

We have seen that pleasure itself eludes description; it is both viscerally concrete and conceptually ineffable. We have also seen that religious discourse is profoundly hedonic, if by hedonic we mean the broad and complex way pleasure has been presented here. Would it be entirely unfeasible to claim, hypothetically, that a significant and perhaps motivational dimension of religious experience is the recruitment of pleasure for specific ideological and theological goals? For example, it may be possible to make the following case based on what we have learned up to now:

1. Pleasure is the ratio between goal ("standard") and present state
2. Pleasure intensity can be felt but is cognitively elusive
3. Due to its linguistic ineffability, pleasure becomes falsely attributed to objects or to goal attainment in a hedonic attribution error, while the true cause, which is the ratio, remains ignored.

Imagine now that the goal is God, pilgrimage, or words of a spiritual master. According to this hypothesis, the pleasure felt by the religious individual is attributed to the divine being, the ritual, or the sacred words, while a psychologist would attribute it to a more complex adaptive process. That would mean that the hedonic discourse we find in religious literature is due to an enormously influential factor that lies just below the level of conscious awareness. Since such pleasure is an aspect of religious discourse, it would be extremely beneficial to understand how the nonconscious adaptive process made its way into cultural religious discourse in all the major religions and what this process consists of. I will not pursue this inquiry just yet; there is too much work to still to accomplish. For instance, what is still missing in this hypothetical construct (1, 2, and 3 stated earlier) is, 4. This is a theory of self: In order to properly explain "religious pleasure," we still need to examine the way that the religious individual is theoretically conceptualized as the agent of actions and the recipient of consequences. This theory of the self is a historical and cultural matter that must be addressed in local contexts.

Furthermore, both religious experience and hedonic regulation – mastery and play pleasure – have a strong historical dimension and must be situated in that context. What that means is that the human understanding and even experience of pleasure have changed over time. One of the most important moments in this history was the Axial Age, the duration in time – mid-centuries of the first millennium BCE – in which mastery pleasure emerged as an explicit theory of positive affect. The theory of an active self emerged as the agent who controls, indeed authors, such pleasure. In more technical terms, some aspects of episodic pleasure became understood as dispositional phenomena – a product of self-psychology. This is the topic of the next chapter.

CHAPTER 3

The Discovery of Mastery Pleasure

Introduction

The previous chapters explained some of the reasons that pleasure is theoretically and popularly misconstrued. I offered an alternative classification system for sorting out the types of pleasure: novelty replenishment, mastery, and play. All three are grounded in human biology, but all three – and especially mastery and play – are largely shaped by culture. In this chapter, I will look at novelty replenishment and mastery diachronically. The question I will attempt to answer is the following: have human pleasures – for example, mastery – been subject to historical change? The answer to this question is a thesis that I will lay out and attempt to defend in some detail: Mastery pleasure – the culturally learned pleasure that derives from self-control – emerged as a theoretical construct – that is, it became the subject of conscious and systematic reflection, in tandem with the broad phenomenon that many scholars have termed the "Axial Age."[1]

This thesis needs to be stated in more precise terms in order to become operational. It is not the mastery pleasure itself that emerged during the mid-centuries of the first millennium BCE. What actually took place was the appearance in written documents of the awareness of some theory of hedonic mastery. The theory was not as well worked out as the post-Axial hedonic philosophies of Plato and Aristotle, but it was an incipient dispositional approach to pleasure and implied the recognition that pleasure is not a simple response to enjoyable external objects or events. Instead,

---

[1] My thesis builds on, but does not fully overlap with, the standard Axial Age cognitive theory discussed in the chapter. The closest resemblance is to the hypothesis of Nicolas Baumard, Alexandre Hyafil, and Pascal Boyer – who propose a change in orientation from short-term materialistic reward to long-term "spiritual" rewards: "What Changed during the Axial Age: Cognitive Styles or Reward Systems?" *Communicative & Integrative Biology*, 8 (2015), available at www.tandfonline.com/doi/full/10.1080/19420889.2015.1046657?scroll=top&needAccess=true (accessed March 10, 2019). This is consistent with A. Norenzayan et al., "The Cultural Evolution," discussed earlier. As noted in the Introduction to this book, I replace "spiritual" rewards with mastery and play pleasure.

pleasure is the product of some internal disposition, perhaps attitude, that can be cultivated and refined through training. And this disposition produces a distinct sort of pleasure: more elevated, longer lasting, and often more intense than the usual sort of pleasure or pleasures.

The Axial Age in which this significant psychological event took place is generally traced to Greece, Israel, India, and China in the primary movement and more broadly in the secondary.[2] In this chapter, I shall look at Greece and India only – with a few comments on Israel – and attempt to identify the emergence of a theory of "mastery pleasure" as a product of the Axial Age transformation. It is important to note here that many cultures and civilizations have not undergone the type of social, economic, political, and intellectual changes linked to the Axial Age: specifically indigenous cultures in the Polynesian islands (including Hawai'i), African cultures, Native American cultures, and so forth. This does not mean that the virtuous pleasures associated with self-control – such as courage, forbearance, and altruism – do not exist there. Missing is the theoretically articulated psychological awareness of these pleasures as a cultural construct and the situating of this construct within a broader salvific conception – be it cosmological or civic. Instead, the mastery pleasure remains implicit and often conceptualized in mythic terms or experienced as the desire to avoid taboo and shame.[3]

In order to make the case for this unusual thesis, it is necessary to invest some time in outlining the cultural features of the Axial Age in Greece and India. This material, based largely on secondary works (S. Eisenstadt, R. Bellah, H. Joas, H. Kulke, Y. Elkanah, J. Heesterman, and others), is familiar and will be provided in general terms only.[4] However, most Axial scholarship focuses on broad macro phenomena, including religious conceptions, while the present thesis focuses on the micro-psychological and hedonic implications. Consequently, I will spend a good bit of space summarizing the theories of Merlin Donald, Peter J. Richerson, Robert Boyd, Jonathan Turner, and others on the biopsychological development

---

[2] Karl Jaspers, *The Origins and Goal of History* (London: Routledge and Kegan Paul, 1953).

[3] Alasdair McIntyre, *After Virtue* (London: Bloomsbury, 2013). McIntyre withholds praise from the post-Enlightenment West because it overturned the Axial Age moral psychology that depended on an overarching ethos.

[4] S. N. Eisenstadt, ed., *The Origins and Diversity of the Axial Age* (Albany: State University of New York Press, 1986); R. N. Bellah, *Religion in Human Evolution: From the Paleolithic to the Axial Age* (Cambridge, MA: Harvard University Press, 2011); R. N. Bellah and H. Joas, eds., *The Axial Age and Its Consequences* (Cambridge, MA: Harvard University Press, 2012). See also the essays, cited later, of J. C. Heesterman, H. Kulke and Y. Elkana in Eisenstadt's edited volume: *The Origins and Diversity*.

of human consciousness. This will constitute the second part of the chapter. To anticipate some of this material, we shall see that the Axial Age transformation emerges in literary cultures where self-reflection and self-criticism became possible.[5]

Both Greece and India offer evidence of the historical moment and the literary corpus where the emergence of the so-called theoretic awareness of mastery pleasure can be traced. In both civilizations, the available initial locus for scrutiny is epic: the *Iliad* in Greece and the *Ramayana* in India. Furthermore, in both civilizations, a more deeply reflective analysis of hedonic psychological states emerges in proximate centuries. In Greece, it is the pre-Socratic thinkers (Prodicus and Democritus) and, in India, the Upanishads and early Buddhist texts. The epics depict the initial appearance of the self-questioning hero while the theoretical texts reveal the reflection on a newly conceived subjective, moral interior that enables self-control in pursuit of highly valued and impersonal goals.

The Axial Age

The Axial Age breakthrough is largely associated with Karl Jaspers's *Vom Ursprung un Ziel der Geschichte* (1949), translated as *The Origin und Goal of History*. Jaspers identified the middle of the first millennium BCE as a turning point, an axis, in terms of social, intellectual, and spiritual history. "Man as we know him today, came into being" thanks to figures such as Confucius, Buddha, the Hebrew prophets, and the Greek philosophers.[6] Jasper's work followed on the heels of Max Weber, Max Scheler, and Georg Simmel – who argued not only for a turning point but for sequential evolutionary stages of human cognition.[7]

The theory of the Axial Age breakthrough has been taken up by numerous later scholars, but few have explained it as systematically as Shmuel Eisenstadt and, most recently, Robert Bellah and Hans Joas. Eisenstatdt was particularly well suited to explore this phenomenon

[5] Daniel A. Mullins, Harvey Whitehouse, and Quentin D. Atkinson, "The Role of Writing and Recordkeeping in the Cultural Evolution of Human Cooperation," *Journal of Economic Behavior & Organization* 90, no. 1 (2013): 141–151.

[6] Bellah, *Religion*, 268.

[7] In Simmel, these were instinct, instrumental rationality, emancipation from purpose, and adherence to an idea for its own sake. See Donald L. Divine, "Note on the Concept of an Axial Turning in Human History," in *Rethinking Civilizational Analysis*, eds., Said Amir Aromand and Edward A. Tiryakian (London: Sage, 2004), 68–69. The Axial Age theory remains highly controversial – as a grand historical narrative. See John D. Boy, "Inventing the Axial Age: The Origins and Uses of a Historical Concept," *Theory and Society* 42, no. 3 (2013): 241–259.

because it required bringing together teams of researchers, and it called for correlating complex sociopolitical, economic, and intellectual developments. This demanded a Weberian effort, and in contemporary terms, coordination of diverse scholars.

The sociopolitical analysis is now familiar: all the societies where the Axial breakthrough took place displayed "literacy, a complex political organization combining central government and local authorities, elaborate town-planning, advanced metal technology and the practice of international diplomacy."[8] The social transition that led to these complex societies can be described in the following terms:

> As society became more complex, religions followed suit, explicating in their own way, the enormous differences between social strata that replaced the basic egalitarianism of forager tribes. Chiefdoms and their archaic kingships require new forms of symbolization and enactments to make sense of the increasing hierarchical division of social classes in terms of wealth and power.[9]

Interestingly, it was the "competition between small states" that created the possibility for the emergence of itinerant intellectuals that functioned outside of centralized priesthoods or bureaucracies and who began to question and critique the accepted meaning of human activity and posit new ways of seeing reality. Seth Abrutyn regards these as religio-cultural entrepreneurs who "are the socio-cultural equivalent to biological mutations, and thus became the unit of adaptivity and selection; group selectionism, then, is less about the content of the cultural assemblage and more about the group's success in imposing pro-social, self-sacrificial, and effervescing relations between members."[10] The key idea that emerged

---

[8] Arnaldo Momigliano, *Alien Wisdom: The Limits of Hellenization* (Cambridge, UK: Cambridge University Press, 1975), 8–9, quoted in Bellah, *Religion*, 268.

[9] Bellah, *Religion*, xix. The scholars working in this area have been keenly aware of the differences among the axial societies (for example, Greece and Israel) both in terms of geopolitical circumstances and in terms of the nature of the axial transformation itself. See, for instance, Johann P. Arnason, S. N. Eisenstadt, and Bjorn Wittrock, "Introduction: Archaic Backgrounds and Axial Breakthroughs" in *Axial Civilization and World History*, eds. Johann P. Arnason, S. N. Eisenstadt and Bjorn Wittrock (Leiden, the Netherlands: E. J. Brill, 2005), 125–126. Nicolas Baumard, Alexandre Hyafil, Ian Morris, and Pascal Boyer argue that economic development ("energy capture") was more influential on the timing of the Axial Age than political complexity or population size: "Increased Affluence Explains the Emergence of Ascetic Wisdom and Moralizing Religions," *Current Biology* 25, no. 1 (2015): 10–15.

[10] Seth Abrutyn, "Religious Autonomy and Religious Entrepreneurship: An Evolutionary-Institutionalist's Take on the Axial Age," *Comparative Sociology* 13, no. 2 (2014): 108. According to Abrutyn (109), the failure of achieving the Axial transformation (in places like Egypt) was the elimination of that social class of potential entrepreneurs (priests).

among the "new type of intellectual elite" was the becoming aware of the necessity to "actively construct the world according to some transcendental vision."[11] Among Axial societies, this resulted in the "emergence, conceptualization, and institutionalization of a basic tension between the transcendent and mundane orders."[12] The Axial breakthrough implied the emergence of competing, alternative visions, social protest, reform, and so forth. This was "closely related to the development of a high degree of "second-order" thinking, which is a reflexivity turning on the basic premises of the social and cultural order."[13]

If the link between sociocultural development and the notion of transcendence is valid, there had to have been significant psychological-hedonic implications to this breakthrough, which will be explained later. Eisenstadt has noted, "purely personal virtues, such as courage, or interpersonal ones, such as solidarity, were taken out of their primordial framework and were combined, in different dialectical modes, with the attributes of resolution of tension between the transcendental and mundane orders. In this way, a new level of internal tensions in the formation of personality were generated."[14] This is precisely the domain of the Axial breakthrough that this chapter explores, and it analyzes the new ways of conceptualizing religious and social motivation along with the psychological rewards which are experienced as mastery pleasure.

India and Greece

The conditions described by Eisenstadt and others apply to a significant extent in the case of India's Axial Age breakthrough. According to Hermann Kulke's formulation: "a dramatic socio-political and intellectual transformation" took place, which "culminated in the 'urbanization' of the Ganges Valley, the simultaneous rise of the first historical kingdoms, and the teachings of the Buddha."[15] The evidence in India for the demographic, economic and ecological changes is scant and ambiguous, coming mainly from the late Rigvedic books (circa 1000 BCE) and the

---

[11] Eisenstadt, *The Origins*, 1.   [12] Ibid.
[13] Ibid., 11; non-Axial societies also evolved cooperative institutions via religious and ritual practices, but without the transcendental visions (and, I think, without the accompanying theories of self and the virtues that accompany that self). See Edward Slingerland, Joseph Henrich, and Ara Norenzayan, "The Evolution of Prosocial Religions" in *Cultural Evolution: Society Technology, Language and Religion*, eds., P. J. Richerson and M. H. Christiansen (Cambridge, MA: MIT Press, 2013), 335–348.
[14] Eisenstadt, *The Origins*, 5.
[15] H. Kulke, "The Historical Background of India's Axial Age," in *The Origins*, ed., S. Eisenstadt, 374.

Brahmanas. Scanter material yet can be gleaned in the early Upanishads. The evidence points to a society that was still mostly rural, consisting of pastoralists and the beginnings of settled farming. Still, Kulke notes: "The texts clearly depict a protracted process of detribalization or 'territorialization' of the tribes and the beginning of social stratification."[16]

This was accompanied by the emergence of small kingdoms in which social stratification reflected the increasing specialization of the priestly class (Brahmins) and an authoritative order in which the role of the king had to be legitimized by the ideology expressed by Brahmins. This late culture of the Brahmanas still did not represent the Axial breakthrough, merely its prelude. As Bellah puts it: "The sacrifice is still embedded in the social world – status is almost everything and the purpose of the rituals was most frequently the improvement of status within a fixed hierarchy."[17]

The Axial breakthrough, with its idea of a transcendental order or reality, would have to come from a class of marginal social elite rather than the establishment. This would have to be the renouncer who abandons the social system with its status and rewards: "The carriers of this breakthrough were renouncers who opted out in a radical strife for a transcendental solution" to the sociopolitical tensions."[18]

Although many scholars point to Buddha as the great exemplar for the Axial Age breakthrough in India, the early Upanishads already hint at the existence of such individuals and clearly elaborate the new conception of reality as Brahman and *atman*. However, it was due to the opening up of the esoteric insight of the Axial breakthrough by the institutional work of Buddhism – and, most effectively, the administration of the Buddhist emperor Ashoka – that the Brahminical establishment as seen in texts such as *Manusmriti*, combined the transcendental values of the Axial transformation with the establishment values of law and order. This was India's secondary breakthrough, and it reflected the enormous impact on such values depicted by the older Sanskrit epics: *Mahabharata* and *Ramayana*. Indeed, a reading of the *Ramayana's* major characters and episodes reveals the "fault lines" of the transformation from pre-Axial archaic society and values all the way to the secondary breakthrough where the

[16] Ibid., 378.
[17] Bellah, *Religion*, 508. See also J. C. Heesterman, "Ritual, Revelation," in *The Origins*, ed., S. Eisenstadt, 395; Damodar Dharmanand Kosambi, *An Introduction to the Study of Indian History* (Bombay, India: Popular Prakashan, 1975), 144–184; Romila Thapar, *Early India: From the Origins to AD 1300* (Berkeley: University of California Press, 2004), 124.
[18] Kulke, "The Historical Background," 390.

Upanishads' esoteric values had become transformed into the social virtues of dharma. This reading will take place later in the chapter.

As in India, the Greek Axial breakthrough was no single event. It was a gradual process with at least three major moments: the development of linear B script (1450 BCE), the Homeric literary production (eighth century BCE), and finally, the philosophical developments that predated Plato in the fifth century BCE.[19] The sociopolitical and economic conditions that drove the breakthrough were also protracted. Some resembled the Indian scene when tribes evolved into city-states, the emergence of organized and relatively hierarchical social units, and the emergence of specialized elites. Other changes did not resemble India at all: for example, high population density, distinct center–periphery relations, intense competition, and international connections.

The first of the two Greek Axial developments was philosophical-scientific, which parallels the transcendental-psychological, moksha-oriented transformation in the Upanishads of India. The second development, which parallels the secondary – dharma – transformation in India, was political and the two did not converge into a comprehensive "coherent map with full-fledged institutional implications."[20] The Homeric deities were not eliminated but transformed into symbols of legitimation of the political and social order of the city-state. Eisenstadt notes that "the development of fully autonomous moral conceptions, transcending the existing social and institutional orders was here, as compared with other Axial Age civilizations, relatively limited."[21]

What that means is that authority did not necessarily shift from the "bearers of office in society: scribes, priests, kings, etc." to some transcendental element such as a supernatural Being or a transcendental order. In other words, no theological conception developed to resolve the new tensions that emerged in the social fabric by means of some transcendental soteriology. On the other hand, a strong and sophisticated second-order thinking – that is, thinking about thinking – emerged in philosophical and moral domains. It is there, even in pre-Socratic times, that questions of agency, motivation, virtue, and goodness develop in a systematic way with hedonic implications.

---

[19] Yehudah Elkana, "The Emergence of Second-Order Thinking in Classical Greece," in *The Origins*, ed., S. Eisenstadt, 45.

[20] Eisenstadt, *The Origins*, 30.   [21] Ibid., 35.

The Axial Age Breakthrough and the Human Mind

The Axial Age theory interests students of religion because it appears to explain the emergence of transcendental conceptions that have dominated the great religions of the world to this day. These include the idea of an entirely Other divine Being or Order, which created or upheld mundane reality but exists in a state of distance or tension with it. The meaningful religious life consists of attempting to bridge this gap or resolve the tension and that accounts, in a general sense, for the great religious soteriologies. Sociologists have been interested in this theory because of the way that religions have helped in organizing worldly affair in a rational attempt to bridge that gap or an irrational attempt to escape the tension by opting out of worldly affairs.[22]

However, the psychological dimensions of the Axial breakthrough have not received the same level of scrutiny until recent times. In his own overview of the Axial Age theory, Robert Bellah has introduced the evolutionary-psychological work of Merlin Donald on the history of human consciousness.[23] This adds a new dimension to our ability to appreciate the psychological underpinning as well as consequences of the Axial breakthrough. Cultural-evolutionary theories are particularly useful in helping us understand the psychological characteristics of near-Axial Age literary figures such as Achilles, Hector, Rama, Ravana, Valin, and others.[24] Furthermore, these theories will allow us to conceptualize the rise of hedonic psychology and philosophy and, more concretely, the relationship between hedonic psychology and both ethics and soteriology. It is essential, then, that such theories receive a brief overview.[25]

The thrust of Donald's argument is that the human mind has evolved over the past two and a half million years in a number of major cumulative

---

[22] According to Max Weber, this rational order first appears in Judaism, *Ancient Judaism*, trans., Hans Gerth and Dan Martindale (New York: Free Press, 1952), 206.

[23] Merlin Donald, *The Origins of the Human Mind: Three Stages in the Evolution of Culture and Cognition* (Cambridge, MA: Harvard University Press, 1991); *A Mind so Rare: The Evolution of Human Consciousness* (New York: W.W. Norton, 2002); Bellah, *Religion*, xvii–xix and *passim*.

[24] Michael Witzel, *The Origins of the World's Mythologies* (New York: Oxford University Press, 2012), 79.

[25] Peter J. Richerson and Robert Boyd, *Not by Genes Alone: How Culture Transformed Human Evolution* (Chicago: University of Chicago Press, 2005); Jonathan H. Turner, *On the Origins of Human Emotions: A Sociological Inquiry into the Evolution of Human Affect* (Stanford, CA: Stanford University Press, 2000); David Sloan Wilson, *Darwin's Cathedral: Evolution, Religion and the Nature of Society* (Chicago: University of Chicago Press, 2002).

stages. The decisive factor in this evolution was what he calls the evolutionary advantages of a "collective mentality."[26] That is, the close linkage
between the human brain and culture, which works in both directions,
has accelerated the rate of human evolution. It should be pointed out that
cultural evolution means different things to different researchers. For
instance, Richerson and Boyd define culture as "information capable of
affecting individuals' behavior that they acquire from other members of
their species through teaching, imitation, and other forms of social transmission."[27] The most basic event in cultural evolution is the acceptance of
a unit of information or cultural variant. Evolution, in this sense, is the
outcome of this aggregate process, and it is not only the group that evolves
but the individual mind too. Other researchers have offered alternative
conceptions that fall in the same general category of cultural evolution. For
example, Linda R. Caporael and colleagues oppose the reductive gene-
based approach of basic biological laws as explanations for cultural developments. They replace this with "scaffolding": "structures and processes
that help individuals or systems acquire new capacities." A greater role in
development relative to population genetics is assigned to "developmental
trajectories experienced by adaptive systems at all scales."[28]

The successive stages of the mind's cognitive development, according to
Donald, which continue to exist as cumulative functional layers in the
modern mind, are the episodic, mimetic, mythic, and theoretic.[29] These
manifest in progressive periods through changes in self-awareness, gestures,
oral traditions, theoretic artifacts, and other increasingly sophisticated
skills.[30] The initial stage places the human mind in a high mammalian
cognitive level, which includes several other species with which we share
mental capacities. It covers a range of perceptual capacities and behavioral
responses and, as we shall see later, many human pleasures represent the
function of the episodic mind as it interacts with the world.

Where humans separate from most other species, excluding one or two
other apes, is the mimetic stage: "The achievements of early hominids
revolved around a new kind of cognitive capacity, mimetic skill, which was
an extension of conscious control into the domain of action. It enabled

---

[26] Donald, *A Mind*, 259.   [27] Richerson and Boyd, *Not by Genes Alone*, 5.
[28] Linda R. Caporael, ed., *Developing Scaffolds in Evolution* (Cambridge, MA: MIT Press, 2014). See
Joseph D. Martin's review in *Acta Biotheoretica* 62, no. 4 (2014): 531–535.
[29] See L. Caporael, "Developing Scaffolds: Introduction," in *Developing Scaffolds*, ed., L. Caporael, 8.
[30] Donald, *A Mind*, 260.

playacting, body language, precise imitation, and gesture."[31] This stage in human development dates to approximately 125,000 BCE and is attested by evidence that shows a variety of new skills such as cutting stones, throwing, manufacturing tools, and, apparently, making intentional vocal sounds. These eventually led to enormous cultural and technological developments – including weapons, tools, boats, complex dwellings, and spoken language.

The third (mythic) transition began about 40,000 thousand years ago "and revolved around a revolution in the technology of symbols." The driver of these developments, Donald argues, was the "externalization of memory": modern humans can "employ a huge number of powerful external symbolic devices to store and retrieve cultural knowledge." While modern culture contains the traces of earlier stages of cognitive evolution, because it rests on the same primate brain capacity for episodic or even mythic knowledge, it has the three added layers: the mimetic, the oral-linguistic, and the external-symbolic layer. In sum, then, "the minds of individuals reflect these three ways of representing reality."[32] The later stages, for example, mythic, did not displace the earlier stages such as the mimetic. The mimetic serves a different function: it regulates the communicative body, language, prosody, and ritual life, while the mythic provides the overall mantel. The mimetic provides the cultural glue while the stories, the mythic, are the main by-products as well as "the principal organizing force, behind the classic form of human culture, the oral tradition."[33]

Mythic bodies of oral narratives influence every phase of life in their societies, and individuals model their lives on mythic figures: "Narratives,

---

[31] Ibid., 261. Mimetics means little without a theory of which gestures (or units of cultural information) are worthy of imitation and of passing on. For instance, Richerson and Boyd describe acceptance (selection) as a complicated process consisting of various modes of transmission – such as "biased transmission" (content-biased, frequency-biased, model-biased), and others. In cultural evolution, the worthwhile information is not the equivalent of Richard Dawkins's memes, which are a sort of cultural phenotype to something genetic and they are not always the product of rational choice theory. See Richerson and Boyd, *Not by Genes Alone*, 66 ff.

[32] Donald, *A Mind*, 262; Donald is only one evolutionary psychologist whose cognitive theory of consciousness and language modifies the constructivist position inspired by L. Wittgenstein, G. Ryle, and others and which has been influential in the so-called ascriptive theory of religion. Merlin Donald, "The Neurobiology of Human Consciousness: An Evolutionary Approach," *Neuropsychologia* 33, no. 9 (1995): 1087–1102.

[33] Donald, *A Mind*, 295.

especially shared life narratives, are the basis of autobiographical memory itself."[34] In combination, the mythic and the mimetic stages of cognitive development "define the self, the tribe, and caste; express how life is to be lived; and specify, usually implicitly or obliquely, what is to be valued."[35]

Donald's scheme does not deal with the Axial Age transformation, but it lays the ground for understanding certain psychological developments that impact hedonic psychology. The latest mythic stages and its product of oral literature introduced one of the significant cognitive changes in the human mind: "Literacy skills change the functional organization of the brain and deeply influence how individuals and communities of literate individuals perform their cognitive work."[36] The key was the written word. The immensely complex neural components of a literate person are acquired with great effort by "decades of intensive schooling" and are not merely the product of natural evolution. While preliterate cultures construct cultural memory by means of external symbols and mimesis in rituals, the literate cultures invent narrative-oriented stories that free up the brain to move beyond rote memorization and rehearsed performance to the domain of meaning.

This makes possible the emergence of the theoretic stage, which is characteristic of the Axial transformation: "External symbolic storage significantly alters the powers of our larger cognitive-cultural system by creating conditions within which formal theoretic systems can emerge." But again, this is a comprehensive and hierarchical system in which the theoretic "wins governance" over culture only by controlling, not eliminating, the earlier cognitive functions of the episodic, mimetic, and mythic.[37]

Hedonic Implications

It is the theoretic stage of cognitive development that made possible the Axial Age transformation. However, it may be useful here to link Donald's biopsychological theory to the theory of pleasure proposed in this chapter — and the entire book. Pleasure consists of three major behavioral-adaptive types: novelty replenishment, mastery, and play. The first type is episodic in depending on external stimuli, and it originates in Donald's

[34] Robin Fivush and Catherine A. Haden eds., *Autobiographical Memory and the Construction of the Narrative Self: Developmental and Cultural Perspectives* (Mahwah, NJ: Lawrence Erlbaum, 2003).
[35] Donald, *A Mind*, 298; Cecilia Heyes, *Cognitive Gadgets: The Cultural Evolution of Thinking* (Cambridge, MA: Harvard University Press, 2018), 2.
[36] Donald, *A Mind*, 302.   [37] Ibid., 323.

first evolutionary stage of the mind's development, the "episodic." Mastery pleasure is far more complex and changes as human social and cognitive skills develop through the mimetic, mythic, and theoretic stages. Mimetic-level pleasure points to the critical role of cultural bonds, via early forms of nonverbal communication, in the production of satisfying acts and events, which are necessary for mastery. It is group cohesiveness or the magnetic pull of social approval that would make, for example, risk taking rewarding and enjoyable.[38] In the mythic stage, a supporting narrative and ritual might come to articulate the way in which a specific culture envisions and approves of risk taking as a form of heroism, as obedience to the voice of a god or as a desire for a great reputation. As the agent, in the late mythic stages – in Bellah's terms, "mytho-speculative" – begins to internalize mythic models, to experience himself in narrative terms, the notion of a goal that justifies the means becomes very meaningful. This is a necessary step in the internalization of cultural values, which is the fount of self-discipline. Without these, mastery pleasure is inconceivable.

In the theoretic stage, the pleasure of risk becomes conceptualized in enormously complex ways that may be expressed in terms of internal motives such as virtue, self-sacrifice, or service to a higher calling. Similar changes alter the way that play pleasure evolves with the increasing complexity of culture and mind. The key change here, as in mastery, is the emergence during the Axial transformation of dispositional theories of pleasure, which open up new ways of understanding the self as agent, the goal of action or soteriology, and – perhaps most importantly – emerging techniques of self-control, which became virtue ethics. These three features of the new hedonics were deeply influenced by the changes of the Axial Age.

As previously noted, Robert Bellah links his analysis of the Axial Age to Donald's theories. The key element is the critical importance of external memory in the emergence of modern human cognition and, more specifically, the progress from graphic invention to script and to literate culture. Bellah identifies Greece as the location where this took place and considers the theoretic stage as the culture where "reflection for its own sake" takes place.[39] This is the same phenomenon that Elkanah identified as "second-order thinking" in his contribution to Eisenstadt's volume on the Axial

---

[38] Gregory Berns, *Satisfaction: Sensation Seeking, Novelty and the Science of Finding True Fulfillment* (New York: Henry Holt & Company, 2005), 82–83; J. Richard Eiser and Russell H. Fazio, "How Approach and Avoidance Decisions Influence Attitude Formation and Change," in *Handbook of Approach*, ed., A. Elliott, 326–327.

[39] Bellah, *Religion*, 273–274.

Age (previously cited). This is not the emergence of rational thinking but the reflection on thought itself. Structurally, it replaces the cognitive function of narrative thinking by positing abstract or theoretical entities as part of the computational process.[40] Conceptually, in thinking about the acting person, about society, and about the cosmos, such modes of cognition led to the Axial insights: "Transcendental breakthrough occurred when in the wake of second-order weighing of clashing alternatives there followed an almost unbearable tension threatening to break up the fabric of society, and the resolution of the tension was found by creating a transcendental realm and then finding a soteriological bridge between the mundane world and the transcendental."[41]

It is this sort of development that makes the hedonic emergence of true mastery pleasure possible. If the early stages of mastery are about restraining the self on behalf of social approval, the axial-stage mastery is now about self-restraint on behalf of a soteriological telos.[42] In fact, the Axial Age revolutionary may actually be the person who derives a deep sense of gratification from going against social or conventional approval. For example, in the Upanishads and early Buddhism, this would be the pleasure of renunciation and, joined with play pleasure, the supreme joys of moksha and nirvana.

Bellah adds an intermediate cognitive stage between the mythic and theoretic, which he calls "mythospeculation." The term comes from Eric Voegelin in reference to modes of thinking that are still deeply steeped in the materials of the cosmological myth.[43] The reference comes from Egypt – an interesting Axial Age precursor where mythical thinking at its most sophisticated and theoretical levels were attained without becoming fully theoretic.[44] That is, the theoretic in Greece and India eventually abandoned the mythical-theological symbols in favor of fully abstract theoretical concepts. In Greece, Hesiod's *Theogony* and *Work and Days* are excellent examples of this.[45] The mythotheoretical stage was universal

[40] See J. Bruner, *Actual Minds, Possible Worlds* (Cambridge, MA: Harvard University Press, 1986), xiii and W. James, *Writings, 1878–1899* (New York: Library of America, 1992), 911.

[41] Bellah, *Religion*, 276.

[42] A. McIntyre, *After Virtue*; Roga Crisp, "Homeric Ethics" in *The Oxford Handbook of the History of Ethics*, ed., Roga Crisp (Oxford: Oxford University Press, 2013), 7. This is what N. Baumard and colleagues called "spiritual newness" – see fn. 1.

[43] See Bellah, *Religion*, 276, and citation with quote at 651 fn. 92.

[44] Jan Assmann, "Axial 'Breakthroughs' and Semantic 'Relocations' in Ancient Egypt and Israel," in *Axial Civilizations*, eds., Johan P. Arnason et al., 133–156.

[45] Glen W. Most, trans., *Hesiod, Theogony, Works and Days, Testimonia* (Cambridge, MA: Harvard University Press, 2006), xxx, xxxviii. Where it comes to pleasure/desire, the creation of Pandora

among complex but archaic political societies such as city-states and kingdoms and is easy to identify in Homeric and Vedic corpora in Greece and India respectively.

This material is relevant for the present work because of all the domains one may discuss relative to the Axial Age – such as politics, economy, and bureaucracy – religious psychology is the topic that encompasses hedonics. This is the area where conceptions of the actor emerge, along with the valued goal of action, the nature of motivation and reward, and so forth. This may be termed a "religious conception" because in pre-Axial stages of cognitive development, human psychology was conceptualized in terms that were related to divinity. Bellah discusses this stage in Egypt – among other places – and provides the following quote:

> You are Amun, lord of the silent,
>   Who comes at the call of the poor,
>   I called to you when I was in sorrow,
>   And you came to save me.[46]

It is possible to find parallels in contemporary cultures, where the poet touches on the internal state of the human mind – often in misery – as a situation of conversation with another powerful but not entirely transcendent entity. The Rigveda 10.33 is a clear example. Here the poet's patron has died and he laments:

> They scorch me all about, like cowives (like ailing ribs).
> Inattention, nakedness, and exhaustion oppress me.
> Like a bird, my attention keeps fluttering here and there.
> Like mice their tails, the cares gnaw at me,
> Your praiser, O you of a hundred resolves.
> At once show mercy to us, bounteous
> Indra, and become like a father to us.[47]

These types of religious poetry are already rich in layers of cognitive achievements, understood in terms of the stages that Donald has outlined. The relationship with god reveals a strong mimetic bond, as though he belonged in the same human society. There is an emerging conception of interiority – that is, human agency – but it lacks autonomy and

---

(and sin) was a divine response to the civilizing act of the theft of fire (*Theogony* 58:91). Before that, "humans had all good things ... delighted in festivities, lacking all evils." (112:97).

[46] Jan Assmann, *The Search for God in Ancient Egypt* (Ithaca, NY: Cornell University Press, 2001), 223, Quoted in Bellah, *Religion*, 245.

[47] Stephanie W. Jamison and Joel P. Brereton, *The Rigveda: The Earliest Religious Poetry of India* (New York, NY: Oxford University Press, 2014), 3: 1429.

boundedness; it is open both to worldly disturbances and to god's intervention. Both examples show the features of that "mytho-speculative"
stage, before the theoretic emerges and begins to formulate a clearer
anthropology or psychology in which the human and the divine agencies
are torn apart by a transcendental abyss.

In the following sections, I will look at works of literature that straddle
the wide dividing line between the mythic and the theoretic stages of
development. The first is the *Iliad*, and the second the *Ramayana*. The
focus, again, is psychology or the conception of agency and human action,
which ultimately frame hedonics. Characters such as Achilles and Hector
on the Greek side and Rama and Valin (or Ravana) on the Indian side will
be considered in some detail. The limited agenda here is to identify the
way that the mythic gave way to the theoretic in terms of the psychological
development of these characters, their virtues and vices, their ethical
attitudes and motivation. While neither text covers hedonic psychology
in any systematic way, they reflect in sharp outlines developments that
took place in their cultural background.

The *Iliad* and the *Ramayana*

The *Iliad* and ancient Greek culture in general have generated a massive
corpus of scholarly literature. There is nothing truly significant that a non-
expert can add, not even to the psychological analysis of mythological
figures like Achilles and Hector.[48] What I intend to do is apply the
cognitive scheme of Merlin Donald to Achilles and Hector in a schematic
manner. In doing so, I rely not only on the text itself (in Robert Fagels's
translation) but rather heavily on the useful introduction to that translation by Bernard Knox.[49]

Knox shows the full range of the cognitive stages of the mind's evolution, shading into each other, from the mimetic through the mythic, and
the mytho-speculative, but not quite the theoretic yet. The mimetic

---

[48] According to Donna F. Wilson's analysis of Achilles's heroic character, much of this vast corpus of
contemporary works revolves around the subject of the hero's rejection of Agamemnon's gifts. Even
the range of theoretical approaches (literary, psychological, sociological, moral, theological) is
daunting. See *Ransom, Revenge and Heroic Identity in the Iliad* (New York: Cambridge University
Press, 2002). It is not my intention to contribute to this immense project but to see whether the
interpretation offered by Knox is consistent with the evolutionary psychology of Merlin Donald.
I am under no illusion that experts in the *Iliad*, who apply psychological modes of analysis to the
character of Achilles, would find this discussion a compelling case for the usefulness of "mimetic"
and "mythic" in explaining Achilles behavior in book 9 of the poem.

[49] Robert Fagels trans., *The Iliad* (New York: Penguin, 1990).

manifests, among others, in that which E. R. Dodds called the culture of shame.[50] Shame, along with more advanced ethics, functions both in the civic bond that holds the residents of Troy together and in the warrior code that both the civic minded Hector and the equally civic minded Odysseus feel bound by:

Hector:

> All this weighs on my mind too, dear woman
>> But I would die of shame to face the men of Troy
>> and the Trojan women trailing their long robes
>> if I would shrink from battle now, a coward. (6.522–6.525)

Odysseus

> Odysseus probed his own great fighting heart:
> "O dear god, what becomes of Odysseus now?
> A disgraceful thing if I should break and run
> Fearing their main force. . .(11.473–11.475)

According to Knox, the city at that point – "The only form of ordered social life they could understand" – was still small enough so the citizens knew one another. There was a cohesiveness and mutual attachment that was still characteristic of the tribe where, as Bellah put it, "egalitarianism is a form of dominance, the dominance of what Rousseau would have called the general will over the will of each."[51] Troy and Odysseus's Ithaca were not egalitarian in the tribal sense, but status and power were not entirely differentiated either. That is where the power of shame moved warriors who had to die or risk socially debilitating shame.

On the other hand, life in a city like Troy – with its wealth, culture, and law – imposed pre-Axial psychological and moral standards: "Inside Troy, the manners of the civilized life are preserved; there are restraints on anger, there is courtesy to opponents, kindness to the weak."[52]

Compare this with the mythic way of conceptualizing the rage of Achilles toward Agamemnon – not to mention Hector, later on – and the way he avoids killing his commander, who had reclaimed Achilles' prize, the lovely Chryseis:

> Should he draw the long sharp sword slung at his hip,
> Thrust through the ranks and kill Agamemnon now?

> Just as he drew his huge blade from its seath,

[50] E. R. Dodds, *The Greeks and the Irrational* (Berkeley: University of California Press, 1951), ch. II.
[51] Bellah, *Religion*, 177.   [52] Bernard Knox, "Introduction," in *The Iliad*, trans., Fagels, 32.

> Down from the faulting heavens swept Athena
> Rearing behind him, Pallas seized his fiery hair
>
> —
>
> "Down from the skies I cam to check you rage
>   if only you will yield. (1.230–1.241)

The poet notes that only Achilles saw Athena – his own mythic way of explaining that the exchange between the hero and the goddess is a psychological event: not external, but not entirely internal either. Indeed, the rage of Achilles is the point in the *Iliad* where so much scholarship focused its interest on Homeric psychology.[53] What sort of a "self" was Achilles, and what was his relationship to the culture and society in which he lived? Even when his father Peleus, as reported by Odysseus, instructs the young to exercise self-restraint, to hold back from strife, it is in order to become honored (9.252–9.259) where honor is certainly the flip side of shame.[54] Furthermore, the rage itself in this archaic psychology is conceived in material terms: as "cholos." In Redfield's analysis, the hostility between Achilles and Agamemnon is due to this substance which, in Achilles's words, "drives a sensible man to harshness; It is far sweeter than honey pouring with one, And in the breasts of men it rises like smoke." (18.107–18.110)[55]

The gods themselves in Homer's world are distinctly mythic personalities, and Achilles, though human, is godlike in terms of the cognitive features he exhibits: the gods recognize and obey no external law or authority other than power, deception, pleasure. Zeus says to Aphrodite:

> Don't provoke me – wretched, headstrong girl!
>   Or in my immortal rage I may just toss you over
>   Hate you as I adore you now with a vengeance . . . (3.480–3.486)

And Achilles demonstrates a godlike, power-driven confidence, harboring no self-doubts, not to mention self-criticism.[56] His dear friend Patroclus died because of Achilles's quarrel with Agamemnon, but he is not racked by guilt. Instead he transfers his rage from that commander to Hector, killer of Patroclus:

---

[53] Wilson, *Ransom*, 1. This is where Julian Jaynes earned his notoriety with his mytho-neurological thesis on the emergence of modern consciousness. *The Origins of Consciousness in the Breakdown of the Bicameral Mind*, (Boston: Houghton Mifflin Company, 2000), ch. 3. No contemporary theory cited in the present work subscribes to Jaynes's ideas.

[54] James M. Redfield, *Nature and Culture in the Iliad: The Tragedy of Hector* (Durham, NC: Duke University Press, 1994), 11; John Carroll, *Guilt: The Grey Eminence behind Character, History and Culture* (London: Routledge and Kegan Paul, 1985), 97.

[55] Redfield, *Nature*, 14.   [56] Knox, "Introduction," 45–46, 53.

"Despite my anguish I will beat it down
    the fury mounting inside me, down by force (18.133–18.134)

However, Homer himself appears to be familiar with the post-mythic man, the civic individual. Hector is such a man and Achilles does finally attain the same level of self-knowledge and, with it, compassion toward others. This happens later, when Priam comes to retrieve his son's body:

He found that, overwhelmed by the sight of Hector,
Wild with grief, Priam might let his anger flare
And Achilles might fly into fresh rage himself,
Cut the old man down.

This self-awareness is new, Knox notes. Achilles can "feel pity for others, see deep into their hearts and into his own."[57] The poem thus concludes with the hero's recognition of human values that are civic – that is, social, other regarding, and dependent on self-knowledge and self-restraint.[58]

Hector is closer to the model of the Axial Age hero – that is, a man acting out of concern for his city and for others.[59] He possesses a simple introspective bent: "He probed his own brave heart" (22.117). But still, what he finds there is the old heroic shame ethos: "If I slip inside the gates and walls, Polydamas will be the first to heap disgrace on me" (22.119). Still, Hector is self-critical in a way that gods – and Achilles – are not: "Now my army's ruined, thanks to my own reckless pride" (22.122). His battle with Achilles, the chase, verbal confrontation and moments before death, the swing between Athena's deception – a mythic psychological moment that describes Hector's confusion – and his final self-knowledge. After all, Athena presented herself in the body of the brother Deiphobus urging Hector to fight. Hector realizes that he was fated to be killed, that his fate was sealed by the gods, but also that, as he meets his doom, he has the freedom to choose how to die: "Well let me die – but not without struggle, not without glory" (22.360).

---

[57] Ibid., 60.

[58] See Hesiod, *Works and Days*, 15: 89 on that archaic distinction, where the terms used are strife (jealousy) and justice and there is no theory of mastery pleasure (self-restraint) yet. But *Works and Days* (287–292) also claims that wickedness is easy to obtain, it is nearby, while excellence is far and hard to reach.

[59] Homeric excellence (*arête*), according to Gosling and Taylor, consisted of aristocratic birth, prowess in battle and the like but gradually evolved into "cooperative virtues" of the sort we already see in Hector. J. C. B. Gosling and C. C. W. Taylor, *The Greeks on Pleasure* (Oxford: Clarendon Press, 1982), 11–12. Redfield relates Hector's social identity, which he holds as the counterpart to Achilles's natural identity, to our own location as the readers of the Iliad today in *Nature*, 27–29.

In contrast, Apollo's speech to the gods about rescuing Hector's body is an indictment of Athena and Hera's vindictiveness but, more so, of Achilles's animalistic (or divine!) nature, which is not fully human: "That man without a shred of decency in his heart . . . his temper can never bend and change – like some lion going his own barbaric way." We have seen that Achilles appeared to change when he met Priam and discovered his own empathy. However, an analysis of the hedonic dimension of that exchange reveals that Achilles did not attain a truly elevated – that is, Axial – level of psychological development. After promising Hector's body back and preparing him to lie in state, Achilles concludes those solemn procedures by declaring: "Now, at last, let us turn our thoughts to supper" (24.708) and, a bit later, "Time to rest, and enjoy the sweet relief of sleep" (24.747). There is nothing in the entire exchange with Priam that suggests mastery pleasure: the satisfaction one achieves from overcoming one's rage, passions, or hostility. There is the exchange of a vast ransom, a great fortune for a dead body, the discovery of empathy, and then the novelty replenishment of a meal and a nap.

These are the sorts of pleasures that the gods indulge in. They enjoy the pleasures of the senses – gifts and food from humans, who thus purchase the loyalty of the gods (24.85) – voyeuristic enjoyment of observing human events (24.120), and the eternal pleasures of a sumptuous lifestyle (24.25). From the hedonic point of view, there is little indication in the life of gods, or in the life of Achilles, of the major Axial transformation in the psychology of pleasure that will emerge into view with the pre-Socratic thought of men such as Prodicus and Democritus in the fifth century BCE.[60]

The Indian epic – the *Ramayana* – enormously popular and influential in India, did not receive the same immense scrutiny among generations of western scholars. And, unlike Homer's *Iliad*, it is the cumulative work of a vast number of unnamed poets, bards, and scholars over a period of centuries during the first millennium BCE. There is no single Rama one could assess psychologically, no single personal vision like Homer's.[61] Here is a different literary world where the contingent features of individual personalities are absent or hidden under poetic formulas that mark individual character with broad strokes. For example, Robert P. Goldman, in

---

[60] *The Odyssey* naturally shows more human pleasures than *The Iliad*. Odysseus's visit in Phaeacia is almost Olympian in its many pleasures. See, for example, Book 9: 1–10.

[61] I am aware of the debates over the singularity of Homer's authorship of *The Iliad*, but nothing there rises to the level of the Ramayana's centuries of indisputable accretions.

discussing the linking of Rama to his brother Lakshmana, argues that the "characters appear to be to a large extent forming, together, a group which itself functions as the hero."[62] The *Ramayana* is vast, and I shall focus on a single episode from the "Kiskindhakanda": Rama's slaying of the monkey king Valin. More specific still, I will limit the material to the exchange between Rama and the dying Valin. The goal is to identify the cognitive stages proposed by Donald at a point in India's literary history where the mythic and mytho-speculative yields to pre-Axial and perhaps Axial transformation.

In Rosalind Lefeber's translation (1994), this material can be found in part 7, sargas 15–25.[63] The episode, in brief, tells the story of the conflict between the two monkeys (*vanaras*): Valin, the head of the monkey kingdom and his brother, Sugriva, who asks Rama for help. Sugriva had unintentionally blocked his brother's passage out of a mountain into which the latter had chased a demon. Assuming that Valin was dead, Sugriva had taken over the kingdom. But Valin was very much alive, and on his return, he exiled Sugriva and took the younger brother's wife as his own. Readers and listeners who are familiar with the *Ramayana* immediately recognize the reverse parallel to Rama's own situation with regard to his own brother Bharata. While both Rama and Bharata were glad to relinquish the throne for a higher principle – that is, honoring promises, respecting an elder, and observing civic order – the monkeys have not separated status from power in kingship or desire from principle in marriage. Rama shoots Valin from a hidden spot, and as the monkey king lies dying, the two debate this act. Valin makes an accusation that Rama was born into a royal and Kshatriya family renowned for virtue (dharma) and violated these norms:

> Conciliation, generosity, forbearance, righteousness, truthfulness, and courage, as well as punishment of wrong doers are the virtues of kings, your majesty . . .
> But you, instead, care only for your own desire. You are wrathful, unsteady, confused about your royal functions, and interested only in shooting your arrows.

[62] Robert P. Goldman, "Rāmaḥ Sahalakṣmaṇaḥ: Psychological and Literary Aspects of the Composite Hero of Vālmīki's *Rāmāyaṇa*," *Journal of Indian Philosophy*, 8 (1980), 150 [149–189].
[63] Rosalind Lefeber trans., *The Rāmāyaṇa of Vālmīki: An Epic of Ancient India, Kiṣkindhākāṇḍa* (Princeton, NJ: Princeton University Press, 1994), IV: 84–107.

You have no reverence for what is right, no settled judgment concerning statecraft; and because you are addicted to pleasure, you are driven by your passions, lord of men.[64]

While Valin entirely mischaracterizes Rama's character and values, he correctly identifies the morality of kings.[65] In fact, his description is an apt definition of the Axial Age polity in which the status of royalty is separated from its power and the primary virtues of rulers involve restraint.[66] This stands in contrast to the clan or tribe where strength, and viciousness, rule. In other words, Valin painted the mirror image opposite of his own *vanara* world. And so, Rama responds:

How can you, who do not understand righteousness, statecraft, pleasure [dharma, *artha*, *kāma*] or even worldly conduct, in your foolishness reproach me here today?

But you violate righteousness and are condemned by your actions. You are engrossed in the pursuit of pleasures and you have not kept to the path of kings.

Learn therefore the reason why I have killed you: You have forsaken everlasting morality and live in sin with your brother's wife.

Out of lust you committed a sinful deed: while great Sugriva is alive you lived in sin with your daughter-in-law Ruma. (18.4–18.15)[67]

In other words, Valin failed to live up to the standards of dharma that bound Rama himself. Acting in pursuit of pleasure while driven by desire leads the actor to a violation of morality. Standing at the head of an animal society did not absolve him. Rama did not kill him for personal gain but in obedience to a general principle of righteousness. He stated two additional factors:

1.   "The self (*ātman*) in the heart of all beings knows good and evil" (18.15). There is an internal moral gauge that informs the actor who possesses self-knowledge.

---

[64] *Ramayana*, 17:25, 29, 30; "addicted to pleasure" is *"indriyaih kāmavṛttaḥ,"* where pleasures are objects of the senses.

[65] *The Ramayana* (1:1) lists Rama's heroic qualities in the following way: "Versed in the duties of life, grateful, truthful, firm in his vows ... benevolent to all beings, learned, eloquent, handsome, patient, slow to anger, free from envy." See also Roderick Hindery, "Hindu Ethics in the *Ramayana,*" *Journal of Religious Ethics* 4, no. 2 (1976): 287–322.

[66] Rama exhibits this quality of self-restraint more than any other character in the epic – certainly more than his father Dasharatha and his brothers Lakshmana and Bharata. The episodes with Kaikeyi – who stole his right to the throne – in book 2 ("Ayodhyakanda") reveal Rama's restraint most clearly, as he is the only character to maintain his respect for the despised woman.

[67] Wife of a younger brother is legally equivalent to the son's wife.

2. "Sins have been committed as well by other heedless rulers of the earth. But when they made atonement, that taint was removed" (18.32). Actions are subject to a universal law of moral retribution and restitution: they do not exist in a meaningless vacuum.

Rama's shooting of Valin from ambush has been the subject of spirited defenses from a variety of sources.[68] However, the best explanation is the simple one: The earliest layers of the epic describe Rama as a prince – not an incarnation of Vishnu. As such, he lacked the power to defeat Valin, who was stronger than Ravana himself but had to keep his promise to Sugriva.

The exchange between Valin and Rama highlights two primary distinctions: The first points to the king as a ruler bound by norms as opposed to the strongman chief bound by the limits of his own strength. The second demonstrates the distinction between the pursuit of pleasure in obedience to desire as opposed to self-restraint and observance of a higher law, which can be known by reason or introspection.

Gregory Alles has posited that the main conflict in the *Ramayana* is between virtue (dharma) and pleasure (*sukha*). Rama exhibits and struggles for the former while the demons act in pursuit of the latter.[69] The monkeys, too, as the story of Valin indicates, are motivated by pleasure and by passions. According to Alles, the ideal human condition is a resonance between dharma and *sukha*, and Rama finally brings this about by destroying the king of the demons – Ravana. While these observation posses merit, they overlook the fact that Rama, as an Axial Age hero, introduces a new type of pleasure. That is, pleasure in the *Ramayana* is not a monolithic concept. The old (demonic, animalistic) pleasure was sensory and driven by desire while the new pleasure, usually termed *sukha*, is the virtuous pleasure predicated on dharma or self-control. This sort of pleasure was not invented in the *Ramayana* but harks back to late Vedic psychology, as seen in the Brahmanas and early Upanishads, and it reaches its apex in the secondary Axial literature of dharma in texts such as

---

[68] Lefeber, 48–49.

[69] Gregory D. Alles, *The Iliad, Ramayana, and the Work of Religion: Failed Persuasion and Religious Mystification* (University Park: Pennsylvania State University Press, 1994), 37–41. As noted in a previous chapter, the pleasure terminology does not consistently reveal the value assigned to the phenomenon. In the *Yoga Sutras* and early Buddhism (in contrast with the *Ramayana*), *sukha* was a positive state of mind. The *Ramayana* uses a variety of other terms for negative pleasures such as *vishaya, kama,* and *indriya,* while *sukha* is also used for pleasure (or joy) as a positive affect (2: 29, 25). But even *kāma* can be positive (2: 31, 25).

Manusmriti, where the observance of dharma is the source of profound pleasure (*sukha*).[70]

Axial Age Hedonic Psychology

It is clear that pre-Axial Greek literature contained no true theory of pleasure. Aphrodite may have been the goddess of pleasure, but even Hector and Priam's limited interiority offered no quarter for self-awareness about the psychological process or events that constitute motivation or explicit hedonic reward. In contrast, by the time of Plato and Aristotle, sophisticated psychological and philosophical theories of pleasure played a major role in ethical thought. The "moment" of transition from the mythic to the theoretic, where it comes to pleasure, is hard to gauge precisely. Sorting it requires a close examination of the pre-Socratic thinkers such as Prodicus (469–399), Democritus (460–370), Aristippus (435–356) and others whose works are available in fragments, or in quotes by later thinkers.[71] A number of general and rudimentary observations apply to these men, as they do to the classical philosophers. The first is that metaphysical commitments, including an understanding of the human self or soul, inform the philosophers' view of pleasure.[72] According to Gosling and Taylor, the Pythagoreans "founded an ascetic way of life on the assumption that the real self was a discarnate soul."[73] Secondly, pleasure differed from feeling and, instead, was a distinct type of attitude. However, the most important feature of hedonic thought was its service on behalf of ethics. Because understanding the good life, the good citizen, and the virtuous man was critically important, a clear distinction emerged between two types of pleasure. In Prodicus, according the Xenophone, the two pleasures are depravity (sensual) pleasure and virtuous or civic pleasure. The former includes sights or sounds that please, scents or touches that

---

[70] Ariel Glucklich, "Virtue and Happiness in the Law Book of Manu," *International Journal of Hindu Studies* 15, no. 1 (2011): 165–190.

[71] Robert Mayhew, *Prodicus the Sophist: Texts, Translations, and Commentary* (New York: Oxford University Press, 2011); Ugo Zilioli, *The Cyrenaics* (New York: Routledge, 2012).

[72] On Democritus's view of the soul as the producer of movement, see Martha Nussbaum, *The Fragility of Goodness: Luck and Ethics in Greek Tragedy and Philosophy* (New York: Cambridge University Press, 2001), 269–270. This sort of metaphysical insight makes an appearance already in Homer. See the Nekuia of *Odyssey* 11 and the discussion in Brad Inwood, "Who Do We Think We Are?" in *The Virtuous Life in Greek Ethics*, eds., Burkhard Reis and Stella Hoffmans (New York: Cambridge University Press, 2006), 234.

[73] Gosling and Taylor, *The Greeks*, 11.

delight, and so forth.[74] In the work that defines these pleasures (*Choice of Heracles*), the hero also faces the option of choosing the course of duty and service to his city-state, and this course offers a distinct set of pleasures:

> The young enjoy the praises of their elders. The old are glad to be honored by the young. They recall their past deeds with pleasure, and they take pleasure in doing their present deeds well.[75]

The distinction that emerges here is between sensory pleasures – one might add killing in battle or enjoying one's power – and civic pleasures, which derive from social approval by city elders. Prodicus adds to this distinction another element. The civic pleasures, that is, being delighted – *euphrainesthai*, "is a condition of learning something and partaking of understanding with the intellect itself."[76] This is not only a hedonic distinction between somatic pleasures and those of the soul (psyche) – but involves a distinction between natural or spontaneous and learned pleasures.[77]

The correct choice in the conflict between sensory and civic pleasures demands the cultivation of the correct attitude, including a selection of a worthy goal – telos – and acquiring the self-control that makes its achievement possible. Hedonic psychology thus shows signs of being a proto-science.[78] This can be seen in Democritus's fragments from *On Contentment*. The author defines contentment as the worthwhile goal in pursuit of which a man must avoid going beyond his power (*dynamis*) and nature (*physis*). Even in the face of good fortune and pleasure, one must practice moderation – that is, exercise self-control toward the right sort of pleasures:

> Those who take their pleasures from their belly, exceeding what is appropriate in food, drink, or sex, to all of them their pleasures are meager and brief, lasting just so long as they are eating and drinking, and their pains are many. For this desire for the same thing is always with them, even when they get what they desire, and the pleasure soon passes, and they have no profit except brief delight; and then they need the same thing again.[79]

---

[74] Zilioli, *The Cyrenaics*, 150–151; David Wolfsdorf, *Pleasure in Ancient Greek Philosophy* (Cambridge, UK: Cambridge University Press, 2013), 13.

[75] Quoted in Wolfsdorf, *Pleasure*, 11; For a full quote from Xenophon *Memorabilia* (2.1.21–2.1.34), see Robert Mayhew, *Prodicus the Sophist: Texts, Translations, and Commentary* (Oxford: Oxford University Press, 2011), 53–59.

[76] Wolsfsdorf, *Pleasure*, 11.

[77] Wolfsdorf (*Pleasure*, 12) attributes this to Plato. That is, Xenophone's version of Prodicus's narrative was influenced by Plato and may not reflect an earlier (pre-Socratic) idea.

[78] Gosling and Taylor, *The Greeks*, 9; Nussbaum, *Fragility*, 94–98.

[79] Quoted in Wolfsdorf, *Pleasure*, 14.

In other words, sensory pleasures fueled by desire are short lived. However, the contrast Democritus emphasizes is not between passing pleasure, along with desire, and stoic suffering. Instead, he emphasizes another – better – sort of pleasure: "self-control increases delights and makes pleasure greater."[80] That sort of pleasure is self-derived and associated with "fine deeds." Walfsdorf calls these "measured pleasures," which derive from or contribute to a contented soul. The man who controls his desire, thus avoiding envy, the source of civic discord, cultivates measured pleasures leading both to contentment and to civic peace.

These earlier theories do not explain the nature of pleasure as such. There is no theory, such as Plato's, that pleasure is the awareness of change from lack to replenishment. However, unlike earlier mythic conceptions, pleasure at least involves an informed conscious choice between the body's responses to the world, which is episodic, and the goals that the soul seeks, which involves some disposition.[81] This is accompanied by an awareness that desire, which is another internal attitude, acts as obstacle to the achievement of the soul's aims, the fount of finer pleasures. There is also the awareness that self-control, the reigning in of desire, enhances these pleasures – that is, that civic-minded and well-trained individuals are those who are able to obtain the best pleasures.

The situation in India's transition from the mythic to the theoretic cognitive (and hedonic) stages both resembles and differs from that of Greece. The *Ramayana* and Rama's *dharmic* character reveal an Axial sensibility, though lacking in systematic theoretic statements. During the mid-centuries of the first millennium BCE, India produced somewhat more clearly elaborated statements on the psychological transformation in the conception and experience of pleasure. These include the Upanishads and early Buddhist sutras, though there are earlier indications of the change in the Brahmanas already.[82]

However, the earliest semi-systematic Axial treatments of pleasure in India, in the early Upanishads, assumed a literary form that makes it inaccessible to non-specialists. The two oldest Upanishads, the *Brihadaranyaka* and

---

[80] Ibid., 16.   [81] Nussbaum, *Fragility*, 94–95.

[82] An excellent but complex example is the story of Sunahsepa in the *Aitareya Brahmana*, 7.13–7.18. This is a much discussed narrative: David Gordon White, *Myths of the Dog-Man* (Chicago: University of Chicago Press, 1991), 82; David Shulman, *The Hungry God: Hindu Tales of Filicide and Devotion* (Chicago: University of Chicago Press, 1993), 87; Asko Parpola, "Human Sacrifice in India in Vedic Times and Before," in ed., Jan N. Bremmer, *The Strange World of Sacrifice* (Leuven, the Netherlands: Peeters, 2007), 164. These and other works focus on sacrifice, magical exchange, linguistic features, and so forth. However, the theme of self-restraint and mastery is clearly discernable in these works.

Chandogya, date roughly to the seventh century BCE – that is, several centuries older than both the pre-Socratics and the early Buddhist sutras. They use complex metaphors taken from the world of the Vedic sacrifice in order to report on new psychological ideas and experiences. Some of these bear on the question of subjectivity – what is the ultimate self? – on action, desire, pleasure, value, and freedom. The archaic ritual terminology hides the radically new insights, and on top of that, these are never systematically expounded. In order to simplify matters I shall glean and organize the most significant hedonic theories in these two old texts according to topic rather than textual development. This will be followed by a brief synopsis of a younger, perhaps post-Buddhist, Upanishad. This is the *Katha Upanishad* where the same ideas become more explicit. While the literary form differs radically from Greek philosophy, it will be possible to draw general observations on the nature of the Axial transformation in the domain of hedonic thought.

The *Brihadaranyaka* and *Chandogya* Upanishads draw a distinction, albeit not always clearly, between simple pleasures, which I have called episodic, and the higher pleasures of the true inner self. The simple pleasures had previously been conflated with objects of desire (*indriyani*) or, more precisely, desires (*kamani*) and are associated with a false understanding of subjectivity. The enjoyer in such cases takes the sensory body-self as the true author of experience. In cultural contexts, the simple pleasures had previously motivated the archaic sacrificial actions, which aimed to obtain satisfying results such as wealth and progeny from the gods who had enjoyed the sacrificial offerings.[83] However, with the Upanishadic transvaluation of the Vedic ritual ethos, one now sees that the sacrifice offers a clue, or even a locus, for self-restraint which is the source of ethics, a new understanding of the self, and higher pleasure. This clue is the gift (*dana*) that the sacrificer offers to the officiating priest.

With the new of understanding of the self, it becomes clear that the mind – that is, conscious intention – governs the performance of actions and responses and absorbs the consequences. This is the foundation of a dispositional understanding of pleasure. Similarly, the adherence to self-restraint that constitutes the practice of both charity and insight into the nature of self ultimately leads to an elevated pleasure that far transcends the simple pleasure of the senses. This, in brief, is the heart of the early

---

[83] There is considerable dispute on the nature and function of the Vedic sacrifice, but its transactional quality is widely recognized. See Harry Folk "The Purpose of Rigvedic Ritual," in *Inside the Texts*, ed., M Witzel, Harvard Oriental Series (Cambridge, MA: Harvard University Press, 1997), 69–88.

Upanishadic hedonic transformation. The textual evidence for it is very rich, but the following brief selection of passages from the *Brihadaranyaka* (BU) and *Chandogya* (ChU) Upanishads should illustrate this insight.

> What a man turns out to be depends on how he acts and on how he conducts himself. If his actions are good, he will turn into something good. If his actions are bad, he will turn into something bad ... And so people say: "A person here consists simply of desire." A man resolves in accordance with his desire, acts in accordance with his resolve, and turns out to be in accordance with his action. (BU 4.4.5)[84]
> On this point there is the following verse:

> > A man who's attached goes with his action,
> > To that very place to which
> > His mind and character cling. (BU 4.4.6)

It is like this. As a man embraced by a woman he loves is oblivious to everything within or without, so this person embraced by the self (*atman*), consisting of knowledge is oblivious to everything within or without.

> Clearly, this is the aspect of his where all desires are fulfilled, where the self is the only desire, and which is free from desires and from sorrows. (BU 4.3.21)
> When a man is hungry, thirsty, and without pleasures – that is his sacrificial consecration; and when he eats, drinks, and enjoys pleasures – by that he performs the preparatory rites; when he laughs, feasts, and has sex – by that he sings the chants and performs the recitations; austerity, generosity, integrity, non-injury, and truthfulness – these are his gifts to the priests. (ChU 3.17.1–3.17.4)[85]
> 'The self (*atman*) that is free from evils, free from old age and death, free from sorrow, free from hunger and thirst; the self whose desires and intentions are real – that is the self that you should try to discover, that is the self that you should seek to perceive. When someone discovers that self and perceives it, he obtains all the worlds, and all his desires are fulfilled.' So said Prajāpati. (ChU 8.7.1)

A more explicit account of the new hedonic insight can be found in the later *Katha Upanishad*.[86] In this text, a boy is sent to the world of Death, the realm of Yama, by his father, whom the boy had criticized for offering unworthy cows in sacrifice. In Yama's dwelling, the Brahmin boy is left waiting for three days due to Yama's absence, and so he is owed three boons. The third boon that Naciketas asks is the truly interesting one:

---

[84] Patrick Olivelle, trans., *Upaniṣads* (New York: Oxford University Press, 1996).
[85] "Without pleasures" is *na ramate*, from the verbal root *ram*, meaning to enjoy.
[86] Olivelle, *Upaniṣads*, 231.

"There is this doubt about a man who is dead. 'He exists,' say some; others, 'He exists not.'" (*Katha* 1.20) The question appears to be about the afterlife, but on a deeper level, this is a question about ultimate reality, the nature of the self, and spiritual liberation. Yama then goes out of his way to avoid answering: He offers the boy sons and grandsons, a long life, extreme wealth, a vast domain of earth, beautiful women with lutes and other worldly joys instead of an answer. "You may ask freely for all those desires (*kāmani*), hard to obtain in this mortal world" (*Katha* 1.25).

But Naciketas is a self-critical Axial Age person, and stubborn: "With wealth you cannot make a man content," he claims, and he explains:

> What mortal man with insight,
> Who has met those that do not die or grow old,
> Himself growing old in this wretched and lowly place
> Looking at its beauties, its pleasures and joys,
> Would delight in a long life? (1.28)[87]

So Death has no choice but to fulfill Naciketas's wish for knowledge. He states:

> The Good (*śreyas*) is one thing, the gratifying (*preyas*) is quite another;
> Their goals are different, both bind a man.
> Good things await him who picks the good;
> By Choosing the gratifying, one misses one's goal. (2.1)
>
> The primeval one (the self) who is hard to perceive,
> Wrapped in mystery, hidden in the cave,
> Residing with th'impenetrable depth –
> Regarding him as god, an insight
> Gained by inner contemplation,
> Both sorrow and joy the wise abandon
> When a mortal has heard it, understood it; (2.12)[88]
>
> When he has drawn it out,
> And grasped this subtle point of doctrine;
> He rejoices, for he has found
> Something in which he could rejoice.
> To him I consider my house
> To be open Naciketas. (2.13)[89]

---

[87] "Would delight at the pleasures" in the text is "pramodān ramet."

[88] Sorrow and joy are *harṣa* and *śoka* respectively. The former is the thrill that is accompanied by the erection of neck hairs.

[89] "Rejoices" is *modate*.

The core of Death's teaching is the existence, in the very core of the individual, of a subjective self that transcends the personality and the function of sensory perception and psychological contingencies. The knowledge of this self brings liberation and is the answer to the question of transcending death:

> Finer than the finest, larger than the largest,
> Is the self [ātman] that lies here hidden
> In the heart of a living being.
> Without desires and free from sorrow,
> A man perceives by the creator's grace
> The grandeur of the self. (2.20)

The Upanishad continues to explain the nature of this inner self and the conditions for obtaining knowledge of this self. Here the authors of the Upanishad recruited material that came from the psychology of contemporary Yoga practice:

> When a man lacks understanding,
> And his mind is never controlled;
> His senses do not obey him,
> As bad horses, a charioteer. (3.5)

In other words the key to realizing the self is discipline and control of the senses. But even choosing the good over the pleasant leads to a finer pleasure.[90] The text is very clear that knowledge of the self (atman) is a hedonic state: "The wise who perceive him as abiding within themselves, they alone, not other enjoy unending bliss (śānti)." (5.13) This sentiment repeats so frequently that it has become self-evident: freedom from the senses, from desires, from attachment to the objects of the world is not anhedonic. On the contrary, it is the highest pleasure imaginable, but a different sort of pleasure.

This material is as familiar to students of Hinduism as the ideas of Plato, if not Democritus and Prodicus, are to students of ancient Greece. However, the focus on hedonics and the comparison between the two hedonic cultures, Greece and India, offer a number of new insights. There are clear similarities and obvious differences, both general and specific. In both cultures, a distinction emerges in the understanding of pleasure between sensory or somatic pleasures and mental pleasure. This distinction

---

[90] Cf. Prodicus's story of "The Choice of Hercules": where Vice attempts to seduce the hero with a promise of (bodily) pleasures, Virtue assures him that though harder, the path of Virtue is pleasanter still. It leads to the firmer pleasures of good reputation and friendship. See Gosling and Taylor, *The Greeks*, 14.

is contingent on an emerging psychology in which the actor's self-awareness, along with his reason or understanding, are decisive and where self-control plays a critical role in regulating pleasure. Another factor that emerges in both cultures is the idea of a telos, a higher goal in comparison with which the mere satisfaction of desire is dwarfed.[91] The *Katha Upanishad* sounded almost Greek in stating that this is the "good" rather than the pleasant, but in fact, the ultimate Upanishadic telos is not ethical but psychological. It is the realization, the experiential knowledge, of the true inner self, and it is liberation from entrapment in endless births and deaths. Nonetheless, in both cultures, the discipline required to obtain the valued goal of action entails some level of self-control and brings about a distinct and more elevated form of positive affect.

Two significant differences between India and Greece should be pointed out. First, the pleasure of the self-disciplined man – using my terms for such pleasures – is mastery pleasure. It is present in both the Greek and the Hindu texts. However, the pleasure of the person who attains knowledge of self (*atma-vidya*), who is liberated, is more than mastery pleasure. It also has a strong element of play pleasure. This will be discussed in a subsequent chapter on play pleasure, where I will show that in the western religions, this type of pleasure developed in later Hellenistic cultures, in Judaism and Christianity. In other words, mystical or spiritual consciousness is saturated with a form of play pleasure.

Secondly, the Upanishadic telos based on knowledge of self, propagated by marginal elite (renouncers, ascetics) rather than the ritual elite of Brahmins, had a profound affect on the normative tradition of dharma. Thus, while Greek civic virtues did not depend on profound cosmological speculations, in India, the equivalent domain – for example, in the *Manusmriti* – was believed to be founded on the transcendental revelation of the Veda. In this secondary Axial development, India resembles Axial Israel after the Deuteronomy revolution, where the concept of covenant, or law, comes to replace the king as source of norms.[92] However, the ideological emergence of Veda as a transcendental source of norms is a secondary Axial development, taking place many centuries after the Upanishads discussed earlier. The key insight to take away from the comparison of India and Greece is the intellectual discovery that pleasure consists of

---

[91] Recall the discussion of goal or "standard" in Chapter 2, where the adaptive underpinnings of pleasure were discussed.

[92] Bellah, *Religion*, 314; see Barbara Holdrege, *Veda and Torah: Transcending the Textuality of Scripture* (Albany: State University of New York Press, 1996).

distinct psychological types, that pleasure depends to a great extent on a subjective mental attitude, and that – in controlling the mind – pleasure itself can be modulated, refined, and elevated. The hedonic product of the Axial Age in Greece and India is the addition as a cultural and psychological concept of pleasure regulation as a worthwhile tool of human development.

Conclusion

This chapter has not touched on the most obvious aspects of Greek theories of pleasure: those espoused by Plato and Aristotle, along with the Hedonists, the Epicureans, and later the Stoics. Instead, I stopped just at the emerging point of the Axial Age transformation, to which these figures belong. To be sure, one can hardly study Christian or Jewish asceticism and moral theology, which are Axial Age phenomena, without examining Greek theories of pleasure and virtue – as centuries of scholars have done. I will touch on some of this in later chapters, as I discuss mastery and play pleasure in religious contexts. However, my focus remains distinct throughout this work. I am interested in the psychological development of pleasure theory and pleasure experience as informed by scientific (adaptive) theories of pleasure. This agenda remains unexplored while the relationship of pleasure, ethics, and theology has seen countless scholarly treatments.

The Axial Age's theoretic developments allowed the elites who led the way to gain an understanding of the proper relationship between the self as the subject of enjoyable experience and the world. The full awareness of dispositional pleasure is a theory of a proper causal psychological relationship. In the absence of such a theory, the subject misattributes his experience of pleasure to the outside world in a number of very specific ways. This is a "pre-Copernican" theory of pleasure, so to speak. And it manifests in what I call a "magical culture." This will be the subject of a separate chapter, following the next.

CHAPTER 4

Philo's Mastery, Plotinus's Play, and the Mystic's Joy

The post-Axial religious and intellectual developments in the Mediterranean region represent one of the most widely studied topics in Christian history. The classical Greek philosophers followed by the Romans, the spread of Hellenistic ideas, and institutions to the Near East – including Alexandria in Egypt, the rise of new political orders, and new religious and philosophical conceptions – have occupied numerous intellectual inquiries. Relevant areas include new theories of the self, psychologies of desire, conceptions of suffering and theodicy, emerging syntheses between transcendental cosmologies, and classical ideas about ethics.[1]

However, it is necessary here to narrow the focus on the transformation and elaboration of mastery and play pleasure within the religious domain. Following the Axial transformation, mastery pleasure grew prominent in Pythagorian, Platonic, Aristotelian, and then Stoic thought. The core insight was the recognition that self-control (*enkreteia*) is a master virtue that not only leads to a good life of justice and virtue but is essential for happiness as well. This moral psychology had a major effect on early Christian thought – as historians of Christianity have pointed out.[2]

The focus here is on a new dimension that mediated between classical ethics and Christian hedonic psychology. It is a refinement of mastery pleasure with the introduction of God as a telos of virtue ethics, the subservience of self-control to that telos in place of a more naturalistic one, such as the Stoic, and the promotion of biblical allegorical interpretation as a new method for making this mediation coherent and practicable. In other words, it is useful to look at the works of Philo of Alexandria in

---

[1] Everett Ferguson, *Backgrounds of Early Christianity*, 3rd edn. (Grand Rapids, MI: W. B. Erdmans Publishing, 2003); Susan Ashbrook Harvey and David G. Hunter, *The Oxford Handbook of Early Christianity* (Oxford: Oxford University Press, 2008).

[2] Kathy L. Gaca, *The Making of Fornication: Eros, Ethics, and Political Reform in Greek Philosophy and Early Christianity* (Berkeley: California Press, 2003).

order to understand how mastery pleasure was recruited and transformed by religious thought.[3]

The scholarly work on Philo is also very substantial and diverse. Once again, the focus of the discussion here is strictly on the way Philo elaborated the theme that I call mastery pleasure. This implies a consideration of how he combined Platonism and Stoicism with Jewish theology in a way that not only ushered a new vision of religious ethics but specifically – and almost explicitly – constructed a method of controlling the desire for novelty pleasure through an elaborate regulatory method in which both mental evaluation and ritual practice played a role. Both methods served a telos that promoted pleasure of a different nature and order of magnitude from the pleasures (*hedone*) he condemned. We shall see that although the goal of a well-lived life – knowledge of and closeness to God – is only indirectly affective, this is a technical aspect of mastery pleasure where the regulating device is never explicitly about pleasure, or even happiness. It does, however, produce a heightened state of positive affect as an essential feature.[4]

Philo in Context

Although Philo of Alexandria (15 BCE–45 CE) has inspired an enormous body of scholarship, very little is known about the man.[5] His distinguished and wealthy Alexandrian family, including his brother and nephew, left a clear historical record as political and economic actors in dealings with Rome and work in Judea. Philo's remarkable influence on religious history is not about the man or his actions so much as his scholarship and massive literary output. His erudition in original Greek literature and culture and his mastery of biblical allegorical interpretation – albeit in translation – placed him at the intersection of Greek, Jewish, and Christian cultures. More specifically, Philo stands as a bridge between these worlds: a middle

---

[3] Adam Kamesar, ed., *The Cambridge Companion to Philo* (New York: Cambridge University Press, 2009); David Winston, trans., *Philo of Alexandria: The Contemplative Life, The Giants and Selections* (New York: Paulist Press, 1981); F. H. Colson, *Philo* (vol. IX), Loeb Classical Library (Cambridge, MA: Harvard University Press, 1985); C. D. Yonge, trans., *The Works of Philo: Complete and Unabridged, New Editions* (Peabody, MA: Hendrikson Publishers, 1993); David T. Runia, *Philo in Early Christian Literature: A Survey* (Van Gorcum Assen, the Netherlands: Fortress Press, 1993).

[4] The link to Aristotle's ethics is clear, but in the present terminology, mastery pleasure depends on self-restraint of novelty in pursuit of a prized goal, which is not itself necessarily hedonic. See *Nicomachean Ethics* I. a.

[5] Daniel R. Schwartz, "Philo, His Family, and His Times," in *The Cambridge* Companion, ed., Kamesar, 9–31.

Platonist – that is, Plato mediated by neo-Pythagorianism and Stoicism, who combined Platonic physics with Stoic ethics in the garb of biblical figures such as Moses and Abraham, along with Jewish transcendental theology. He fashioned a universalistic religious ethic, which proved enormously influential in patristic Christianity, specifically in the works of Origen (185–254 CE) and Eusebius (265–340 CE).[6]

Philo's work touched on numerous topics and ideas, but the ethical views that he espoused in his synthesis of Stoicism with biblical interpretation that directly bear on our theme include notions of divine transcendence, the primacy of self-control (*enkrateia*) as the foremost of virtues, and – especially – his work on the community of Therapeutae in *The Contemplative Life*, with emphasis on a description of their banquets.[7]

On the matter of God's transcendence, the pressure that developed in the life of the Babylonian Jewish Diaspora to disassociate God from concrete ties to a place, to Judea, the Temple in Jerusalem, was an old one, not the invention of Philo. The biblical references to "God in Heaven" are largely postexilic – that is, the products of that Babylonian exile.[8] In Philo's case, this impetus to delocalize God is tied to, and served by, the allegorical reading of the Bible and Judaism in general. Hence, he argued, what is grander than the Temple for God than the "vision-seeking mind?"[9]

But here, too, Philo was not the first. In fact, as we have seen in a previous chapter, the allegorical understanding of the gods as psychological entities was already ancient in Philo's time: Theagenes of Rhegium (sixth century BCE) and Anaxagoras (ca 500–426 BCE) already applied this approach to the Homeric gods in the service of psychological ethics.[10] But in Philo's case, this was a transcendental God with Platonic elements, set off against material nature, and also a universal God who is accessible to "all who practice wisdom either in Greek or barbarian lands."[11] This is important, not only as a matter of theology but the ethics that shape the work in Philo about mastery pleasure. Hence, "the virtuous man, the final

[6] Runia, *Philo*, 180–184, 227–231; the *Studia Philonica Annual* offers more than twenty scholarly articles each year including such works as David Konstan's "Of Two Minds: Philo on Cultivation," 22, no. 1 (2010): 131–138, which touches on our theme.
[7] *The Contemplative Life* (*De vita contemplative*), in D. Winston, *Philo* 41–57; Jean Danielou, *Philo of Alexandria*, trans., James G. Colbert (Cambridge, UK: James Clark & Co., 2014).
[8] Lester L. Grabbe, *Ezra-Nehemiah* (London: Routledge, 1998), 11.
[9] Daniel R. Schwartz, "Philo, His Family," 26.
[10] Michael W. Herren, "Classical Exegesis – From Theagenes of Rhegium to Bernard Silvestris" *Florilegium* 30, no. 1 (2013): 59–102.
[11] *On the Special Laws* (*De specialibus legibus*), 2.44.

product of this quest, thus finds himself in a spiritual kinship with God."[12] In other words, proximity (in mind, not body) to God is a telos, a goal, and also a gauge for one's moral and spiritual progress – along with the affective implications. But although God is more than mere allegory for a particular psychological trait, He is profoundly implicated in the supreme delight that results from success in this path.

Central to Philo's moral psychology were the concepts of human freedom and the exercise of self-control. Indeed, man was potentially above nature, although not divorced from it. Man is *methorios*, Philo claimed. He exists on the border between material and spiritual realities, between time and eternity, between evil and good. That is, although man is disfigured by sin and limited by death, he does posses the freedom of choice to be good.[13] And as a thinking being, man can attain proximity to God and to Godlike virtue.

In this sense, Philo sharply broke away from his Stoic predecessors. He argued that there was a gap between nature and the transcendent, which man can aspire to overcome. This is because man was created superior to the animals (Genesis 1:26–27). But in order to realize his superiority, he must come to know the sinful alienation from God as the condition in which he finds himself.[14] The Stoics, in contrast, posited a natural harmony in nature and man's place in nature, which could be realized through what they called *oikeitosis*.[15] This was the pursuit of a sort of self-interest, accompanied by a broader concern for the totality of existence. Thus, the Stoics viewed infancy as a natural state that is followed by gradual adaptation – according to Cicero, this was *conciliatio* – to one's true nature leading to harmony.[16] In contrast, for Philo, the infant was no such perfect natural being, and maturing was actually a move away from nature.

The psychological theory that underlies the view of human nature was elaborated in a variety of ways, including a detailed account of human emotions and dispositions, which were known as "passions." Philo

[12] Carlos Levy, "Philo's Ethics," in *The Cambridge Companion,* ed. A. Kamesar, 146–174, 149.
[13] "For nature has created all men free." *On the Contemplative Life,* quoted in *The World,* 704; See also *Every Good Man Is Free* (*Quod Omnis Probus Liber sit*). And see Cristina Termini, "Philo's Thought within the Context of Middle Judaism," in *The Cambridge Companion,* ed., A. Kamesar, 95–123, 103.
[14] Levy, "Philo's Ethics," 146–147.
[15] Ilaria Ramelli, *Hierocles the Stoic: Elements of Ethics, Fragments, and Excerpts* (Atlanta, GA: Society of Biblical Literature, 2009), xxxv.
[16] Ramelli, *Hierocles,* xxxv, xlviii; Marcus Tullius Cicero, *On Moral Ends,* trans., Raphael Woolf (Cambridge, UK: Cambridge University Press, 2001), 1995.

accepted the seven Stoic passions: four bad ones (desire, fear, sadness, pleasure – *hedone*) and three good (joy, caution, wishing). However, he modified their meaning and mutual relationship. Commenting allegorically in *Questiones in Genesim* 2.57 on Genesis 9.3: "Every reptile that lives shall be for you for food." There is a contrast there between the bad and good passions: "Alongside sensual pleasures there is the passion of joy. And alongside the desire for sensual pleasures, there is reflection. And alongside grief there is remorse and constraint. And alongside desire, there is caution."[17]

These negative passions run rampant in childhood as excitements, desires and pleasures, but they can be controlled via *enkrateia* and *kartereia* (endurance).[18] Philo did not discover these, nor did the Stoics. As noted in a previous chapter, Prodicus (465–395 BCE) made them famous in his narrative on the choice of Heracles. But one cannot avoid thinking about Freud in the way Philo applies these in relationship to the maturing process of children. And, more importantly, Philo attached them to biblical narrative and transcendental theology in the way that he allegorically interpreted key passages that allegedly represent these essential virtues.

For example, in "On the Special Laws" (Spec.) 1.8–1.11, Philo takes the biblical divine injunction on male circumcision as a sign for the elimination of superfluous pleasures. This interpretation repeats in *De Migratione Abrahami* 92, where God, the Lawgiver acting as the best of all physicians for the distempers and maladies of the soul, excises all pleasures and passions. But not only physical pleasure symbolically dissolves under the circumcision knife. It is pride, too, the pride that comes from forgetting that God Himself governs reproduction.[19] Similarly, the passion of desire, which is often viewed as the source of every base passion, receives a similar treatment under the rubric of the tenth commandment ("thou shalt not covet" [Exodus 20:17]).[20] Philo applies this to food laws which Moses legislated "to encourage the virtue of *enkrateia* (self-control)" and improve human relations by means of frugality and temperance. These same virtues, especially self-control, are also promoted by setting aside the first fruit of the season (Spec. 4.98–4.99).

---

[17] Trans., C. Levy, "Philo's Ethics," 157; Albert C. Geljon and David T. Runia, *Philo of Alexandria on Cultivation: Introduction, Translation, and Commentary* (Leiden, the Netherlands: E.J. Brill, 2013), 22.
[18] Geljon and Runia, *Philo*, 190.
[19] Termini, "Philo's Thought," 116; Levy, "Philo's Ethics," 159–161.
[20] Termini "Philo's Thought," 120.

This allegorical reading of scripture in order to wed biblical narrative to Stoic and Platonic ethics is probably the most famous aspect of Philo's work. Indeed, the identification of the matriarch Leah with reason as a precondition for the acquisition of virtue and Rachel as the struggle against the senses and irrationality represents a pillar of Hellenistic Judaism.[21] Little of this played any role in the evolution of Rabbinic Judaism in the Mishnah and Talmud, but it did profoundly influence patristic Christianity.

And Philo's contribution to middle Platonism prominently included the idea of a transcendent and reigning God. The purpose of the biblical allegory, among others, was to link this conception of divinity with Stoicism in such a manner that the ultimate goal of virtue becomes knowledge of and proximity to God. The mastery pleasure (joy, *chara* in Philo) that empirically attended the achievement of such a goal could thus be attributed not only to *enkreteia* but to God Himself. This is a critical development: pleasure (*hedone*) itself was understood as a negative passion. If mastery pleasure was to be celebrated, it had to be separated from such a passion, despite its good feel, and attributed to something that was not of the negative passions. While some of the positive passions, such as hope, describe an attractive state of mind, a far more intense feeling of joy had to be ascribed to an agency such as God.

The Philonic theory receives an anthropological illustration, perhaps verification, in his vivid description of the "Therapeutae" (Healers) community of the Mareotic Lake outside of Alexandria in *The Contemplative Life*.[22] Specifically, the comparison in that work between pagan Greek and Italian banquets and that of the Healers tells the story of passions, self-control, virtue, and supreme mastery pleasure in the company of God.[23]

In this brief work, Philo dedicated the bulk of his comments to the comparison between those banquets that celebrate uncontrolled pleasure with a banquet that celebrates knowledge of God and regulated passions.[24] However, the text begins with a description of the Therapeutae – their

---

[21] Levy, "Philo's Ethics," 154.

[22] David Winston, trans., *The Contemplative Life* (*De vita contemplativa*), 41–57. Joan E. Taylor and Philip R. Davies deny Philo was referring to an Essene-like community but writing about a small group of elite Alexandrian Jews whose virtue he was extolling rather than simply describing. "The So-Called Therapeutae of De Vita Contemplativa: Identity and Character," *Harvard Theological Review* 91, no. 1 (1998): 3–24. See also David M. Hay, "Things Philo Said and Did Not Say about the Therapeutae," *SBL 1992 Seminar Papers* (Atlanta: Scholars Press, 1992), 672–683.

[23] *The Contemplative Life* in trans., David Winston, *Philo of Alexandria: The Contemplative Life, The Giants, and Selections* (New York: Paulist Press, 1981), 39–58.

[24] In Exodus, Book 1, Philo applied the same criteria to the Passover Seder in his commentary from the biblical text, which points to the change from youthful ignorance and intemperance to maturity, patience and moderation.

daily routine, intellectual habits, and forms of worship. Philo wrote that the Therapeutae were healers who healed "souls mastered by grievous and virtually incurable diseases inflicted by pleasures and lusts, mental pains and fears, by acts of greed, folly, and injustice."[25] They were able to "exercise their sight, aim at the vision of the 'Existent,' and soar above the sense-perceptible sun and never abandon this post which leads to perfect happiness."[26] Their devotion is such that they always remember God, even in their dreams.

Twice a day, at dawn and evening, the Healers pray. In the morning, they pray for a joyful day – that is, that their minds be filled with celestial light. In the evening, they pray that their soul be "relieved from the disturbance of the senses and objects of sense" so that they are able to search for the truth.[27] They conduct their prayers and meditation in an empty room – a "sacred chamber" in their modest homes, where nothing can be found but books.

Between these two prayers, in addition to their work, they study the scripture in an allegorical manner as a spiritual exercise. It is possible that this exercise is designed not only as an intellectual practice but as a way of measuring and evaluating their present state of mind using criteria derived from the allegorical reading of scripture. This is how Philo writes about the matter: "For the whole of the Law seems to these people to resemble a living being with the literal commandments for its body, and for its soul the invisible meaning stored away in its words."[28] That is, the hidden meaning, the soul, is the standard to which their own internal experiences ought to be matched.

Throughout the day they practice moderation and self-control: "They lay down self-control as a sort of foundation of the soul and on this build the other virtues."[29] For example, they do not take food or drink before sunset (darkness being the time for attending to the body). When they do eat, they consume bread and salt (sometimes hyssop too) and drink water. They shun satiety as a "treacherous enemy" of both soul and body. Some of the healers go a step or two further. They "so revel and delight in being banqueted by wisdom, which richly and lavishly supplies her teachings, that they hold out [against eating] double that time and scarcely every sixth day partake of necessary sustenance."[30]

Philo writes in considerable detail and rather explicitly, as he describes the Greek and Italian banquets, which he sets up as a sharp contrast with

---

[25] *The Contemplative Life*, 42.   [26] Ibid., 43.   [27] Ibid., 46.   [28] Ibid., 55.   [29] Ibid., 47.
[30] Ibid.

that of the Healers. The two Greek banquets are those of Socrates at the house of Callias and Agathon; Philo describes them as sexual in nature, that is, dealing with "love" in every conceivable combination: "The greater part is taken up with common and vulgar love, which not only robs men of courage ... but produces in their souls the disease of effeminacy."[31] The theme of uncontrolled sexuality continues in the description of the Italian banquet, with its sexual exploitation of (male) slaves, the reckless consumption of food and drink, and the luxurious trappings. Philo describes the banquet as "unleashing the lusts whose reduction would be to our advantage ... For one may well pray for what are most to be deprecated, hunger and thirst, than for the lavish abundance of food and drink found in festivities of this kind."[32]

All of this vivid imagery sets the tone for the description that follows, of the Healers' banquet: "I shall set in contrast with them the festal gatherings of those who have dedicated their own lives and themselves to knowledge and contemplation of the realities of nature, in accordance with the most sacred instructions of the prophet Moses."[33] The men are nothing like the Roman and Greek partygoers. They are "garbed in white and radiant," solemn and quiet as they enter the hall, where they seat on modest wooden furniture with simple side cushions. The order of seniority is determined not by age but by years in spiritual practice. And they pray to God.

The women, who during weekly Shabbat service are screened off from men, enter too – they, too, modestly and solemnly: "Eager to enjoy intimacy with her [Wisdom], they have been unconcerned with the pleasures of the body, desiring a progeny not mortal but immortal, which only the soul that loves God is capable of engendering unaided."[34] The feast itself is no different from ordinary days – bread, salt, and water and perhaps hyssop as well. The pleasure comes from other aspects of the banquet: The president leads an inquiry into holy scripture – conducted with the help of allegory and offered modestly, with little display of individual brilliance. The audience listens quietly, focused and intent on his words. The president follows this by singing a hymn of praise to God –

---

[31] Ibid., 51; on Socrates's banquets, see Heda Segvic, *From Protagoras to Aristotle: Essays in Ancient Moral Philosophy* (Princeton, NJ: Princeton University Press, 2008), 37. Maren R. Niehoff, "The Symposium of Philo's Therapeutae: Displaying Jewish Identity in an Increasingly Roman World," *Greek, Roman, Byzantine Studies* 50, no. 1 (2010): 95–116 (100).

[32] *The Contemplative Life*, 51. Katherine M. D. Dunbabin, *The Roman Banquet: Images of Conviviality* (Cambridge, UK: Cambridge University Press, 2003), 58; Francois Lissarrague, Andrew Szegdy-Maszk, *The Aesthetics of the Greek Banquet: Images of Wine and Ritual* (Princeton, NJ: Princeton University Press, 1990).

[33] *The Contemplative Life*, 52.   [34] Ibid., 53.

a complex composition, in which the community appears to have developed a high level of sophistication.[35] The others gradually join in: "men and women alike were filled with divine ecstasy, formed a single choir, sang hymns of thanksgiving to God their savior."[36] In such a way, they continue till dawn, "intoxicated with the exquisite intoxication and then, not with heavy head or drowsy eyes, but more alert than when they came to the banquet, they stand with their faces and whole body turned to the east ... they pray for a joyous day, truth and acuity of thought."[37]

Philo concludes the work by offering a glowing praise of the Healers who, he writes, "through contemplation and life have secured for themselves the most fitting prize of nobility, which excels all good fortune and attains to the very summit of joy."[38] This joy (*eudaimonias*) is what I have been calling mastery pleasure, although the word *hedone* could never apply to it. To begin with, Philo clearly assumes that pleasure is a dispositional matter. It is made possible by sense perception, but it is not the direct effect of sense perception. Perception is either good or evil according to the virtue or sinfulness of the perceiving subject – it depends on moral disposition.[39] In contrast, pleasure (*hedone*) itself is caused by sinful disposition – which is represented by the snake in Genesis: the allegorical embodiment of pleasure. That is, pleasure is intrinsically evil as the product of a sinful passion. Defeating pleasure (as sin) requires, beyond self-control (*enkrateia*) and endurance (*kartereia*), the assistance of God. Philo uses poetic imagery, which clearly owes to the image of the banquet, in order to express this pleasure and its source:

> And, when the happy soul holds out the sacred goblet of its own reason, who is it that pours into it the holy cupfuls of true gladness, but the Word, the Cup-Bearer of God and Master of the feast, who is also none other than the draught which he pours – his own self free from all dilution, the delight, the sweetening, the exhilaration, the merriment, the ambrosian drug ... whose medicine gives joy and gladness?[40]

---

[35] Joachim Braun, *Music in Ancient Israel/Palestine: Archaeological, Written and Comparative Sources* (Grand Rapids, MI: William B. Eerdmans Publishing, Co., 2002), 274.

[36] *The Contemplative Life*, 56.   [37] Ibid., 57. Taylor and Davies, "The So-Called," 7, 8.

[38] *The Contemplative Life*, 57.   [39] Winston, *Philo*, 226–227.

[40] *De Somniis*, 2.249, trans., Colson and Whitaker in David T. Runia and Gregory E. Sterling eds., *Studia Philonica Annual XXVI, 2014* (Atlanta: Society of Biblical Literature, 2014), 145. F. H. Colson and G. H. Whitaker, *Philo* vol. V, Loeb Library (Cambridge, MA: Harvard University Press, 1988), 554: *charas* and *efthymia* are terms of inner affect that are free of the sensual connotations indicated by *hedone*.

In *De migratione* 118–199 on Genesis 12:3, Abraham states to God: "In you all the tribes of the earth will be blessed," which Philo interprets as the "transformation of the bad passions into the good ones."[41] And in *De somniis* 1.173, God assures Jacob that he need not suffer fear, which is a negative passion.[42] The activity of an external and transcendent agency alongside the psychological and moral discipline by means of which pleasure is transformed into joy is a characteristic of mastery pleasure in Philo. The positive affect is still a measurement of present state in relation to end-state (goal or telos), but that telos is an ideological and moral construct. It is the proper disposition that eliminates novelty pleasure (*hedone*) and replaces it with something else. Mastery pleasure is the achievement of progress in lowering the gap between end state – the attainment of truth, wisdom, "Existent" – and present state. That present state may include hunger, fatigue, or even pain. The body feeling, as Philo noted with regard to perception, is not what determines the (mastery) pleasure; it is the "ratio" or relation of goal to present state, and it is experienced as a movement toward God.

Plotinus and Play Pleasure

While Philo provides an important case study for an Axial Age religious theorist on the subject of mastery pleasure, his material does not offer anything that a modern reader – certainly one familiar with Greek thinkers – would find surprising or counterintuitive. His idea of mastery pleasure as an affect produced by psychological discipline and a transcendental goal is rather straightforward. Plotinus (204–270 CE) provides a striking contrast with this. Like Philo and many others, Plotinus was familiar with the usual excoriation of sensory pleasures, or what I call novelty (e.g., *Enneads* I.4.12). But that is not the focus of the present discussion.

Plotinus has been far more influential in Christian theological history than Philo. Indeed, he is one of the leading figures in the history of mystical theology. The literature on Plotinus himself and on Neoplatonism as a whole is vast and exhaustive.[43] However, the subject of pleasure in the work of Plotinus and, more importantly, the subject of play pleasure

---

[41] Levy, "Philo's Ethics," 161.   [42] Ibid., 160.

[43] Richard Dufour, *Plotinus: A Bibliography, 1950–2000* (Leiden, the Netherlands: E. J. Brill, 2002); Lloyd P. Gerson, ed., *The Cambridge Companion to Plotinus* (Cambridge, UK: Cambridge University Press, 1996); Algis Uzdavinys, *The Heart of Plotinus: The Essential Enneads* (Bloomington, IN: World Wisdom, 2009); David J. Yount, *Plotinus the Platonist: A Comparative*

have eluded modern scholarship and remain paradoxical and difficult.[44] Play pleasure will be the exclusive focus of the discussion in these pages, and broader, more familiar topics will only be broached inasmuch as they illuminate that specific subject. The chapter will conclude with a discussion of modern applications of this theme: play pleasure and spiritual pursuits.

A clarification is in order here. One normally thinks about the subject of religion and play, or play pleasure, in terms of rituals, games, theater, contests, festivals – and while Plotinus discussed some of these (art and theater), the play pleasure we seek in his work has little to do with these topics.[45] It is true that many of these religious contexts often involve play pleasure, but they are also dominated by novelty and mastery pleasures. The mere fact that a pleasurable religious event involves games does not necessitate the presence of play pleasure or even play itself.[46] As we shall see in the following pages, play is both a state of mind and a distinct but disputed objective reality, while a game, like a ritual or contest, can be an overly reified conception of some types of conduct that may have absolutely nothing in common with the playful hedonic state of mind.

Furthermore, the genius of Plotinus's elucidation of play pleasure has little to do with rituals and "games" and is rather the domain of what may loosely be called "mystical experience."[47] This is what I set out to show here: that a most forceful early cultural elaboration of play pleasure comes from the domain of mystical theology and can be found in the work of Plotinus. However, this material is far from straightforward and requires a rather lengthy theoretical exposition on Plotinus's understanding of play, on play itself, and on play pleasure in mystical theology. It is well known that Plotinus may be the godfather of the notion that "all the world is a

---

Account of Plato and Plotinus' Metaphysics (London: Bloomsbury, 2014); Raoul Mortley, *Plotinus, Self and the World* (Cambridge, UK: Cambridge University Press, 2013); Lloyd P. Gerson, "Plotinus," in *Stanford Encyclopedia of Philosophy*, https://plato.stanford.edu/entries/plotinus (accessed March 14, 2018). Stephen MacKenna, trans., *Plotinus The Enneads* (London: Penguin, 1991).

[44] Works on Neoplatonism and pleasure are available, but the category of what I call play pleasure is not part of the discussion. See, for example, Gerd van Riel, *Pleasure and the Good Life: Plato, Aristotle and the Neoplatonists* (Leiden, the Netherlands: E. J. Brill, 2000).

[45] Johan Huizinga, *Homo Ludens*, was the decisive work in linking play and game-like contexts. Play pleasure is more specific.

[46] Two examples: The Passover Seder can be playful but is more likely to involve the novelty pleasure of food and the mastery pleasure of Haggadah reading and discussion. The dawn purification bathing in the Ganges in the winter is a great display of mastery but no play.

[47] For Plotinus's dismissal of rituals, see Naomi Janowitz, *Icons of Power: Ritual Practices in Late Antiquity* (University Park: Pennsylvania State University Press, 2002), 17.

stage," made famous by Shakespeare.[48] The idea is that conventional reality is ultimately unreal and therefore not truly serious. But in order to build on this familiar axiom, we need to explain the following:

1. How does Plotinus's concept of play compare with current understanding?
2. What is the relationship between play and play pleasure?
3. How does play pleasure manifest in the work of Plotinus, and how, more broadly, in mysticism?
4. Is Plotinus tapping into a universal feature of religious psychology such that similar notions can be found elsewhere, for instance, India or in the modern world?[49]

In order to begin this investigation into the insights of Plotinus, it is necessary to briefly review the fundamentals of play and play pleasure. According to Johan Huizinga, whose groundbreaking work in *Homo Ludens* argues that play has acted as one of the most significant factors in the formation of human culture, play in general can be summed up in the following way:

> We might call it [play] a free activity standing quite consciously outside "ordinary" life as being "not serious," but at the same time absorbing the player intensely and utterly. It is an activity connected with no material interest, and no profit can be gained by it. It proceeds within its own proper boundaries of time and space according to fixed rules and in an orderly manner.[50]

If there is one feature of play that can be regarded as the "essence of play," Huizinga argued, it is fun – a surprisingly tricky word that corresponds (very loosely) with the Dutch word *aardigkeit*.[51]

Since Huizinga wrote this in the 1930s, a great deal of more precise psychological and biological data has been added to the analysis of play, and few experts buy into the grand theory of play as the foundation of culture or even as such a distinct and clearly bounded area of human action

[48] R. Mortley, *Plotinus*, ch. 3.
[49] The evidence for the India link is not yet conclusive but very strong. See Paulos Mar Gregorios, ed. *Neoplatonism and Indian Philosophy* (Albany: State University of New York Press, 2001); J. Filliozat, "La doctrine des brahmanes d'apres Saint Hippolyte," *Revue de L'Histoire des Religions* 130, no. 1 (1945): 59–61; Corenelia J. Vogel, "On the Neoplatonic Character of Platonism and the Platonic Character of Neoplatonism," *Mind* 62, no. 1 (1953): 43–64. If play pleasure is a universal psychological by-product of the activity that generates "mystical" experiences, then a direct cultural contact between Plotinus and India may seem superfluous as a causal matter.
[50] Huizinga, *Homo Ludens*, 13.   [51] Ibid., 3.

and feeling. There is a strong consensus today that play is difficult to define because the boundaries between play and non-play have been questioned by recent analyses in a variety of fields. For example, the distinction between serious and non-serious as a criterion of distinction is patently imprecise.[52] Victor Turner has already acknowledged this in 1983 and attempted instead to analyze "playfulness" – the attitude that may accompany either game or any other activity: "Yet, although 'spinning loose' as it were, the wheel of play reveals to us ... the possibility of changing our goals and, therefore, the restructuring of what our culture states to be reality."[53]

Richard Schechner offers six parameters by means of which play may be defined, at least on a spectrum: structure, process, experience, function, ideology, and frame. Play may take place in a designated space, extend to a designated amount of time, produce a distinct experience, and so forth. However, the parameters are not defining criteria but qualities that can be instantiated in distinct ways in different contexts and cultures. The boundaries remain fuzzy. For example, it is possible to be in a playful mood during an academic department meeting, and it is also possible to become angry or sad during a chess game. Within Schechner's six parameters, a scholar may focus on distinct dimensions such as the player's willingness to embrace multiple cognitive realities as a matter of ideology or as a cognitive exercise.

Andre Droogers, like Schechner, has chosen to focus on this aspect of play – that is, the acceptance of multiple realities. This implies the freedom to maintain such multiplicity, even contradictions, simultaneously. Incidentally, for Droogers, this is also an epistemological recommendation for the scholar-researcher who can also be playful in her methodological eclecticism. Unlike the "tool box" approach to theorizing, in which one tool is selected at one time, here multiple perspectives are retained simultaneously, even at the cost of apparent contradictions.[54]

However, there are two aspects of play theory that need to be highlighted in the context of mystical experience as play pleasure. The first is

[52] Schechner, *The Future*, 24. The work of Huizinga (early twentieth century) is naturally long-since superseded, as noted in Chapter 2 of this book. But it generated enormous interest beginning perhaps in 1958 with Roger Caillors, *Man, Play and Games*, trans., Meyer Barush (Urbana: University of Illinois Press, 2001). The sort of work that is published in the field of play and games today is Anthony D. Pellegrini and Peter K. Smith, *The Nature of Play: Great Apes and Humans* (New York: Guilford Press, 2005).

[53] Victor Turner, *The Ritual Process*, 234, quoted in Schechner, *The Future*, 25.

[54] Andre Droogers, Peter B. Clarke, Grace Davie, Sidney M. Greenfield, and Peter Versteeg, *Playful Religion: Challenges for the Study of Religion* (Delft, the Netherlands: Eburon Delft, 2006), 75–96.

hinted at in the Turner quote given earlier. His expression "spinning loose" resonates with Hans-Georg Gadamer's understanding of play as *Spielraum*, that is, the leeway or free play in a piece of machinery or in the play of light or waves.[55] This is a more "objective" understanding of play than the experiential approach – the third in Schechner's list. Play is defined by the loose to-and-fro motion of some reality. This may impose a certain experiential response in those who enter this space, but play is not defined by the attitude itself. This position will be discussed later in the book, but it has clearly influenced religion theorists, such as Dan Handelman and David Shulman, in their analysis of Hindu theological conception of Shiva's paradoxical play with the world.[56] The play offers a gateway or transition into paradoxical spaces where both the category and its opposite are maintained in an ostensibly impossible juxtaposition. Both are true and both are false – the play is the endless motion across such boundaries back and forth within the domain of play space.

Gregory Bateson, who came up with this insight in 1955, wrote that if the Epimenides paradox ("All Cretans are liars") is fed into a computer in order to be solved, the answer is an infinite series of yes ... no ... yes ... etc.[57] The play does not contradict the non-play but defines a space where both – as cognitive opposites – take turns being true and false. The consequence is not a stasis between cognitive categories but a dynamic play where a pluralistic simultaneity dominates the mind.

However, the *Spielraum* conception is not merely a tolerance for paradox, as the Hindu theological theories suggest. Nor is it merely about multiple cognitive conceptions, held simultaneously, in the face of apparent contradictions and inconsistencies. Just as importantly, play as *Spielraum* is subversive in relation to power and social hierarchy. The play deals with social and psychological categories that organize the distribution of power in society and the internalization of such arrangements in the individual participant.[58] Hence, in discussing the nature of pleasure involved in play situations, it is significant that in shaking up social and psychological categories, a sense of exhilarating and structured depersonalization takes

[55] Hans-Georg Gadamer, *Truth and Method* (London: Continuum, 1989), 101–110.
[56] Don Handelman and David Shulman, *God Inside Out: Siva's Game of Dice* (New York: Oxford University Press, 1997), 42. Schechter's research is also based in India. Indeed, Hinduism lends itself most easily to ludic theological theories. See also Kinsley, *The Divine Player*, and Jack Hawley, *At Play with Krishna*.
[57] Gregory Bateson, "A Theory of Play and Fantasy" in *Steps to an Ecology of Mind* (New York: Ballantine, 1972), 175–191.
[58] Droogers, *Playful*, 86–87; Turner, *Ritual Process*, ch. 3. A later chapter will show how this plays out during a paradoxical festival such as the Hindu Holi.

place. Interestingly, all of the theorists who have discussed play (Gadamer, Bateson, Turner, Droogers, etc.) have neglected to examine the pleasure that play excites. An inductive approach to this question – via the testimony of religious players, such as mystics – can produce useful information.

If one were to pick a quality of play that leads us closer to an understanding of play pleasure, that quality is attentive freedom. Peter Gray elaborates on this freedom in the following way:[59]

1. Play is self-chosen and self-directed. That is, play is free; one chooses to play and plays freely.
2. In play, means are more important than the end. For instance, if you play soccer or chess specifically to win, perhaps to get paid, the playful attitude is diminished relative to some other motivation.
3. The rules of play are not dictated by physical or, indeed, external necessity but emanate from the minds of players.
4. Play is "imaginative, non literal, mentally removed in some way from 'real' or 'serious' life."
5. Play involves an active and alert but non-stressed frame of mind.[60]

None of these important characteristics touches directly on pleasure. However, Gray adds the following: "The joy of play is the ecstatic feeling of liberty. Play is not always accompanied by smiles and laughter ... but play is always accompanied by a feeling of *yes, this is what I want to do right now*."[61] This is the same state of mind that Kay Redfield Jamison describes in great detail in her book *Exuberance* as "a feeling of free or unimpeded movement ... involving fun and amusement and characterized by swift, exuberant, irregular or capricious motions; and a springing, flying or darting to and fro, a joyous gamboling and frolicking about."[62] Indeed, the biopsychological underpinning of such a distinct feeling of wonderful arousal, is the activation of the SEEKING system described in Chapter 2, based on the work of Jan Panksepp and others.[63]

---

[59] Peter Gray, *Free to Learn: Why Unleashing the Instinct to Play Will Make Our Children Happier, More Self Reliant and Better Students for Life* (New York: Basic Books, 2013), 140. The cognition that Droogers and Bateson analyzed is an aspect of such a notion of freedom.

[60] Items 2 and 5 relate to the pleasure described as "flow" in Chapter 1 of this book: Mihaly Csikszentmihalyi, *Flow: The Psychology of Happiness* (New York: HarperCollins, 2008).

[61] Gray, *Free*, 141.

[62] Kay Redfield Jamison, *Exuberance: The Passion for Life* (New York: Vintage, 2004,) 42. The "darting to and fro" is the somatic equivalent of the mind's *Spielraum*.

[63] Antonio Alcaro and Jaak Panksepp, "The SEEKING Mind."

In sum, any play situation – such as game, ritual, or contest – involves complex motivations, goals, feelings, and affects. The player may wish to prove himself, defeat a despised opponent, win some money, impress friends, or pursue any number of other ends. When the focus is on fun and the pleasure is play pleasure – rather than novelty and mastery, which figure in many play situations – none of these extrinsic factors are involved. Play is free and autonomous; it exists in a multiplicity of simultaneous frames of existence, including those that may appear divorced from reality. The play pleasure remains intrinsic to that realm of the playful mood and what makes it play is its free energy and logical flexibility.

It is important to take note of the ontological and metaphysical assumptions underlying these general criteria for distinguishing play, at least in games, from other activities. The notion that game play is fantasy and therefore somehow unreal, while work and other goal-oriented activities are real, is merely conventional.[64] Briefly put, this distinction rests on functionalist assumptions of a social, economic, or cultural nature.[65] That is, the criterion here is that play is not work – it does not contribute to our survival. But this flies in the face of potentially subversive conscious experiences of the player for whom the ontological frames that undergird cultural assumptions are dynamic if not permeable. That is, that which determines the autonomy or freedom of play does not rest on our assumption about separate frames of reference that players obey by remaining in one domain and rejecting the other. Play is not simply freedom from the bonds of the real; it is the rejection of the distinction between real and unreal as necessary, along with the constraints and intentions that apply to one or the other. Recall that play is not entirely free of internal constraints: the rules of play are binding in their own way too. Indeed, in play the relationship can be metaphysically toyed with or reversed: one can argue that ordinary everyday reality such as work and school are ultimately unreal and that the play situation – for example, surfing – is what is truly real. Play pleasure would be the function of the real (surfing) and would be absent in the unreal – work and school. The surfer would experience the freedom of play pleasure due to her awareness of the boundary she has

---

[64] This observation clearly takes us to the work of Wittgenstein, *Philosophical Investigations* (1953) and the immense wake that followed. For one recent example, see John Searle, *The Construction of Social Reality* (New York: Simon and Schuster, 2010).

[65] This can be illustrated by theologians who have defined work. For instance, Miroslav Volf, *Work in the Spirit: Toward a Theology of Work* (New York: Oxford University Press, 1991), 10–11: "Work is honest, purposeful, and methodologically specified social activity ... apart from the need for the activity itself."

crossed between one domain, the unreal, and the other – the real. However, in play, both are kept in view simultaneously

In other words, play pleasure is not the function of escaping objective
reality into a realm of fantasy freedom; it is the function of being aware of
moving dynamically from constraint to freedom and back and that awareness of the to and fro itself is what separates the experienced joy from
solemnity.

The Metaphysics of Plotinus

The general metaphysical and psychological scheme in the philosophy of
Plotinus is familiar and fairly simple to summarize.[66] At the core of his
philosophy is an ontological hierarchy at the root of which is the "One" or,
in Platonic terms, the "Good."[67] This is the simplest and most fundamental existent, the underpinning of all apparent multiplicity. It defies conceptualization and description, lacking all intelligible attributes. Next in
the hierarchy is "Intellect," which emanates or derives from the "One." In
contemporary jargon, one may possibly say that the Intellect is the most
basic emergent from the utter simplicity of the "One," although this is not
meant in an evolutionary or, indeed, temporal sense. The Platonic
"Forms" on which the discrimination of empirical properties is based is
located in the "Intellect." In other words, the "Intellect" is the function of
intelligibility while the "One" is simply the principle of being, and in its
cognitive function Plotinus, calls this the "Demiurge" (*demiourgos*). The
"Demiurge" is the "Intellect" facing the world of matter, so to speak, rather
than its source.[68]

Then there is the "Soul," the driver of desire for those things external to
the Intellect, which it faces as "Demiurge." The "Soul" makes life possible
by its attraction to survival in the pursuit of food or sleep as the objects of
desire. As such, the "Soul's" desire contrasts with the desire of the Intellect,
which is satisfied by contemplation of the "One," as it is an internal form
of desire. Below the "Soul," so to speak, is matter – that is, the raw or
unformed principle of existence. Matter is evil in the sense of lacking the
"Forms" that link the activity of the "Intellect" to the "One," the latter

[66] L. P. Gerson, "Plotinus," in *Stanford Encyclopedia*; Jennifer Yhap, *Plotinus on the Soul: A Study in the Metaphysics of Knowledge* (Selinsgrove, PA: Stanford University Press, 2003), 11–18; D. Yount, *Plotinus*, ch. 1.
[67] D. Yount, *Plotinus*, ch. 1, 148, fns. 4, 5.
[68] For example, *Enneads* III.7.12; D. Yount, *Plotinus*, 85–89; L. P. Gerson, "Introduction," in *Cambridge Companion to Plotinus*; Mortley, *Plotinus*, 40.

being the ultimate goal of human life. However, matter is not rejected as evil within the philosophy of Plotinus the way it is in Gnosticism.[69] Indeed, the "Demiurge" actually derives pleasure in appreciating the beauty of matter – but only inasmuch as such beauty reflects the model ("Form") that the empirical fact somehow resembles.

This entire scheme may read like a mythological account of creation, resembling Plato's *Timaeus*, but represents a subtle reflection on both ontology and epistemology. Human beings instantiate the process described before inasmuch as they embody material existence, along with the potential to approach the "One" by means of the contemplative work of the Intellect.

Plotinus's understanding of the world as play is predicated on the ontological and cognitive distinction between material existence outside of the Intellect and the Intellect's own contemplative turning toward the "One."[70] The former – matter – is ultimately unreal in a cognitive sense, while the latter is that which gives us knowledge of the real. It is important to bear in mind that matter is not ontologically unreal; it is, after all, "caused" by the One. Instead, matter is lacking in the order imposed by the Forms.[71] Life in the material world, thus, is not unreal; it just lacks the epistemological validation of the Intellect, which means that it is something like a show: It is related but not identical to the reality outside the theater.

Plotinus wrote a great deal about human life and actions as a sort of play (*paidia*): "The only difference, we may imagine, between men and brutes is that men are allowed to recognize that they are playing."[72] We are normally ignorant of the fact that we are at play and that when we admire something, like a lover with the beloved, it is the model behind the manifest that arouses such emotions as love or admiration. The world of our experience is thus like a theater. But Plotinus often wrote about this fantastic situation in violent metaphors in order to capture the nonrandom quality of the experienced world of play and the animalistic quality of a life trapped in material nature as play: "The animals devour each other . . . all

[69] Th. G. Sinnige, *Six Lectures on Plotinus and Gnosticism* (Dordrecht, the Netherlands: Springer, 1999), 73; A. Uzdavinys, *The Heart*, 77.

[70] R. Mortley, *Plotinus*, 2–4.   [71] D. Yount, *Plotinus*, 118–119.

[72] Kevin Corrigan notes that Plotinus identifies play with the external and seriousness with internal reality. See his *Reading Plotinus: A Practical Introduction to Neoplatonism* (West Lafayette, IN: Purdue University Press, 2004), 137; Stephen R. L. Clark, "Plotinus: Body and Soul," in *Cambridge Companion*, ed. L. Gerson, 282, citing *Enn*. III.2.17.49. See also *Enn*. I.4.8, III.2.15–2.16, 18.

is war without rest."[73] Or in the case of humans, "Men directing their weapons against each other under doom of death yet neatly lined up to fight as in the pyrrhic sword-dances of their sport – this is enough to tell us that all human intentions are but play."[74]

While this violence is a play, God is the dramatist or the playwright, and the "Soul" is the actor, Plotinus argues (*Enneads* III.2.17). However, the blame for this miserable condition of humans "falls on matter dragging them down." And, "what does it matter when they are devoured only to return in some new form? It comes to no more than the murder of one of the personages in a play; the actor alters his make-up and enters in a new role. The actor, of course, was not really killed."[75] The parallel in the Sanskrit *Bhagavad Gita* is striking: "Who thinks this [self] can be a slayer, who thinks that it can be slain, both of these have no [right] knowledge: it does not slay, nor is it slain." And beyond this: "As a man casts off his worn out clothes and takes on other ones, so does the embodied [self] cast off its worn out bodies and enters new ones."[76] The comparison with Hindu ideas about reincarnation and moral retribution (karma) are clear and have been attributed by historians to Plotinus's visit to Persia, where Hindu ideas had taken hold: "Just so the Soul, entering this drama of the Universe, making itself part of the Play, bringing to its acting its personal excellence or defect . . . receives in the end its punishment or reward."[77]

The similarity with Hinduism does not end there. As in India, this condition, called *samsara* in Sanskrit, is highly unappealing but can be overcome by contemplation that reveals this state of affairs and opens up the possibility of attaining freedom from bondage by realizing the ludic nature of existence.[78]

---

[73] *Enn.* III.2.15 translated by Stephen Mackenna and B. S. Page in classics.mit.edu./Plotinus/enneads .html (accessed February 2, 2017).

[74] Ibid.

[75] *Enn.* III.2.15.22–23, trans., Mackenna and Page. It is the serious man who recognizes that what appears serious (a weapon) is a mere toy or replica of the truly real in "*Nous.*" Roman T. Ciapalo, "Seriousness and Playfulness in Plotinus' Enneads" (1978). Master's Thesis. Paper 2971. http:// ecommons.luc.edu/luc_theses/2971 (accessed December 5, 2018).

[76] *Bhagavad Gita* 2.19; 2.22, trans. R. C. Zaehner, *The Bhagavad-Gita: With a Commentary Based on the Original Sources* (London: Oxford University Press, 1976).

[77] *Enn.* III.2.15.22–23. Paulos Mar Gregorios, ed., *Neoplatonism and Indian Philosophy* (Albany: State University of New York, 2002). In comparison, the *Brihadaranyaka Upanishad* (3.2.13) states (from the mouth of Yajnavalkya): "A man turns into something good by good action and into something bad by bad action." For further consideration, especially touching on karma, see Gananath Obeyesekere, *Karma and Rebirth: A Cross Cultural Study* (Delhi: Motilal Banarsidass, 2006), 287–307.

[78] R. Mortley, *Plotinus*, ch. 7; A. Uzdavinys, *The Heart*, 118–119; *Enn.* III.8.1.

The goal or telos of life is attaining "Likeness with God" (*Enneads* I.2.2). As a path to escape the life of play, Plotinus, like Plato, recognized two types of virtues: civic (*politikai aretai*) and purificatory (*kathartikai aretai*).[79] We have seen the former earlier and discussed their affective outcome as mastery pleasure. Plotinus wrote: "They ennoble us by setting bound and measure to our desires and to our entire sensibility."[80] But unlike purificatory virtues, they are only partially efficacious in advancing to the highest goal. They do not lead to full autonomy from existence in the play world. It is only the purificatory virtues (*kathartikai aretai*) that lead humans to the likeness of God:

> As the Soul is evil by being interfaced with the body and by coming to share the body's states and to think the body's thoughts, so it would be good, it would be possessed of virtue, if it threw off the body's moods and devoted itself to its own Act – the state of Intellection and Wisdom.[81]

This is a return to the pure function of the "Intellect" and the turning of its work away from matter, via the "Soul," to its true origin within the One. This is what Plotinus describes as a "Divine Act" – the "Soul" discovers its likeness to God. Certain existential features define this state of the Intellect's union with the "One": "If the quester has the impression of extension or shape or mass attaching to that Nature he has not been led by Intellectual-Principle which is not of the order of such things."[82] The "One, in its utter simplicity, lacks any empirical features. Indeed, like Brahman of the Hindu Upanishads, it transcends discursive description: "We should put neither a This nor a That to it."[83]

This indescribable realm is entirely separate from the experiential world, which had been characterized as a play: "In sum, we must withdraw from all the external, pointed wholly inwards; no leaning to the outer; the total of things ignored."[84] This is not a negation of existence, a total escape from feeling, or even perception. Rather, it is purification and a liberation, which is made possible by turning inward to see the underlying unity by means of a higher faculty, the Intellect. The result is not the emptying of

---

[79] David J. Yount, *Plato and Plotinus on Mysticism, Epistemology and Ethics* (London: Bloomsbury, 2017), 153–154; the concept of "philosophic" virtue in Yount is in Uzdavinys discussed as purificatory virtue, *The Heart*, 47.

[80] *Enn.* I.2.2 in Uzdavinys, *The Heart*, 50.   [81] *Enn.* I.2.3 in Uzdavinys, *The Heart*, 51.

[82] *Enn.* VI.9.3 in Uzdavinys, *The Heart*, 211.

[83] Compare this to the statement in the *Brihadaranyaka Upanishad* (3.9.26): "About this self (*ātman*), one can only say "not – , not – ." The expression "*neti neti*" is often translated as "not this, not that," but Olivelle's is the precise literal translation.

[84] *Enn.* VI.9.7 in Uzdavinys, *The Heart*, 213.

consciousness or draining of emotion: "It is sound, I think, to find the primal source of Love in a tendency of the Soul toward pure beauty, in a kinship, in an unreasoned consciousness of friendly relationship."[85]

That "Love" is "inborn to the Soul" and thus true art, which Plotinus described as "story and picture," expresses heavenly love. (*Enneads* VI.9.10) Paradoxically, the domain of aesthetics can point to a way out of life-as-play, and art, read allegorically, can demonstrate the way that the Divine enters human life. It is such an allegorical reading that points to the Soul as the "Aphrodite of heaven" (*Enneads* VI.9.10). Much of Plotinus's analysis of the affective dimension of the life of the Soul as it engages with the Intellect is an allegorical reading of Greek mythology such as the *Symposium* myth – particularly the love relationship of Zeus and Aphrodite. In brief terms, the relationship between Intellect and Soul describes her birth as the penetration of the Reason-Principle (function of the Intellect) into the Soul, which is the "garden of Zeus." (*Enneads* III.5.9) Plotinus calls this *Poros* and explains it as "the lavishness, the abundance of beauty."[86] He elaborates: this is the "Nectar-drunkenness":

> Poros intoxicated is some Power deriving satisfaction outside itself: what then can we understand by this member of the Supreme filled with Nectar but a Reason-Principle falling from a loftier essence to a lower? This means that the Reason-Principle upon "the birth of Aphrodite" left the Intellectual for the Soul, breaking into the garden of Zeus."[87]

This drunkenness on divine nectar is not a complete or permanent union but the product of fleeting moments and is certainly not available to everyone but only "those who see with the Soul's sight" (*Enneads* I.6.4). What Plotinus extensively and vividly describes, then, is the pleasure that those individuals derive who experience the world by means of these higher faculties of the soul into which the Divine has penetrated. They perceive the real behind the unreal and delight in Beauty and Love and feel a drunken intoxication that can only be compared to the nectar of the gods. To use my terminology, this is play pleasure.

In the metaphysics of Plotinus, play is unreal existence, and the real is not play but seriousness. Play is conventional, which the religious actor in pursuit of God ought to recognize and transcend. How can the mystic's

[85] *Enn.* III.5.1 in Uzdavinys, *The Heart*, 97.
[86] Uzdavinys, *The Heart*, 109; Corrigan, *Reading Plotinus*, 153; John R. Bussanich, *The One and Its Relation to Intellect in Plotinus* (Leiden, the Netherlands: E. J. Brill, 1988), 81; Jennifer Yhap, *Plotinus on the Soul: A Study in the Metaphysics of Knowledge* (London: Associated University Presses, 2003), 48.
[87] *Enn.* 3.5.9 in Uzdavinys, *The Heart*, 108–109.

highest pleasure be play pleasure then? Recall that play and play pleasure are not the same as game and the pleasure of games. It is the dynamic movement in the *Spielraum* – Gadamer's term – between several simultaneously held notions. The Neoplatonic mystic must first realize that conventional reality is but a play or a theatrical reality.[88] Play pleasure depends on disrupting epistemological seriousness in order to make possible the movement toward the Divine. That movement takes the form of exploration, which is a journey toward one place without having entirely left the original point of departure.

However, in order to see how the mystic had accessed play pleasure in a robust and novel way, we need to apply the criteria described earlier in the chapter for play pleasure, bearing in mind that neither Plato nor Plotinus would recognize the biological concept of "play pleasure."[89] This means that we should set aside the ontological distinction between "play" or *paidia* (the external world of matter) and the realm of Platonic "Forms" – the "Real." We can certainly ignore the term "play"; one might as well call it *maya* – the Hindu concept of unreality, if anything at all.[90] The key is not ontological but psychological: participants in the domain of the "garden of Zeus" are aware of moving between two realms that are not actually two bounded domains because one of them, *paida*, is merely conventional. Operating in that paradoxical space, they are unconstrained by any material or social necessity; they are endlessly fascinated, even awed by the experience; they are fully energized, enraptured by nothing at all outside of the situation at hand. The talk about the "One," "Intellect," "Soul," etc., need not detract from the basic psychological fact that this is the play attitude, following the five criteria outlined earlier for the attitude described as the play attitude: freedom, intrinsic value, mental, separateness, arousal. The player need not be a mystic but could just as well be a surfer describing a great wave or a soccer player in the flow of a game.

[88] Play, like *lila* in Hinduism, is the gateway to contemplative insight. For a stunning affirmation, see Jean Amery's words about his time in the death camp: "for the greatest part the intellect is a *ludus* and that we are nothing more" and "before the camps we were nothing more than *homines ludentes*." *At the Mind's Limits: Contemplations by a Survivor on Auschwitz and Its Realities*, trans., Sidney Rosenfeld and Stella P. Rosenfeld (Bloomington: Indiana University Press, 1980), 20.

[89] Arman D'Angour, "Plato and Play: Taking Education Seriously in Ancient Greece," *American Journal of Play* 5, no. 3 (2013): 293–307; Gavin Ardley, "The Role of Play in the Philosophy of Plato." *Philosophy* 42, no. 161 (1967): 226–244.

[90] The Hindu devotional concept of *lila* (divine play), which is highly diverse, shares some of the connotations associated with the Greek *paidia*. See William Sturman Sax, *The Gods at Play: Lila in South Asia* (New York: Oxford University Press, 1995); Daniel Kealey, "The Theoria of Nature in Plotinus and the Yoga of the Earth Consciousness in Aurobindo," in *Neoplatonism*, ed., P. Gregorios, 175 (173–186).

The Pleasure of Exploring

As a cognitive state of mind, play often manifests in the form of exploration pleasure. Exploration is the mind's pursuit of its own intrinsic play pleasure and can manifest in a variety of ways. For example, researchers have seen mice give up the food rewards of solving a maze puzzle in favor of just exploring the maze for their own pleasure – that is, satisfying curiosity or seeking novelty.[91] For humans, this can be a new path in the woods, pursuing new knowledge, or a new way of seeing what we already know. Exploration and discovery are two sides of the same coin, both elicited by play pleasure – that is, by pursuing the intrinsic rewards of the activity itself. This applies in any field of human endeavor, including in a very prominent way both science and religion. Consider the following statements: "The day has passed delightfully. Delight itself, however, is a weak term to express the feelings of a naturalist who, for the first time, has wandered by himself in a Brazilian forest." The writer, Charles Darwin, in Brazil in 1832, is expressing a feeling that any child in a dazzling new playground would feel.[92] But the pleasure of exploration is even more basic than childhood play, as David Livingstone described it in 1866: "The mere animal pleasure of travelling in a wild unexplored country is very great."[93] The feeling of the pleasure itself is hard to describe, driven as it is by dopamine saturation in specific circuits, though it manifests in ways we all understand. Lynne Medsker, who is a digital artist, describes it in the following way: "I lose track of time, reality slips away, and I am absorbed into the creation that blossoms on the screen before me."[94] The total absorption in the other task, the temporary loss of self-awareness, the disappearance of time: none of these are hedonic descriptions, strictly speaking, but all of them describe the cognitive evaluations that accompany hedonic tone of exploratory play pleasure.

---

[91] D. H. Brant and Lee J. Kavanau, "Unrewarded Exploration and Learning Complex Mazes by Wild and Domestic Mice," *Nature*, 204 no. 4955 (1964): 267–269; Cardyn Johnson and Linda Wilbrecht, "Juvenile Mice Show Greater Flexibility in Multiple Choice Reversal Learning Than Adults," *Developmental Cognitive Neuroscience* 1, no. 4 (2011): 540–551.

[92] Robin Hanbury-Tenison ed., *The Oxford Book of Exploration* (Oxford: Oxford University Press, 2005), 353.

[93] Hanbury-Tenison, *The Oxford Book*, 178.

[94] Gary Singh, "The Joy of Exploration and Discovery," *IEEE Computer Graphics and Applications* 33, no. 1 (2013): 4–5; M. T. Bardo, R. L. Donohew, N. G. Harrington, "Psychobiology of Novelty Seeking and Drug Seeking Behavior," *Behavioral Brain Research* 77, no. 1 (1996): 23–43; it may be tempting to link mystical pursuit with dopamine driven novelty seeking, but (1) absent empirical research this is highly speculative, and (2) the mystical pursuit (and scientific exploration) are usually preceded by rigorous self-discipline, which is associated with mastery pleasure.

These are the feelings of having fun. In the field of physics, no one has given this more attention than Richard Feynman: "Another value of science is the fun called intellectual enjoyment which some people get from reading and learning and thinking about it, and which others get from working in it."[95] For Feynman, the whole point of doing science is that feeling – the self-rewarding satisfaction of exploration and discovery: "I don't see that it makes any point that someone in the Swedish Academy decides that this work is noble enough to receive a prize – I've already got the prize. The prize is the pleasure of finding the thing out, the kick in the discovery ... these are the real things, the honors are unreal to me."[96]

Interestingly, it is probably this pleasure of the intellectual challenge that drives Feynman, who was an atheist, to describe scientific discovery as a game of chess with God in which the human player must discover the rules as he proceeds further into the game.[97] There is something profoundly theological, perhaps even mystical, in this sentiment that links the scientist, mutatis mutandis, with someone like Nicholas of Cusa (1401–1464 CE), who did believe in God and wrote:

> For such harmony would draw to itself our Soul's reason, because it is all reason, just as infinite light would attract all light; thus freed from the sensible, the soul would not without rapture hear this supremely concordant harmony with the ear of the intellect. Here we could derive great pleasure from contemplating not only the immortality of our intellectual and rational spirit ... but also the eternal joy into which the blessed ones are taken, when they are freed from the things of the world.[98]

In a significant sense, the mystic is much like the scientist. He seeks to know that which is unknown in terms of pre-existing human experience, or experience of an ordinary nature, and will go wherever he is led by his mind's own desire to know and attain the pleasure of discovery. Plotinus already knew about this.

The "Intellect," in Plotinus's conception, is the instrument that perceives "traces" of the "Good" and strives to know it in fullness. Knowing that the world of ordinary experience is a poor reflection of "Being" – a

---

[95] Richard P. Feynman, *The Pleasure of Finding Things Out* (Cambridge, MA: Perseus, 1999), 143. The parallel pleasures of scientific and religious awe is a familiar theme explored by Paul Bloom, *How Pleasure Works: The New Science of Why We Like What We Like* (New York: W. W. Norton, 2010), 212–213.

[96] Feynman, *The Pleasure*, 12.   [97] Ibid., 13–15.

[98] H. Lawrence Bond trans., *Nicholas of Cusa: Selected Spiritual Writings* (New York: Paulist Press, 1981), 129.

mere play of shadow – the "Intellect" seeks its pleasure in discovery beyond.

> But as one that looks up to the heavens and sees the splendor of the stars thinks of the Maker and searches, so whoever has contemplated the Intellectual Universe and known it and wondered for it must search after its Maker too. What Being has raised so noble a fabric? And how? Who has begotten such a child, this Intellectual Principle, this lovely abundance so abundantly endowed?[99]

This joy of pursuing the Good comes from the play pleasure characterized by its essential freedom due to seeing through the ordinary. The Intellect is free inasmuch as it acts as the guiding force for those who "possess or pursue the Good, which standing above them all, must manifestly be the only good they can reasonably seek."[100] I believe that stripping away the Platonic and Neoplatonic terminology, here is a perfect description of the scientist, like Feynman, who regards the search for scientific truth as an autonomous and free activity, a sort of play and a source of deep gratification. It remains to be seen whether this attitude can be found in the words of other mystics or whether Plotinus was unique in this regard.

The Surfer and the Convert

In this final section, I will make the case that, inasmuch as we are focusing on the play pleasure of mystics or other religious actors such as those undergoing spiritual conversion rather than the "game" itself, there is little difference between the mystic and the surfer. The dynamics of the play, the process that the mystic and the surfer engage in, is homologous: parallel in conception but overlapping in form. This includes, among other features, the target, the goal or purpose, the search, the training, esotericism, the discovery of the hidden nature of the Other, the altered states of consciousness, the joy.

The play as process is virtually identical in many respects, and the pleasure of the play is thus almost identical. This is true even when the surfer is not on an explicitly spiritual quest.[101] For that reason, I have intentionally avoided those surfing books that consciously speak of surfing in spiritual terms. Such authors are imitating or adopting spiritual frameworks such as Zen or dharma with which they interpret or even prefigure

---

[99] *Enn.* III.8.11, Uzdavinys, 135.   [100] *Enn.* VI.8.7, Uzdavinys, 205.
[101] Examples of "spiritual" surfers are manifold. For example, see Greg Gutierrez, *Zen and the Art of Surfing* or Bethany Hamilton, *Soul Surfer.*

their surfing experiences. In contrast, William Finnigan's Pulitzer-winning autobiography *Barbarian Days* sets up no such framework.[102] The author tells the story of his life in plain narrative terms with no recourse to some religious paradigm in which he comes to understand his surfing – certainly not in any conscious way. This allows me to conduct a comparison of play as structure – or, rather, process – without resorting to theology at all. Similarly, C. S. Lewis's story of his conversion, *Surprised by Joy*, the account of his surrender to God, is not yet a Christian story, properly speaking.[103] It is the play process of an English intellectual still lacking the terminology of grace, revelation, incarnation, or any other Christian term of mystical theology that might overwhelm or obscure the process of the personal play.

C. S. Lewis's journey to conversion – finding God – ran through erotics, mythology, materialism, "Joy," and philosophical idealism and ended with acquiescence to God, though not yet the Christian God. As he put it in his conversion narrative, it was very much a search for the Other and an effort to fight off the efforts of that Other to draw him in. And it was certainly a game – or, rather, a number of games. There was chess, he writes; the more pieces on the board he lost, the closer was God's victory. But there was also the Shakespearean stage play constantly reminding us that Lewis could no more know God than Hamlet could know Shakespeare. There was archery – God slinging arrows of Joy at Lewis – and, not least, wave surfing!

Is it a mere coincidence that C. S. Lewis was fascinated by waves, not having been to the shores of Hawai'i, where surfing was a traditional sport and a cliché for spiritual pursuits? Lewis describes surf bathing, near to his defeat in the chess match with God, as "mere rough and tumble, in which the waves, the monstrous, emerald, deafening waves, are always the winner, and it is at once a joke, a terror, and a joy to look over your shoulder and see (too late) one breaker of such sublime proportions that you would have avoided him had you known he was coming."[104] Could he be talking about God here, who will defeat him in that other game – chess? Could it be anything else? After all, nearer yet to the end of his play, when Lewis realized the difference between "True Joy" and its imprint on his mind – the obstacle to finally surrendering to God – the metaphor again was the wave and its imprint on the sand.[105] If one ever needed a

[102] William Finnegan, *Barbarian Days: A Surfing Life* (New York: Penguin Books, 2015).
[103] C. S. Lewis, *Surprised by Joy: The Shape of My Early Life* (New York: Harper One, 2017).
[104] Ibid., 223.   [105] Ibid., 267–268.

justification for comparing a spiritual book to a surfer's autobiography, this is would be it.

As play goes, surfing and chess have a great deal in common. Both eschew linear movement; the trajectory is a zigzag and even includes retreats. Lewis's intellectual play certainly involves progress toward a goal, but the journey was hardly direct or steady. Motion was its chief characteristic, and doubt, coupled with interest or curiosity, were its energizing forces.

For a flavor of the play in Lewis's account, I pick up the narrative in the chapter entitled "Check," a word no chess player likes to hear from his rival. As he continued to analyze the feeling of profound joy, Lewis reports abandoning mythology: "Finally I woke from building the temple to find that the god had flown."[106] He had earlier turned nostalgia into a sort of idolatry, expecting the "Desirable" to appear in the temple that he built for the mythical god. Lewis was on the verge of discovering that "God cares only for temple building and not at all for temples built."[107] His error, Lewis notes, was confusing the living with the dead, not realizing that, in the words of the angel to the women at the Sepulcher: "He is arisen." As a boy he, had looked for prayer to produce certain thrilling states of consciousness, and these were the false gods in the temple. But living itself, that which Levinas would later call "Infinity," is what God wanted from him. And thus, thrill had to be a by-product of that other activity: "Only when your whole attention and desire are fixed on something else," rather than one's own mental state, can one expect the Holy.

The search that led him through erotics, mythology, and exotic states of consciousness now led him to holiness and, paradoxically, it was right next to him: "For the first time the song of the sirens sounded like the voice of my mother or my nurse."[108] It had always been next to him but required quickness in order to be seized, a quickness Lewis as player lacked. The joy remained, even grew, but was de-exoticized: "For now I perceived that while the air of the new region made all my erotic and magical perversions of Joy look like a sordid trumpery, it had no such disenchanting power over the bread upon the table or the coals in the grade."[109] The Other, which Lewis consistently called "bright shadow," came out into the real world, transforming all common things, remaining itself unchanged by them.

The realization that temple building rather than the gods in the temple represented the difference between authenticity and mental projection

---

[106] Ibid., 204.　　[107] Ibid., 295.　　[108] Ibid., 220.　　[109] Ibid., 222.

placed the Holy in the reality of everyday. This is where Lewis found "awe," which must be characterized as a deeply spiritual emotion. He realized that "in deepest solitude there is a road right out of the self" and onto something truly objective, not a mental construct. Joy accompanied the "moments of clearest consciousness," when one is aware of the "fragmentary and phantasmal" nature and longs for a reunion with what is true. When, in the Trinity term of 1929, Lewis "gave in" and was brought into the embrace of God "kicking, struggling, resentful and darting his eyes in every direction for a chance to escape," what did he find? What was the great apotheosis of his conversion? He writes: "There was no strain of music from within, no smell of eternal orchards at the threshold, when I was dragged through the doorway."[110] It was still "mere Theism," not yet the Christian God.

Based on the document Lewis has given us and that of Plotinus, it is possible to construct a descriptive grid that applies to the game, the dynamics of play and the hedonic conditions that apply in these contexts. The grid is not complete but still useful:

The game: Language, Cognitive, Contests, Athletic-Physical, Explorations, Tests

Play dynamics: Order, Tension-Release, Anticipation-Fulfillment, Motion, Change, Chance, Rhythm

Hedonic Conditions: Freedom, Difficulty, Mastery, Absorption, Arousal, Curiosity, Discovery, Intrinsic Reward

To give an example of how detailed such a grid can become, consider the first item: some language games that may engage players: paradoxes, counterfactuals, parables, riddles, dilemmas, jokes, fantasy, puzzles, simulation, mimicry, rhyming and alliteration, metaphors, aphorisms, anagrams, gematria, etc.[111]

Both Plotinus and C. S. Lewis employ language games to express themselves as they move about in the space that is a sort of wiggle room between the perfectly mundane and the perfectly sacred, which are not truly separate nor truly other than separate. This is how the joy of surfing

---

[110] Ibid., 282.

[111] Taken as play, word games are the very soul of religious discourse: "I am always at work and at rest in stillness"; "and you are spiritually crucified and you die every day for my sake." Rik van Nieuwenhove, Robert Faesen, S. J., and Helen Rolfson, eds., *Late Medieval Mysticism of the Low Countries* (New York: Paulist Press, 2008), 223, 224; "Now take the bees, son. They prepare the honey by gathering nectar from a variety of trees." *Chandogya Upanisad* 6.9.1.

can also be discussed even where there is no effort to describe it as religious. It is merely attendant on a specific sort of play.

The surfer, like Finnegan, who dedicates himself fully to his play, is a scholar of the ocean. If the ocean were God, the surfer is a theologian. Finnegan writes that the iconography of surfing as a creature of summers is wrong – it is a winter sport: "That's when the big storms occur, usually at higher latitudes. They send forth big waves."[112] Indeed, those waves coming at the end of a long chain as a result of some atmospheric event are "quick and violent." At times, when all the conditions are right, "the best breaks have a Platonic aspect – they begin to embody a model of what surfers want the wave to be."[113] Once the waves arrive, they are closely studied, not just for physics but also for their personality: "The wave had a thousand moods, but in general it got better as it got bigger."

The dedicated surfer does not passively wait for those waves with "sparkling depths and vaulted ceiling" to come to him. One goes searching, and young Finnegan, having saved his hard-earned money, traveled to all the distant places where he could surf the best waves for a particular time of year. He writes: "I was twenty-five and I had never been to the South Seas. It was time for a serious surf trip, an open-ended wave chase. Such a trip felt strangely mandatory."[114] Finnegan never used the word pilgrimage – that was not his game – but the search for those great waves was dedicated and costly. The ocean itself, the wave he was seeking, was a sort of God. It was not a sublime loving God, but something subtler. And the field of play with such a God was no chessboard:

> Everything out there was disturbingly interlaced with everything else. Waves were the playing field. They were the goal. They were the object of your deepest desire and adoration. At the same time, they were your adversary, your nemesis, even your mortal enemy. The surf was your refuge, your happy hiding place, but it was also a hostile wilderness – a dynamic, indifferent world. At thirteen, I had mostly stopped believing in God, but that was a new development, and it had left a hole in my world, a feeling that I'd been abandoned. The ocean was like an uncaring God, endlessly dangerous, power beyond measure.[115]

Mastering this environment required a great deal of "long, patient practice and sometimes luck."[116] The wave did not abide liars or pretenders – it could be unforgiving. Finnegan wrote that the surfer, as a matter of survival, had to know his own limits, both physical and emotional.

---

[112] Finnegan, *Barbarian*, 147.   [113] Ibid., 203.   [114] Ibid., 48.   [115] Ibid., 18–19.
[116] Ibid., 209.

Too much adrenaline or too much testosterone could mean the difference between life and death. The correct play was that fine line between caution and abandonment – it was a place of mastery.

The play sometimes produced terror, as when Finnegan discovered he had mounted a wave during a shallow low tide, and a fall could easily mean death. But more often, there was pleasure or even bliss and rapture:

> When a wave finally came to me, I took it. The floodlights switched on in the middle of my first turn. I tried to look ahead, tried to see what the wave had in store down the line and plan accordingly, but I was surrounded by turquoise light. I felt some rapture of the deep. I looked upward. There was a silver, sparkling, ceiling. I seemed to be riding a cushion of air. Then the lights went out . . . I couldn't remember the wipeout. All I remembered was the rapture.[117]

It's important to emphasize that Finnegan is not trying to hint at some hidden theology. Although he had studied for a while with Norman O. Brown at University of California Santa Cruz, he dropped out to go surfing and was later rejected by the professor. The episode involves a description of a young man surfing through a tube with his hands reaching out like a crucifix, while he and his friends were high on drugs.

Neither Lewis nor Finnegan engage the reader with sentimentality. Both are restrained writers. And while Lewis spends a great deal of words on "Joy" and Finnegan on thrill, neither wallows in particularly emotional introspection. The great Other of C. S. Lewis is God (or "bright shadow") while Finnegan's is the ocean. They both play with that other as an ambiguous adversary, sometimes frightening at other times the giver of joy. For both writers, the play is life's all-consuming search, which requires rigorous and persistent training leading to a dispassionate, almost sober study of truth, the occasional altered consciousness, moments of joy, and even self-forgetfulness. Both are sustained by a powerful fascination and attraction to their play and to the other player. C. S. Lewis is both a climber and a surfer of ideas and doctrines, as well as a loser in a chess game, while Finnegan is a rider of water mountains.

The comparison rests on structural correspondences in the dynamic of the play in which each was involved. Play pleasure is the product of such dynamic forms and, therefore, is neither purely mystical nor athletic.

---

[117] Ibid., 142.

CHAPTER 5

Pleasure, Play, and Magical Thinking

Introduction

According to Max Weber and Axial Age proponents, pre-Axial societies displayed a human–divine homology, direct ritual-sacrificial reciprocity between humans and nonhuman agencies, an emphasis on the material nature of these exchanges, and a magical conception of the world.[1] Beyond such generalities, one can also add more specifically that pleasure theory was entirely episodic – that is, lacking dispositional theories or conscious cultivation of mastery pleasures – and there was no theoretic view of the self as an autonomous agent.

In Greece, the *Iliad* displays some of these features in a variety of concrete situations, and in India, the *Rigveda* shows human interaction with gods taking place along similar lines. In both cultures, heroic virtues are highly prized, and they demand self-control and mastery over fear, but there is no theory of mastery pleasure, which both attributes the virtues to the inner agent and counts the self as the source of the mastery pleasure. For example, when Hector finally stops to fight Achilles – a suicidal decision – this is due to the deception perpetrated on him by Athena, not some appeal to virtue – that is, the product of a genuine internal deliberation.

Similarly, we know that there are contemporary societies and cultures where the Axial breakthrough did not take place, and similar – so-called archaic – religious and psychological characteristics have persisted. This might include societies that have been isolated until recently (including indigenous Hawai'i) but even some communities within Axial civilizations, such as tribal groups in remote Indian locations, where human interaction

---

[1] Max Weber, *Essays in Sociology* (Oxon: Routledge, 2007), 350. This includes so-called tribal and archaic religions about which much of the sociology of religion (Durkheim, Weber, Malinowski) and the history of religions (G. Van der Leeuw, Joachim Wach, B. Kristensen, M. Eliade) developed their theories.

with spirits (*bhut-prets*), ghouls (*rakshasas*), and godlings (*devatas*) is common. In such settings, one continues to see the "magical" worldview functioning in a variety of ways, and episodic and pre-theoretic views of pleasure still holding sway. Heroism and stoicism can be found there too, but these virtues may be inspired by external agencies and are not theoretically related to some dispositional view of mastery pleasure or a conception of the self as autonomous agent that must overcome the feeling – the "passion" of fear or the sin of selfishness.[2]

However, what is even more significant than identifying archaic or exotic religions today is Merlin Donald's theory that earlier stages of cultural evolution remain functional in the design and function of the modern mind. That means that even American Christians or Jews have retained the neurofunctional basis of the episodic, mimetic, and mythic cultures. That is, one can still find, for example, mimetic factors in the way we feel or mythic factors in what we believe. Furthermore, magic still acts as a compelling force, if not in our worldview as magical belief, certainly in some emotional component of our social interaction as magical thinking.[3] The literature on social and affective cognition bears this out, as we shall see. The general point is that we are still bound together in tight reciprocal expectations in the manner – if not intensity – of ancient mimetic groups.

It may be necessary to draw two distinctions here. First, the bonds that mimetic culture describes on Donald's theory do not constitute the same causal explanation of sociality as the genetic theories of individual evolution where the prisoner's dilemma or rational choice theory accounts for our prosocial behavior.[4] Donald's is just one culture-first theory of group cohesiveness.[5] Second, Marcel Mauss has fathered a variety of gift-exchange theories where reciprocity is a rather advanced cultural product

[2] Frederick M. Smith, *The Self Possessed: Deity and Spirit Possession in South Asia, Literature and Civilization* (New York: Columbia University Press, 2006), 253 and passim.

[3] Merlin Donald, *Origins of the Modern Mind: Three Stages in the Evolution of Culture and Cognition* (Cambridge, MA: Harvard University Press, 1991), 356; Eugene Subbotsky, *Magic and the Mind: Mechanisms, Functions, and Development of Magical Thinking and Behavior* (New York: Oxford University Press, 2010), 7.

[4] I am oversimplifying the picture, of course. The two approaches are kin selection and reciprocal altruism. For the first, see W. D. Hamilton's ground breaking, "The Evolution of Social Behavior," *Journal of Theoretical Biology* 7, no. 1 (1964): 1–52; for the latter, see R. L. Trivers, "The Evolution of Reciprocal Altruism," *Quarterly Review of Biology* 46, no. 1 (1971): 35–57. For a recent iteration, see Martin A. Nowak and Roger Highfield, *Super Cooperators: Altruism, Evolution and Why We Need Each Other to Succeed* (New York: Free Press, 2011).

[5] Other cognitive-evolutionary theories would take a different approach to the persistence of magical thinking in the modern world. For example, Lee A. Kirkpatrick, *Attachment, Evolution, and the Psychology of Religion* (New York: Guilford Press, 2005), 293, focuses on attachment theory, which has vivid developmental implications.

involving social capital leading to mutual obligations and, ultimately, forms of governance. Like rational choice theory, the theory of the gift-exchange is extremely familiar to researchers in a variety of fields, including religious studies.[6] However, the mimetic theory touches on a more primitive or foundational level of human, or even nonhuman, mutuality. It is gestural as mimicry and affective as empathy, before cultural evolution emerges as a social context where competing interests need to be resolved by means of ritualized exchanges. On this theory, when I see you crying, I feel moved, perhaps even to tears, not because I consciously wish for you to do the same. And when you smile at me, I smile before I realize that I have smiled. In other words, mimesis is not a theory of social transactions but a theory of a brain that evolved to function in a group setting.[7] And while the brain has evolved higher cortical functions over time, the older functions have not disappeared.[8]

Magic Theory

All of this has made it possible to generate a new theory of what "magic" means and how it works, but keeping in mind the distinction between magical belief and magical thinking. On this theory, magic belief is an attributional conception that emerges in the mythic – that is, post-mimetic – culture to explain the certainty that a result will follow, or has followed, an act where the certainty itself develops from the mimetic force of social-magical thinking. By "social thinking," which is at the root of magical thinking, I mean emotional cognition that develops and perpetuates human interaction without the use of abstract or conceptual categories. To be more specific, what we normally call "magic" and which I have here described as attribution, is magical belief while the emotional cognition that produces the need for attribution is magical thinking. This distinction will figure prominently in the present chapter.

---

[6] Nicholas Baumard and Pascal Boyer reject prisoner's dilemma for a "biological market" of signaling and reputation to explain reciprocity as an evolutionary disposition. "Explaining Moral Religions," 272–280; Marcel Mauss, *The Gift: The Form and Reason for Exchange in Archaic Societies* (London: Routledge, 2002); Wendy James and N. J. Allen, *Marcel Mauss: A Centenary Tribute* (New York: Berghahn Books, 1998).

[7] Donald, *A Mind*. The majority of religion brain research deals with religious experience, not the social implications of neurofunction. See Ralph W. Hood Jr., Peter C. Hill, and Bernard Spilka, *The Psychology of Religion: An Empirical Approach* (New York: Guilford Press, 2009), 62–65.

[8] In cognitive function, this manifests via dual processing, which D. Kahneman made famous in *Thinking Fast and Slow* (Part I). See Baumard and Boyer, "Explaining," 275.

One may ask, what does this theory have to do with pleasure, or does pleasure contribute to this magical worldview in any way? It is important to bear in mind that mimesis is a socially adaptive product of cultural evolution, and it has a hedonic dimension. "Adaptive" refers here to the approach/avoid theories discussed in an earlier chapter. Mimesis contributes not only to social cohesiveness but to cognitive and emotional coherence as well. It feels good when these are maximized and bad when it fails to achieve these goals or, in its absence, social isolation results. However, the mythic mind does not recognize pleasure as a function of adaptive choices; pleasure is attributed to external agencies of a mythic nature or some other, perhaps more abstract force. As a result of this misattributed hedonic dimension of mimesis, magic has to be either good or bad; malevolent or benevolent. It must account for those things that make us feel good or those that make us feel bad.[9] It is not a hedonically neutral force such as, to give a contemporary example, the force that regulates the prime lending rate or weather systems. In other words, in order for a magical worldview to be compelling, it must have salience, and that comes from the hedonic dimension of mimetic culture.

In order to see how this psychological theory of magic comes together, we need to assemble three areas of research, which initially appear unrelated: (1) Relate Merlin Donald's theory to contemporary cognitive theories: Donald may be wrong about the historical terrain of his cultural-evolutionary theory, but it may still be the fact that human cognition and affect today are highly social in the way that he describes the mimetic culture. It is necessary to look at this question – of social and affective cognition – in order to strengthen the theoretical model of magic offered here. (2) Examine social-anthropological theories of magic, which de-exoticize the phenomenon by regarding it as irreducibly social. (3) Overview theories of childhood magic where – like anthropology – magic is not a mere category error in ignorant minds but a distinct cognitive processing that deals with social actors rather than with conceptual categories. It will become clear that magical belief loses its grip on the developing child when

---

[9] It actually feels better to know that a pregnancy ended badly due to the work of a witch than to think that it was random chance. The witch may be evil, but the explanation, the cognitive coherence, is satisfying. Bertram Gawronski, "Back to the Future of Dissonance Theory: Cognitive Consistency as Core Motive," *Social Cognition* 30, no. 6 (2012): 652–668. Similarly, the unpleasant feeling of disgust associated with contagion – magical thinking about certain substances – is highly adaptive. Paul Rozin, "Toward a Psychology of Food and Eating: From Motivation to Module to Marker, Morality, Meaning and Metaphor," *Current Directions in Psychological Science* 5, no. 1 (1996): 18–24. See also Steven Pinker, *How the Mind Works* (New York: Norton, 1997), 381.

learning introduces familiarity with scientific conceptions but that magical thinking persists, especially under conditions that are hedonically salient – for example, stress, anxiety, and discomfort.

Social and Affective Cognition

It may be useful to recall that what Merlin Donald called mimesis is not identical to imitation. Rather, mimesis is "an analogue style of communication that employs the whole body as an expressive device."[10] It manifests as pantomime, imitation, gesturing, sharing attention, ritualized behavior and many games. Mimesis is not only the foundation on which human language was initially scaffolded as a neural development but as a complex and binding social development as well. This is due to the fact that mimesis made possible the refinement of a variety of skills, public motoric displays of perceived or remembered episodes, social coordination, non-linguistic gesture and pantomime, and reciprocal emotional display or mirroring.[11] Indeed, other researchers have agreed that imitation – an aspect of mimesis – and "especially imitation of complex behavioral patterns, constitute the 'social glue' that make us successful social animals."[12]

The agenda for linking magical thinking to mimetic culture is not a historical but a psychological one: What does research say concerning the relationship between individual cognition and those factors that make us irreducibly social animals such that the child or the pre-Axial culture individual cannot help but think in reciprocal social terms, and how is such social thinking also an affective phenomenon?

The most fundamental psychological approach requires a modeling of brain processes that underlie complex social modes of cognition – and currently, this implies connectionist models. Without going into much detail, connectionist models treat "the processing involved in perceptual

---

[10] Donald, *A Mind*, 240. This is something that Darwin himself already noted: *The Expression of Emotion in Man and Animals* (New York: Oxford University Press, 1998), 19; See Mark L. Knapp, Judith A. Hall, and Terrence G. Horgan, *Nonverbal Communication in Human Interaction*, 8th edn. (Boston: Wadsworth, 2007), 44; Albert Mehrabian, *Nonverbal Communication* (New York: Routledge, 2017).

[11] Susan Hurley and Nick Chater, "Introduction," in *Perspectives on Imitation: From Neuroscience to Social Science*, eds., Hurley and Chater (Cambridge, MA: MIT Press, 2005), 42.

[12] A. P. Dijksterhuis, "Why We Are Social Animals: The High Road to Imitation as a Social Glue," in *Perspectives*, eds., Hurley and Chater, 208. On the relation between imitation and social cognition, see also Michael Tomasello, Ann Cale Kruger, and Hilary Horn Ratner, "Cultural Learning," *Behavioral and Brain Science* 16, no. 3 (1993): 495–511.

and cognitive tasks in simple neuron-like units."[13] In briefest terms, simple processing units are activated and in turn activate other units ("nodes"): the pattern of connection affects how the activation spreads – all of this without higher executive control. According to Yuichi Shoda and Walter Mischel, the key to activation is salience. It does not matter what an individual believes or what goals he holds, his behavior will not be affected unless there is an activation of the relevant units or nodes:

> we started with the assumption that the social behaviors reflect the activation of relevant cognitive and affective units connected in a network that characterizes each person. That is, each person is assumed to be characterized by a stable and distinctive network that guides and constrains the activation of the set of cognitions and affects that are potentially accessible. Furthermore, the activation of some of these units is in response to the presence of psychologically salient features of situations.[14]

Affective and social cognitive studies demonstrate and explain the social nature of salience as driving behavior and thought and increasing social commitments by a variety of methods.[15] For example, sexual desire and jealousy facilitate reproduction and child rearing, gratitude signals cooperation or reciprocity, guilt does the same while acting as a self-directed signal, anger can be related to social policing, and so forth.[16]

The role of emotions and affects (including pleasure and pain) in thinking and behavior has emerged as a significant area of study in the wake of behaviorism's decline and, following that, the cognitive revolution. Most researchers today assume that emotion, to put it bluntly, is, in fact, a type of cognition. This does not require a conscious awareness of some computation, however. Indeed, in the case of affective thinking, "we propose that basic affective stimuli can act via unconscious processes to directly alter the target's incentive value."[17] The judgments triggered by salient activation of nonconscious affective processes can be independent of the conscious ones, which means that thinking is not locked into linguistic forms of communication. Hence, the expectation of reciprocity that accompanies some act of giving need not be construed as a conscious

---

[13] Stephen J. Read and Lynn Miller, eds., *Connectionist Models of Social Reasoning and Social Behavior* (New York: Routledge, 1998), ix.

[14] Yuichi Shoda and Walter Mischel, "Personality as a Stable Cognitive-Affective Activation Network," in *Connectionist Models*, eds., Read and Miller, 184 (175–208).

[15] Joseph P. Forgas, ed., *Affect in Social Thinking and Behavior* (New York: Psychology Press, 2012).

[16] Dacher Keltner, E. J. Horberg, and Christopher Oveis, "Emotion as Moral Intuition," in *Affect in Social Thinking*, ed., Forgas, 162–163.

[17] Piotr Winkielman and John Cacioppo, "A Social Neuroscience Perspective on Affective Influences on Social Cognition and Behavior," in *Affect in Social Thinking*, ed., Forgas, 53.

culturally articulated value such as the Maussian theory of the gift suggests. The expectation itself is an affect that could have been activated by entirely nonconscious but highly salient social events – for instance, a mother's nurturing behavior.

Some researchers are beginning to examine these social events. For instance, Craig Smith and his colleagues have developed a relational model of appraisal theory, which means that they examine the information that allows a subject to appraise his situation as positive or negative and the affect as pleasant or unpleasant relative to goals.[18] The underlying assumption is that a variety of social processes such as seeking support, sharing emotion, and emotional negotiation with others influence the way individuals appraise and modulate their experience of well-being. This, too, is an implicit process.

De-Exoticizing Magic

These new psychological theories of social and affective cognition resonate with current anthropological theories of magic as a social but non-occult practice. For a number of generations, the study of magic in remote cultures focused on the exotic and the strange, often in pursuit of vast theories of human rationality ("mentality"), evolution, and sociality.[19] Contemporary scholars are far more cautious. Bruce Kapferer cites Evans-Pritchard as indicating that Azande magical practice was "an everyday, practical knowledge, thoroughly different from scientific rationalism as idealized – a practice completely unconcerned with contradiction and system coherence of the scientific sort."[20]

Magical practice, Kapferer adds, is akin to the "natural attitude" of phenomenology – that is, it is grounded "in ordinary experience mediated through cultural categories."[21] That natural attitude does not mean that the anthropologist is not interested in cognition ("practical reason") but that he recognizes that "there is no singular or ultimate form of practical reason," which is due to the fact that reason is entirely social in its nature.

[18] Craig Smith, Bieke David, and Leslie Kirby, "Emotion-Eliciting Appraisals of Social Situations," in *Affect in Social Thinking*, ed., Forgas, 94–96.

[19] This can still be seen in Jeffrey Burton Russel's article "Witchcraft," in *Encyclopedia of Religion*, ed., M. Eliade (New York: Macmillan, 1987), 415–423.

[20] Bruce Kapferer, ed., *Beyond Rationalism: Rethinking Magic, Witchcraft and Sorcery* (New York: Berghahn Books, 2003).

[21] Kapferer, "Introduction," 6; Subbtosky calls this state of mind "phenomenalistic" in *Magic*, 143. This probably originates in Piaget's understanding of the child's mind.

Kapferer concludes – correctly, I believe – that "this social grounding, extending from the ideas of Durkheim and Mauss, is vital in the psychological dimensions of magical and especially witchcraft, experience."[22] Consider the following case of witchcraft accusation:

> Santa Fe, May 13, 1708
>
> Doña Leonor Dominguez, native resident of this Province, wife of Miguel Martin, appears before your lordship in due form and manner according to law, and of my own will affirm: that being extremely ill with various troubles and maladies which seemed to be caused by witchcraft, having been visited by persons practiced and intelligent in medicine, who gave me various remedies, which experiments were followed not only by very slight improvement but also every day increased my sufferings and supernatural extremity, and although I am a catholic Christian, by the goodness of God, I know that there have been many examples in this Province of persons of my sex who have been possessed by witchcraft with devilish art, as is well known and perceptible in Augustina Romero, Ana Maria, wife of Luiz Lopez, and Maria Lujan, my sister-in-law, and other persons, the effect being the same in one case as in the others, which has been seen to ensue in some of them [by means of some small inquiry] upon their health, as they declare: Wherefore, I cite them, and having just suspicions of certain [persons] notorious for this crime [mutilated] some things.[23]

According to the editor:

> What starts as an accusation of witchcraft lodged by a Spanish colonist against three Indian women reveals itself as a complicated web of interactions, in which the accuser, Doña Leonor Dominguez, believed her husband, Miguel Martin, to be sexually involved with one of the accused women, Angelina Pumazho. The trial exposes the entangled lives of Spaniards and Indians in colonial New Mexico, only a few years after the Spanish returned to the province following their expulsion in the wake of the Pueblo Revolt. Witchcraft featured in these new relationships, providing a way for Doña Leonor to articulate her anger.[24]

What appears irrational to the contemporary outsider is, in fact, a failure to see the distinct logic of a social practice and social-affective cognition. The accusation of witchcraft could never be considered authoritative unless it spoke to a form of social reasoning that implicitly rested on social relationships. Kapferer states: "Reason, always a social practice, is limited

---

[22] Kapferer, "Introduction," 6.
[23] Alison Games, *Witchcraft in Early North America* (Lanham, MD: Rowman & Littlefield Publishers, 2010), case 12.
[24] Ibid., case 12.

by this self-same social factuality and can never establish a 'pure' perfect form of it in social contexts. Magic and witchcraft are particular manifest-ations of this fact."[25] This is the same terrain covered by religion theorists like Proudfoot and McCutcheon, in the discussion of religious experience, who claimed that there is no pure religious experience away from the manner in which a given culture formulates the contours of various conceptions and ideas that constitute individual belief and thinking on religious matters.[26]

Other anthropologists developed and elaborated the sort of social con-ditions that shaped the nature of magical thinking. For example, Mary Douglas's theories on the grid and the group – with its close examination of boundary setting, personal control, and freedom – illuminate a concep-tual distinction between witchcraft and sorcery.[27] It is the social situation in which one is identified as intrinsically, perhaps unconsciously, a witch as opposed to the fully aware specialist who is a sorcerer.

It is possible that the powerfully persuasive and persistent dimension of witchcraft and sorcery is a psychological dimension that is usually only implicitly discussed in social anthropology. Kapferer states:

> Sorcery is a public reaction, and the dangerous, volatile potentially rebounding quality of its revengeful force (sorcery in effect, embodies the dangers of reciprocity and the transgressive potentiality of sociality) is one impetus behind both its ritual control and the social marginalization of its practitioners who must bear sorcery's risks.[28]

The key concept is "dangers of reciprocity." Kapferer understands this in terms of Durkheim and Mauss as the conscious awareness of mutual obligations, of social capital and its violation, guilt, anger, vindictiveness, and so forth. This is undoubtedly true for cases of attribution of misfor-tune to hypothetical agencies – the sorcerer. However, there are noncon-scious attributional forces at work too, as Douglas's theories indicate. These include the hedonic appraisal of a situation as miserable and the

[25] Kapferer, "Introduction," 7.
[26] Russell T. McCutcheon, "Introduction," in *Religious Experience: A Reader*, eds., Craig Martin and Russell T. McCutcheon (Sheffield: Equinox, 2012); Wayne Proudfoot and Phillip Shaner, "Attribution Theory and the Psychology of Religion," *Journal of the Scientific Study of Religion*, 4, no. 4 (1975): 317–330.
[27] Mary Douglas, *Natural Symbols: Explorations in Cosmology* (London: Routledge, 2003), 117. The internal fuzziness of the group also manifests in a psychological cosmology where the self is regarded as permeable and thus subject to the influence of others like the witch or the sorcerer. See Marylin Strathern, *The Gender of the Gift: The Problem with Women and Problems with Society in Melanesia* (Berkeley: University of California Press, 1988).
[28] Kapferer, "Introduction," 12.

psychological response to salient activators, which are responses to social contexts by means of adaptive feelings and actions. The magical theory that emerges attributing one's condition to a human agency is the mere instantiation of affective and social cognitions, which Donald characterizes as mythic, that energize social theories of malevolent agents and forces.

Hence, the certainty that reciprocity is an effective force, on which both witchcraft and sorcery beliefs are based, is the place where magic theories must focus their attention. It is the place where the mimetic function of the modern mind, coupled with the yet more advanced mythic function, produce the visceral certainty of reciprocity along with the attributional theorizing based on cultural theories about dangerous actors. These actors are rarely random, but their special location in the social grid is a matter for another theory. In order to look at this more basic psychological dimension of magic, it is necessary to look at the magical world of children, where the evolutionary strata of the human mind undergo a developmental recapitulation.

Childhood Magic

Among the many things that infancy presages about the adult world, nothing stands out more sharply than magical thinking. The truth of the matter is that a phenomenon as widespread and tenacious as magic has its hidden roots deep within our infancy. But the source of magic, unlike what the famed cognitive psychologist Jean Piaget believed, is not the sheer ignorance of newborn infants and young children. Our propensity to engage in magical thinking is not entirely a matter of the infant's failure to understand causality, the permanence of objects, the separation between the mind and the physical world, or the limited reach of words. These are eventually overcome, while magic remains, both as thinking and – more rarely – as belief. Instead, we need to look at the social and affective life of the infant for an explanation of magic. Her new world is not only external objects, mind, and language; it is also, perhaps primarily, a world that is constructed and that achieves coherence through social interaction with caregivers and later other children within increasingly complex social settings.[29] And it is also the world of a deep psychic immersion where, if

---

[29] Melissa A. Koenig and Paul L. Harris, "The Role of Social Cognition in Early Trust," *Trends in Cognitive Sciences* 9, no. 10 (2005): 457–459; Fabrice Clement, Melissa Koenig, and Paul Harris, "The Ontogenesis of Trust," *Mind and Language* 19, no. 4 (2004): 360–379. On trust and magic see Wilfried Ruff, "Entwicklung religiöser Glaubensfähigkeit," *Forum der Psychoanalyse: Zeitschrift für Klinische Theorie & Praxis* 21, no. 3 (2005): 293–307.

all goes well, reality itself is an extension of the self. All cognitive abilities emerge in a social and emotional universe, as the Russian psychologist Lev Vygotsky demonstrated.[30] However, that which we define as magical thinking is especially so. To put the matter succinctly, the origins of infantile magic are attachment and trust.

The scientific study of the infant's mind began with Piaget's recording of his own children's development, a work that continues to impress researchers today, although much has been revised. Piaget was fascinated by the philosophical problem of how a world comes to be known, organized coherently into space, time, causality, and substance. He did not believe that these categories were innate – the so-called nativist perspective – but that they developed as the infant internalized her own movements. It was body movement in space and time that become mental representations, and this takes a fairly long time, up to 18 months, to develop, in stages. Piaget called these representations "schemas," and for him, they were the basic elements of knowledge: they filter and give meaning to sensations.[31] In short, the schemas allow humans to adapt. They do so by a twofold process of assimilation – that is, perceiving reality based on pre-existing knowledge and accommodation, changing internally to fit the outside world. The first is conservative and the second, more adventurous, explorative – the engine of change. Adaptation enables increasingly sophisticated learning as children go through stages of cognitive growth: sensorimotor, preoperational, concrete operational, and formal operational. These reflect a general movement away from egocentrism and magical omnipotence, where the infant can only understand her world with the aid of her own motor activity, toward a de-centered and more scientific view of external reality.

Piaget argued and demonstrated that young children hold mistaken beliefs about the relationship between their own mind and external reality.[32] He made the case for "magic by participation between thoughts and things" as a belief that thinking or wishing can change the physical world. Likewise, performing a procedure like counting to ten can influence other events, or using one object to influence another ("magic by participation between objects") is possible. Two generations of psychological researchers

[30] L. S. Vygotsky, *Mind in Society: The Development of Higher Psychological Processes* (Cambridge, MA: Harvard University Press, 1980). See also Sara Meadows, *Parenting Behavior and Children's Cognitive Development* (East Sussex: Psychology Press, 1996), 24–28; Greenspan and Shanker, *The First Idea*, 59–60.

[31] Jean Piaget, *The Psychology of the Child* (New York: Basic Books, 2000), 140 and passim.

[32] Ibid., 18–19.

have set out to examine these early assumptions – most of them confirming the observations.

Contemporary researchers such as Gopnik, Meltzoff, and Kuhl, who cite a large number of experiments, recognized the broader implications of infantile thinking. They followed Piaget in linking infants to the "superstitious" quality of adult magic.

> In fact, much of what we think of as magical, irrational thinking in adult life may really reflect the same sort of confusion between physical and psychological causality. Shamans and magicians say special words, wave their hands in particular ways, and take care in choosing particular garments in order to influence events in their world.[33]

The researchers conclude that "Magical procedures" of this type, whether in adults, are, in fact, ineffective, but believing in them may not really be irrational – just mistaken.[34]

In other words, given the confusion between the categories of objects and persons, or between mind and world, and the invisibility of this error, it is useless to seek effective causal relationships – but it is not entirely irrational. And so, if the baby can make Mommy raise her hands by raising her own, why not do the same with the dog, or a duck? Or if the baby sees an elephant in a book, why not make it appear in the toy box or in the room? Indeed, the study of infantile magical thinking tends to focus on such category lapses and confusion, driven by emotion. It so happens that other psychologists who study magical thinking share this view that there is something superstitious about such thinking. Piaget himself identified childhood "animism" as falsely assigning to inanimate objects like the moon (category 1) the same property that people (category 2) have – that is, a spirit.[35] These ideas are distant heirs to the colonial-period anthropologists who had written that animistic savages who engage in "magical practices" were being infantile – there appears to be some crossinsemination between two distinct scholarly disciplines. And so many of the experiments that have been set up to study children's magical thinking were designed to isolate and examine such magical phenomena as the cognitive crossover between distinct categories of thought.

The most widely studied forms of category confusion have been mind–world (and vice versa); mind-mind (that is, false control over other minds); word–reality (spells and false power of words). The underlying types of

---

[33] Alison Gopnik, Andrew N. Meltzoff, and Patricia K. Kuhl, *The Scientist in the Crib: What Early Learning Tells Us about the Mind* (New York: William Morrow, 1999), 76.
[34] Ibid.   [35] Piaget, *The Psychology*, 110.

behavior identified by psychologists have been discussed as wish fulfillment and false causality. This area of psychological study has seen a great deal of recent work, but the leading researchers have been Jacqueline Woolley, who has focused on wishful thinking Eugene Subbotsky, whose extensive research has covered by far the widest range of magical phenomena Stuart Vyse and others.[36]

The present analysis is based largely on Subbotsky's work, whose approach has been the most consistent with contemporary anthropology – that is, open ended and avoiding the magic-is-superstition worldview: "Because magical reality deals with meaning, emotions, and communication, it can peacefully coexist with, and productively complement, scientific reality."[37]

Indeed, according to Subbotsky, the magical attitude is not just a matter of confusion between conceptual categories; it need not even be regarded as a merely cognitive matter, narrowly understood. Observing his child early on in life, Subbotsky observed: "What impressed me most about my son's attitude was not that he was strongly overestimating his abilities and generally ignorant of the limitations of reality; rather, it was his absolute confidence in the idea that nature would be kind to him."[38] The category error, if indeed it exists, is not what is most salient to this observer. Instead, it is the emotional and interpersonal nature of such a magical attitude that matters most.

In order to understand this type of magic, it is necessary to revisit the distinction between magical thinking and magical belief. The former, Subbotsky explains, confines magical characters and events to the imagination while magical belief extends these characters and events to the real physical world.[39] While the observations of Piaget and contemporary followers in regard to childhood magical thought apply to magical beliefs, which diminish and disappear as children mature and acquire scientific knowledge, the case of magical thinking is entirely different. According to Subbotsky, adolescent children continue to be engaged in magical

---

[36] Subbotsky, *Magic and the Mind*; see also Eugene Subbotsky, "The Permanence of Mental Objects: Testing Magical Thinking on Perceived and Imaginary Realities," *Developmental Psychology* 41, no. 2 (2005): 301–318; J. Woolley, "The Development of Beliefs about Direct Mental-Physical Causality in Imagination, Magic, and Religion," in *Imagining the Impossible: Magical, Scientific and Religious Thinking in Children*, eds., K. S. Rosengren, C. N. Johnson, and P. L. Harris (Cambridge, UK: Cambridge University Press, 2000), 99–129; Jacqueline D. Woolley, Katrina E. Phelps, Debra L. Davis, and Dorothy J. Mandell, "Where Theories of Mind Meet Magic: The Development of Children's Beliefs about Wishing," *Child Development* 70, no. 3 (1999): 571–587; Stuart A. Vyse, *Believing in Magic: The Psychology of Superstition* (New York: Oxford University Press, 2014).
[37] Subbotsky, *Magic*, 14.   [38] Ibid., ix.   [39] Ibid., 163.

thinking, which is not unlike the magical thinking of five- or six-year-old children.[40] The focus is no longer on fairy tale characters, but it does transfer to characters from fiction, cinema, and popular culture. Under the right circumstances, such thinking can even be found among adults, as we shall see.[41] Indeed, several researchers have noted that even magical beliefs, which are culturally suppressed but never altogether eliminated, may emerge in conscious awareness when the psychological and social cost of suppressing them is greater than removing the suppression. Witchcraft and scapegoating maybe one such case, and the thought pattern of the narcissist may be another such case.[42] Both cases involve the selection of salient information that confirms a judgment, ascription, or attribution that has already been made on the basis of magical thinking: for example, waking up in the morning with a backache must be due to the sorcery, curse, or evil eye of a neighbor one has slighted the previous week.

Subbotsky has studied the subject of magical thinking from a much broader perspective, in which all cognition is social and emotional and, therefore, reflects evolutionary psychological developments:

> On one hand, rather than being a host for wrong beliefs and superstitions, magical reality [thinking] provides a person with coping strategies for problems that are beyond the reach of scientific thinking. Because magical reality deals with meaning, emotions and communication, it can peacefully coexist with, and productively complement, scientific realty.[43]

This is consistent with the observation of psychologists like Bettelheim, who studied magic and fantasy extensively and sympathetically. Bettelheim had argued that rich fantasy life – the magic realm – "provides the ego with an abundance of material to work with" as it develops modes of coping with reality.[44] Other, more contemporary researchers have shown that

---

[40] Ibid., 164.
[41] As noted, magical beliefs also persist as a theory that accounts for events that have already taken place; see E. E. Evans-Pritchard, *Witchcraft, Oracles and Magic among the Azande* (Oxford and New York: Clarendon, 1977), ch. IV.
[42] It is difficult to fully explain the 1980s devil-worship hysteria in the United States or cases such as the McMartin preschool trials without taking into account the effect of stress on magical thinking. Mary de Young, "The Devil Goes to Day Care: McMartin and the Making of Moral Panic," *The Journal of American Culture* 20, no. 1 (1997): 19–25; Sandra Bosacki, *Social Cognition in Middle Childhood and Adolescence: Integrating the Personal, Social and Educational Lives of Young People* (West Sussex: Wiley Blackwell, 2016).
[43] Subbotsky, *Magic*, 14.
[44] Bruno Bettelheim, *The Uses of Enchantment: The Meaning and Importance of Fairy Tales* (New York: Knopf, 2010), 119.

stress increases the persuasive power of magic beliefs, hence helping to explain the possible function of magic.[45]

However, in the case of magical thinking, which is far more pervasive after early childhood, the matter is even clearer. Magic humanizes the world by enriching the imagination. It makes it possible to read the world more quickly for the purpose of relating to it and to others in the process of coping. Magic (thinking), Subbotsky argues, makes the "inanimate world more understandable and humane."[46] But this is an emotional and social relationship, not a scientific one, and the function of coping, in the case of magical thinking, should not be construed in a technological sense. The reason that this coping is effective is the close relationship between the so-called laws of magic, especially reciprocity, and the nature of cognition as an emotional and social phenomenon: "Our emotional and communicative reactions are literally based on the laws of sympathetic magic."[47] There is nothing here about supernatural causality, but the empathetic reciprocity I have discussed earlier in this chapter underlies both magic and emotional and social reactions.

On Subbotsky's understanding of magic, unlike those of Piaget and theorists who emphasize category confusion – that is, false causality – social and emotional cognitions are at play in magical thinking. This view is consistent with Gluckman, Evans-Pritchard, Bruce Kapferer, and contemporary anthropologists who have de-exoticized magic and regard it as the product of social forces.

But there is another dimension of childhood magic that helps us link it to anthropological theories and, more importantly, religious experience and religious hedonics. This dimension is the role of childhood play, role playing, and fantasy. These are the contexts where magical thinking or fantasy and pleasure intersect as the school for training the future religious mind in the process of refining, elevating, and perpetuating pleasure.

Childhood play is one of the best places to study the link between cognition and emotion or, more broadly, affect, and the comparison with primate play demonstrates the biological (adaptive) roots of the phenomenon.[48] The studies that explore the true significance of play in the

---

[45] Giora Keinan, "Effects of Stress and Tolerance of Ambiguity on Magical Thinking," *Journal of Personality and Social Psychology* 67, no. 1 (1994): 48–55; Vyse, *Believing*, 160–161.

[46] Subbotsky, *Magic*, 173.   [47] Ibid., 173.

[48] G. Burghardt, *The Genesis of Animal Play: Testing the Limits* (Cambridge, MA: MIT Press, 2005); Anthony D. Pellegrini and Peter K. Smith, "Play in Great Apes and Humans," in *The Nature of Play: Great Apes and Humans*, eds., Pellegrini and Smith (New York: Guilford Press, 2005), 3–2; Renfrew et al., eds., *Ritual, Play and Belief*, 9–22.

cognitive development of children had to await the demise of behaviorism with its mechanistic stimulus-response theories. Contemporary researchers look at human beings from birth as "information-seeking creatures, curious and exploratory, striving to organize and to integrate novelty and complexity but also attempting to anticipate and match prior learning with new material. When they can integrate novelty and complexity with such pre-established schemas, they feel comfortable, indeed, show the ... smile of predictive pleasure."[49] Childhood play is a highly evolved form of behavior that serves these tasks and does so while maximizing – and, indeed regulating – pleasure.

Researchers agree that it is very difficult to define play with great precision. However, as Peter Gray notes, play cannot be defined by the overt actions but by the motivation and mental attitude.[50] With two people pounding a nail, one could be working, the other playing. The following characteristics, Gray adds, apply to play in most cases: Play tends to be a self-chosen and self-directed activity where means are more highly valued than ends. Although play contains rules, these are created by the minds of the players rather than being dictated by external necessity such as legal or economic. Play involves fantasy – that is, it is imaginative and non-literal and removed from "serious" life. In ideal circumstances, play involves active, alert, and non-stressed states of mind – that, in fact, is what it means to act "playfully."[51] Furthermore, social play is highly transactional and communicative, and it is most enjoyable when play cooperation is at its highest.

Just as he was interested in childhood magic, Piaget was also interested in play. He linked play to cognitive development and identified three primary stages: sensorimotor play in infancy in which objects are manipulated and dropped in order to produce pleasurable effects. This is followed by fantasy or pretend play, from about fifteen months to six years and, after that, symbolic games with rules.[52] However, from a typological perspective, researchers divide play into fantasy or pretend, sociodramatic, rough and tumble, rule-based games, and others. Indeed, play can be used

[49] Jerome Singer, "Imaginative Play in Childhood: Precursor of Subjunctive Thoughts, Daydreaming, and Adult Pretending Games," in *The Future of Play Theory: A Multidisciplinary Inquiry into the Contributions of Brian Sutton Smith*, ed., Anthony D. Pellegrini (Albany: State University of New York Press, 1995), 189–190.
[50] Gray, *Free to Learn*, 136.   [51] Ibid., 139.
[52] Jean Piaget, *Play, Dreams, and Imitation in Childhood* (London: Routledge, 1999), ch. V.

as a tool for understanding a wide variety of cultural practices, including rituals and – as we have seen – mysticism.[53]

There is no dispute that play is a universal aspect of childhood, and numerous studies have shown its significance in contemporary hunter-gatherer communities. In fact, play appears to be a distinct form of childhood culture, even if Piaget's developmental classification is not accepted as universal. Given this fact, it is somewhat surprising that researchers have been unable to agree on the function play has as a natural aspect of human development. To begin with, different types of play have distinct consequences. For example, pretend play relies on and develops meta-representational skills – objects standing for something else – while sociodramatic play may utilize and develop sophisticated language, and rough-and-tumble play demands inhibition of violence and aggressive feelings. All of these serve as a sort of school for enculturating children and allowing them to adapt to adult society. However, other researchers have argued that these forms of play are not essential for acquiring social skills, which can be developed and honed in other contexts different from play.[54] Hence, if play is universal, there must be some other function – for example, allowing parents to leave the children on their own as they attend to other important tasks.

I believe that it is essential to take into account the affective dimension of play in order to begin to understand its biological and sociocultural functions. As Gosso and colleagues put it, ultimately, "play is just fun," and that simple fact is key.[55] From a neurobiological perspective, play is the arousal of what Moskal and Panksepp call the SEEKING system, which mediates a certain kind of emotional-behavioral state that includes vigorous investigative sniffing, exploration, foraging, and – in hunting species – predatory urges.[56] The arousal of this system is the fun, or the experienced pleasure, not necessarily the actions performed. Exploratory or play arousal are intrinsically pleasurable, as Moskal and Pansksepp noted, but that is not the only pleasure in childhood games. Gosso and colleagues state: "Fun and enjoyment are suggestive of fluency and full mastery of the

[53] Bellah, *Religion*, 91–97; Ritual play will be discussed in the context of the Hindu Holi festival and the Jewish Tikkun Kelali ritual in Chapter 7.

[54] Peter K. Smith, "Social and Pretend Play in Children," in *The Nature of Play*, eds., Pellegrini and Smith, 188.

[55] Yumi Gosso, Emma Otta, Maria Morais, Fernando Ribiero, and Vera Dusab, "Play in Hunter-Gatherer Society," in *The Nature of Play*, eds., Pellegrini and Smith, 242.

[56] Jaak Panksepp and Joseph Moskal, "Dopamine and SEEKING: Subcortical 'Reward' Systems and Appetitive Urges," in *Handbook of Approach*, ed., A. Elliot, 68.

tasks at hand. The repetitive character of many forms of play, which might be taken as drilling, may well be either simple fun or something that goes beyond the technique and allows other subtler psychological experiences to emerge."[57]

Seemingly, the repetition, which leads to the loss of novelty, should diminish the pleasure of playing, and some researchers have argued that this is a learning process that enables the child to adapt to the routine of adult life. However, I believe that there is more going on here and that the play pleasure includes the other two types: novelty and mastery. Vygotsky has remarked on this in his own way:

> The ... paradox is that in play [the child] adopts the line of least resistance – she does what she most feels like doing because play is connected with pleasure – and at the same time she learns to follow the line of greatest resistance by subordinating herself to rules and thereby renounces what she wants, since subjection to rules and renunciation of impulsive action constitute the path to maximum pleasure in play. Play continually creates demands on the child to act against immediate impulse. At every step the child is faced with a conflict between the rules of the game and what she would do if she could suddenly act spontaneously ... Thus, the essential attribute of play is a rule that has become a desire ... The rule wins because it is the strongest impulse. Such a rule is an internal rule, a rule of self-restraint and self determination ... In this way a child's greatest achievements are possible in play, achievements that tomorrow will become her basic level of real action and morality.[58]

The concept that Vygotsky did not explicitly state is the one I have previously discussed as mastery pleasure. Not only does the child master a behavioral skill, which gives her a feeling of achievement, in learning to master her need for novelty – which is in conflict with the rules – she acquires a new type of pleasure: mastery pleasure. However, she enjoys the process of refining her enjoyment because it takes place within the game.

In sum, play brings together in childhood culture – and sometimes for adults as well – the full spectrum of benefits that characterizes magical thinking and pleasure. Play is the domain of the mind, created by the imagination. It is subjunctive, describing not just what is but what is possible. It is largely cooperative and depends on strong reciprocal relationships with the other players, and it is, perhaps above everything else, pleasurable. The game does not bore, even after it has been played over and

---

[57] Gosso et al., "Play," 242.   [58] Vygotsky, *Mind in Society*, 99–100.

over again, because novelty gives way to mastery and because the game is wondrous – it requires some other player who is not the self – and it is magical.[59] Play is the place where magical thinking dominates, but not in the sense of the mind influencing physical reality. The game is the children's version of a Harry Potter world of fantasy where the players are characters who move and act together to perpetuate states of mutual delight.

As we go back to the beginning of this chapter and pre-Axial religion, magic-play pleasure takes its place in a variety of contexts that defy Greek philosophy, Israelite prophetic ethics, or Christian contemplative monasticism. This realm – which is not merely of the distant past – can be termed "archaic" or "pagan spirituality," as some feminist theologians have termed the broad spectrum of beliefs and practices. According to Rosemary Ruether, this type of religion "focuses on the renewal of the earth and human life within the changing seasons."[60] While several prominent feminist theologians ("thealogians") argued for the idea of a primordial matriarchy and Goddess spirituality that was obliterated by patriarchy and male theology, Reuther argues on behalf of a continuity between pagan spirituality, prophetic ethics, and contemplative religion. Both sides of this debate agree that the matriarchal religions possessed distinct features, which were somewhat consistent with the way Max Weber had described pre-Axial religion. These characteristics still apply in feminist spirituality and have been recently described by Selene Fox of the Circle Sanctuary:

> I am Pagan. I am part of the whole of Nature. The Rocks, the Animals, the Plants, the Elements, and Stars are my relatives. Other humans are my sisters and brothers, whatever their races, colors, genders, sexual orientation ... Planet Earth is my home.[61]

The quote calls to mind the way that Eugene Subbotsky described the relationship he perceived between his young son and the universe: "What impressed me most in my son's attitude ... was his absolute confidence in the idea that nature would be kind to him; that the elements (water, air, gravity) were aware of his presence in the universe, accepting his divine

---

[59] I am using a terminology based on Emmanuel Levinas, though his phenomenological reflections are not derived from empirical studies but from introspection and the reading of other phenomenologists. Still, I believe he captured much of what is enjoyed in mutual play with others, which psychologists recorded using other means. Emanuel Levinas, *Totality and Infinity: An Essay on Exteriority*, trans., Alphanso Lingis (Pittsburgh, PA: Duquesne University Press, 1969).

[60] Rosemary Radford Ruether, *Goddess and the Divine Feminine* (Berkeley: University of California Press, 2005), 2.

[61] Quoted in Ruether, *Goddess*, 293.

right to be there."[62] Both of these quotes are about magic – understood not as supernatural causal thinking but as a social and emotional way of thinking and relating to the world.

However, while some "thealogians" have assumed that the magic was lost to patriarchal theology – and, with it, the celebration of natural pleasures – Ruether shows the continuities in great detail. This helps us understand the function both of pleasure and magic in the religious experiences that dominate Axial religions. The case of Song of Songs, which has already been discussed in the Chapter 1 of this book, will be used as an example of this line of investigation. That chapter touched on McGinn's analysis of Origen and Gregory of Nyssa as mystical theologians who incorporated the erotics of the Hebrew Song of Songs as metaphorical tools for spiritual insights. This is extremely familiar terrain that need not be repeated here. Furthermore, traditional Jewish hermeneutics, beginning with R. Akiva, also famously reads the text allegorically as the relationship between God and his chosen people.[63]

But the biblical text is already just the second station of this erotic text. Most scholars situate the poetry in a widely distributed pre-Israelite erotic culture – such as Egyptian secular love poems.[64] Samuel Kramer links the Song of Songs to ancient Near Eastern sacred marriage rituals with the specific association of Inanna and Dumuzi in the background.[65] Ruether notes, however, that while the ancient sexual magic of the sacred marriage had to do with the renewal of nature in the spring, the Song of Songs had lost that ritual connection. Still, "the lush language of love in vineyards and gardens of agricultural abundance . . . may well have provided conventions for the celebration of young love, tropes which then passed into secular poetry."[66]

This is an extremely useful link, but the flaw in Ruether's analysis is the conventional distinction between ritual magic as the presumed cause of nature's rejuvenation and the metaphorical linking of love to nature. We have seen that anthropologists and psychologists today often reject this occult understanding of magic and have replaced it with theories about

---

[62] Subbotsky, *Magic*, ix.

[63] Ariel Bloch and Chana Block, *The Song of Songs: A New Translation* (Berkeley: University of California Press, 1995), 30.

[64] Michael V. Fox, *The Song of Songs and the Ancient Egyptian Love Songs* (Madison: University of Wisconsin Press, 1985).

[65] Samuel Noah Kramer, "The Biblical Song of Songs and the Sumerian Love Songs," *Penn Museum: Expedition*, 5, no. 1 (1962): 25.

[66] Ruether, *Goddess*, 89.

social and emotional cognition. Within these theories, the social factors at the root of emotional cognition account both for matters of natural fecundity and human love. It is not only that human sex is believed to cause natural growth – a magical belief – but that both sex and nature are felt to be governed by a single law and a single certainty: the fact of reciprocity that underlies magical thinking. Both contexts, human love and nature, are also saturated with positive and negative affect because they are about flourishing or failure to flourish, about reproduction or sterility, perhaps even trust and betrayal. As the erotic poems journey from the ancient Near East wedding to Christian mystical theology, they do not become reduced to mere tropes. The essential affective force that animates them survives and flourishes although the nature of the social function and the quality of the pleasure undergoes change. Moreover, the wedding and the fertility rite, which were the cultural games in which the poems expressed pleasurable magic, give way to new ritual contexts – new games – and new forms of affective consciousness.

This transition from pre-Axial archaic religion, matriarchal or not, to Axial religion is not confined to matters of fertility, sexuality, or love. For example, in the feeding of the dead on the Dia de Muertos in Mexico and in the *Pindapradana* rituals of India, one sees ancient rituals involving food and a reciprocal magical relationship with the dead that later on gives way to national and even legal performances.[67] There is no reason to assume that the pleasure of symbolic feeding should disappear altogether, but it has certainly been the case that the nature of that pleasure has changed over time.

---

[67] Stanley Brandes, *Skulls to the Living, Bread to the Dead: The Day of the Dead in Mexico and Beyond* (Malden, MA: Blackwell Publishing, 2006).

CHAPTER 6

Church-Sect Theory and Pleasure

Introduction

A broad theoretical argument underlying this book is that hedonic regulation in cultural contexts was useful for the survival and prospering of groups in evolutionary and historical times and that religious beliefs and actions played a major role. "Hedonic regulation" – to repeat the discussion from Chapter 2 – is the curtailment of novelty pleasures and promotion of mastery pleasure.

One of the best ways to test this theory is to examine the hedonic implications of church-sect theory. Such work builds on Reinhold Niebuhr's adaptation of Ernst Troeltsch's *The Social Teachings of the Christian Churches* (1931).[1] In Ralph Hood's paraphrase of Niebuhr: "He suggested that persons who are dissatisfied with the commonness and permissiveness of churches as they successfully appeal to the masses seek more demanding criteria for membership."[2]

The broader group that is rejected is the "church" or, in contemporary terms, denomination. The selective group is the "sect." The former is inclusive and natural in the sense that one is born into a denomination. In contrast, sect is exclusive and voluntary – one is not usually born into a sect. There are numerous examples of such a distinction among religious groups in Christianity, Judaism, Islam, Hinduism, and other traditions.[3]

---

[1] Ernst Troeltsch, *The Social Teachings of the Christian Churches*, 2 vols., trans., O. Wyon (New York: Macmillan, 1931). See Rodney Stark and Roger Fink, *Acts of Faith: Explaining the Human Side of Religion* (Berkeley: University of California Press, 2000), 259–276.

[2] Hood et al., *The Psychology of Religion*, 246.

[3] Barbara R. Walters, "Church-Sect Dynamics and the Feast of Corpus Christi," *Sociology of Religion* 65, no. 3 (2004): 285–301; Darren E. Sherkat, "Investigating the Sect-Church-Sect Cycle: Cohort-Specific Attendance Differences Across African American Denominations," *Journal of the Scientific Study of Religion* 40, no. 2 (2001): 221–234.

In this chapter, the sects that will be discussed are the Jewish Qumran sect, the Hindu Pashupata and Aghori sects, and the Christian Bruderhof sect.

Denominations and sects differ in regard to their status relative to the so-called mainline culture in which they both exist. The focus of this inquiry is the degree of tension or antagonism between the religious group – denomination and sect – and the host culture in a variety of areas. According to Benton Johnson, a church accepts the social environment in which it operates, and the degree of tension is minimal.[4] In contrast, the sect rejects the broad sociocultural environment, and thus, the degree of tension is maximal. The areas of tension, antagonism, and separation vary. They can include family, marital relations and sexuality, food behavior, sleep, dress and comportment, education, work, economics and property values, and others. An economics style theory proposes that in the interest of increasing or decreasing membership a group can increase or decrease the tension with the norms of the host culture.[5]

Church-sect theory can be tested, that is operationalized, through surveys of mainstream denominations such as Presbyterian compared with groups like the Mennonites or Amish. Such work has utilized data on gambling, censorship, and dancing in the domain of action and rejection of Darwin, belief in the Devil, and expectation of Jesus's return in the domain of belief.[6] The church-sect theory is consistent with evolutionary theories that posit tolerance of effort, and even pain, as a condition for enhancing group cohesiveness in competitive environments.[7] But a number of questions arise in connection with this theory: Does the church-sect theory apply only in the case of religious groups? What about military, athletic, academic, and other types of groups? If the pattern is broader, what precisely is the role of religion in this dynamic? Is it possible that the comparison with denominational groups and tension with the host culture is not based on religious doctrine or faith but on something more fundamental in evolutionary terms? And why would a splinter

---

[4] Benton Johnson, "On Church and Sect," *American Sociological Review* 28, no. 4 (1963): 539–549.
[5] Roger Finke and Rodney Stark, "The New Holy Clubs: Testing Church-to-Sect Propositions," *Sociology of Religion,* 62 (2001), 175–189.
[6] William Sims Bainbridge and Rodney Stark, "Sectarian Tension," *Review of Religious Research* 22, no. 1 (1980): 105–124. See Hood et al., *The Psychology,* 252.
[7] Brock Bastian, Jolanda Jetten, and Laura J. Ferris, "Pain as a Social Glue: Shared Pain Increases Cooperation," *Psychological Sciences* 25, no. 11 (2014): 2079–2085; Richard Sosis and Candace Alcorta, "Signaling, Solidarity and the Sacred: The Evolution of Religious Behavior," *Evolutionary Anthropology* 12, no. 6 (2003): 264–274; Harvey Whitehouse, "Rites of Terror: Emotions, Metaphor and Meaning in Melanesian Initiation Cults," *Journal of the Royal Anthropological Society* 2, no. 4 (1996): 703–715.

religious group not seek to increase its size and recruit members – that is, by softening the tension with mainline culture? Is it true that sectarian groups seek to avoid growth – and is that a clue to understanding the precise role of religion in the context of church-sect theory? Specifically, can one support the thesis that the doctrine of radical salvation and elevated moral requirements for redemption, characteristic of sects, require a change in human nature that cannot possibly be met by the "common man" – the member of the denomination?

As we consider church and sect groups, it is important to note that there is a very substantial typology of nonreligious groups and multiple disciplines that analyze group formation, organization, dynamics, and so forth. For example, there are political groups, military groups, academic and student groups, sports groups, economic and labor groups, and many others. Some groups are voluntary, like sects, while others are natural, like denominations. Some have initiatory rituals, again like sects, while others are merely based on finances – say, country club membership. Some nonreligious groups are largely moral in character – for example, charity volunteer groups or volunteer firefighting units – while others exist for the sake of entertainment, competition, or profit. Multiple disciplines are utilized to understand such groups, ranging from evolutionary and cognitive psychology, organizational psychology, several subfields within sociology, economics, anthropology, and others.[8] Some of these disciplines have even been utilized in the study of religious groups. To give one example, Laurence Iannaccone is an economist who has explored the dynamics of religious groups from a variety of economic perspectives, including rational choice theory and statistics, and has been influential on the work of Stark and Finke, who are also leaders in the cognitive study of religious groups.[9]

Some of the factors that explain the formation and perpetuation of religious groups overlap with those of nonreligious groups. However, the present study focuses on a distinct feature of religious psychology: hedonic control. The agenda is to determine, first of all, what do religious sects share as common features, and how are these features different from those

---

[8] Mary Godwyn and Jody Hoffer Gittell, eds., *Sociology of Organizations: Structures and Relationships* (Los Angeles: Sage Publishers, 2012); Michael A. Hogg and Scott Tindale, eds., *Blackwell Handbook of Social Psychology: Group Processes* (Malden, MA: Blackwell, 2001).

[9] Laurence R. Iannaccone "Introduction to the Economics of Religion," *The Journal of Economic Literature* 36, no. 3 (1998): 1465–1495. See especially, Laurence R. Iannaccone, "Sacrifice and Stigma: Reducing Free-Riding in Cults, Communes, and Other Collectives," *Journal of Political Economy* 100, no. 2 (1992): 271–297.

of large denominational groups. Second, is there any distinctly religious factor that explains not only the organization of the group but also the way that some affects are curtailed or rejected while others are promoted?

In order to examine these issues, it may be useful to look at the hedonic dimension of the antagonism or tension between sectarian and denominational groups and mainline cultural norms. A distinct thesis emerges from such an examination: sects maintain a far greater hedonic antagonism with mainline culture where novelty pleasure is concerned, which places pressure in the direction of decreasing group size. However, such groups promote mastery pleasure to a significantly greater extent than the large groups, and that fact is actually consistent with the rejection of novelty pleasure. The rigorous regulation of novelty pleasure – that is, acceptance of pain and discomfort, austerity, deprivation, and hard labor – is a social unifier for an exclusive group as long as such conditions are described and experienced as conducive to a different sort of pleasure, which these groups describe as joy and I call mastery pleasure.[10]

This hypothesis goes beyond the surveys of Finke and Stark and needs to be tested experimentally with the aid of social psychologists. In the present context, it is merely illustrated and elaborated by means of three historical examples: the Essenes or Qumran Sect from ancient Israel, the Hindu Pashupata sect and Aghori group in modern times, and the Anabaptist splinter group Bruderhof in North and South America. Focusing on hedonics the following agenda will be pursued: In terms of novelty pleasure, what is the tension between these groups and their host cultures? Given the sharp antagonism anticipated, is there a compensatory mechanism to increase group cohesiveness and viability – that is, mastery pleasure? The three cases will demonstrate how mastery pleasure complements the severe excoriation of novelty pleasure and compensates for the weakened survival viability in such groups caused by the diminished demographic strength.

In other words, the analysis will show that in religious-evolutionary terms, the renunciation of novelty pleasure coupled with the promotion of mastery is a positive motivator for well-being in difficult circumstances as well as group-oriented altruistic behavior. It is important to note that mastery pleasure is also – though to a lesser extent – prized in denominational religious groups where it also functions as a psychological motivator for prosocial behavior and softens the need for divine surveillance in advanced (post-Axial) cultures. The examination of sects is useful in

[10] For a discussion of "joy" in relation to "pleasure," see Chapter 1 of this book and the Conclusion.

religious history because it demonstrates the function of mastery pleasure in extreme cases where situational factors do not favor small-group survival.

The Historical Cases

The first fact that emerges in the search for historical and textual illustrations of the church-sect theory is the sheer complexity of the data. In fact, Stark and Bainbridge questioned the conceptual viability of such a sharp distinction between church and sect.[11] Empirical research among contemporary groups can address isolated topics by means of questionnaires that touch on gambling, eating, sleep, and similar areas of behavior. Ancient texts do not provide such isolated data, and even if they did, this is no clear evidence for actual practice.[12] Their strongest feature is the language of sharp rejection of comforts and pleasures on behalf of austerity, physical effort, and selflessness. Similarly, the hedonic terms used are not always easy to translate to modern English idiom because they are steeped in ancient psychological notions, are not used consistently, and are subjective to the given author, who uses them in either Hebrew or Sanskrit.

Moreover, a multidimensional comparison of several textual-historical cases is probably too ambitious for a single chapter.[13] The following comparison does not yield a comprehensive church-sect analysis but on the single dimension of novelty vs. mastery pleasure – that is, on the matter of affect regulation – the comparison is fruitful and can yield useful insights for those who wish to use this in the assessment of the relative function of biological and cultural factors in the dynamics of religious groups.

For the sake of clarity, the presentation of the three cases – the Qumran Sect, Pashupata and Aghori, and Bruderhoff – will follow a consistent pattern:

[11] Rodney Stark and William S. Bainbridge, "Of Churches, Sects and Cults: Preliminary Concepts for a Theory of Religious Movements," *Journal for the Scientific Study of Religion* 18, no. 1 (1979): 117–131.

[12] Jutta M. Jokiranta, "Sectariansm of the Qumran 'Sect': Sociological Notes," *Revue de Qumran* 20, no. 2 (2001): 223–239, 238.

[13] There are several dimensions one may wish to examine. To give the example of social structure alone: egalitarian vs. hierarchical, voluntary vs. birth, exclusive vs. inclusive, small vs. large, unique legitimacy vs. pluralistic, and several others. See E. Troeltsch, *The Social Teachings*, vol. 2, 604, and passim.

1. What is the social relationship of the sect to its denominational "rival" and to the mainline culture of its time?
2. How do sectarian texts deal with hedonically relevant topics such as work, comfort, ethics and virtue, and pain?
3. What is the ultimate affective telos described and promoted by each sect in this discussion?

The pattern that will emerge from this survey will be consistent, in general terms, with church-sect theory: the three groups intentionally set themselves apart from, and at odds with, contemporary Judaism, which was priestly, and Hellenized, mainstream Shaivism in India and Anabaptist Protestantism in South and North America. All three were far more rigorous in their moral demands, and all were more severe in their anhedonic pronouncements and forms of conduct. That is to say, all three reinforce the hypothesis that as sects they stand in tension with mainline cultural norms – more so than the denominational religions of their time and place. At the same time – and this is a new contribution to the church-sect theory – all three promote a supreme telos that is described in highly affective terms, in a variation of what we would call "joy," "ecstasy," "euphoria," or similar terms. This highly positive affective state is described as closely related to the virtues and the struggles of sectarian life, but it also serves as a goal, the great psychological accompaniment of spiritual salvation. The hedonic material is indirect, as one would expect, and is couched in the language of sin and vice associated with sensory or sensual experiences, but the pattern is not difficult to detect. The discussion will begin with the Qumran Sect.

Qumran Sect

The Qumran Sect, which is also often referred to as the Dead Sea Sect, came to light in the middle of the twentieth century, when the so-called Dead Sea scrolls were discovered in the caves above Khirbat Qumran on the Northwest shore of the Dead Sea. Eleazar Sukenik of the Hebrew University was the first, in 1948, to link the finding to the group described in the texts.[14] This was a Second Temple group that isolated itself from Jerusalem and mainstream Judaism of second century BCE leading up to 70 CE and the destruction of the temple by the Romans.

---

[14] Magen Broshi, *Hamegillot Hagenuzot, Qumran ve-Hasi'im* (Jerusalem, Israel: Yad Ben Tzvi Publication, 2010).

The question of exactly who constituted this group is still debated among scholars, especially due to the apparent disparity between the literary sources and the scrolls and archeological evidence.[15] The literary sources include Josephus, Philo, and the Roman historian Pliny, all three discussing the "Essene" groups located in a number of places throughout Judea and the Galilee.[16] One theory, "The Qumran Essene Hypothesis," posits that the Qumran community was an Essene group while an equally forceful argument differentiates between the rather monastic Essenes and the desert community that consisted of families. The latter position also looks at evidence from Josephus that the Essenes were sun worshipers and rejected temple sacrifices while the Qumran scrolls reject sun worship and take the sacrifices for granted. On this view – based on scroll texts – Qumran may have been a Sadducee splinter group and distinct from the Essenes. However, the authority of Josephus and Philo can certainly be questioned when taking into account the fact that they had no direct access to either the Essenes or the Qumran group and were writing for Greco-Roman audiences and may have tailored their information accordingly.

Furthermore, the scrolls ("Damascus Document" and "The Rule of the Community") point to a distinction within the Qumran sect itself. They distinguish between the family-oriented and somewhat looser community and the stricter voluntary group called *yahad*, which was all male, celibate, and difficult to access. That *yahad* was conceptualized as a "kingdom of priests," a "house of perfection," and its members were "men of perfect holiness." This points to the difficulty of dividing the religious groups into merely "church" and "sect," for it turns out that there may be intermediary subdivisions in between.[17]

This is not the place to fully survey this debate, let alone take a position. It is safe to note, at a minimum, that there was a great deal of similarity between the external literary sources on the Essenes and the scrolls on the Qumran community on a number topics of central interest to the subject

[15] Gabriele Boccaccini, *Beyond the Essene Hypothesis: The Parting of the Ways between Qumran and the Enochic Judaism* (Grand Rapids, MI: William B. Erdman, 1998); Lester L. Grabbe, *Judaism from Cyrus to Hadrian*, 2 vols. (Minneapolis, MN: Fortress, 1992); Simon J. Joseph, *Jesus, The Essenes, and Christian Origins: New Light on Ancient Texts and Communities* (Waco, TX: Baylor University Press, 2018).

[16] Josephus, *Jewish Antiquities*, books 18–19, trans., L. H. Feldman (Cambridge, MA: Harvard University Press, 1996); Philo of Alexandria, *Quod Omnis Probus liber sit*, 75–91, *De Vita Contemplativa* (see Chapter 4); Pliny the Elder, *Natural History* (New York: Penguin 1991), 61; See also Todd S. Beall, *Josephus' Description of the Essenes* (Cambridge, UK: Cambridge University Press, 2004).

[17] Allison Schofield, *From Qumran to the Yahad: A New Paradigm of Textual Development for the Community Rule* (Leiden, the Netherlands: E. J. Brill, 2009), 142.

at hand: Both groups were highly ascetic, rejected material goods, emphasized purification, entirely subserved the individual to the community, insisted on initiatory practices, and were very rigorous in their moral demands.

The following observations are based on a reading of the Dead Sea scrolls (both in the original Hebrew and in translation) without consideration of the "Qumran Essene Hypothesis" because the hedonic sectarian values are shared by the Essenes, as reflected in the external sources and the Qumran group.[18] The Qumran community was isolated near the northwest shore of the Dead Sea in Khirbat Qumran. It is important to note that the water of the lake is highly saline and useless for supporting farming, bathing, or drinking. The community subsisted in a hot and isolated environment, remaining aloof from a denominational context (Sadducee Judaism) or mainstream Second Temple Judaism with its strong urban Hellenizing trends between the second century BCE and 70 CE.[19]

The textual material and paraphrases illustrate the sect's views on pleasures, those regarded in this book as novelty, and its promotion of virtues that depend on the active rejection of these pleasures through effort and discipline. This will be followed by texts that promote the highly prized affective states that I regard as mastery pleasure.

The Qumran sect was grounded in biblical Judaism based on Mosaic law but offered a new covenant – that is, one that was available to initiates who "were to be reckoned among God's elect." Election in the Torah implied an obligation deriving from being a party to the covenant. Deuteronomy 7.6, 11, states: "You shall therefore be careful to do the commandments, and the statutes, and ordinances." In broad denominational Judaism, one entered "the congregation of the chosen primarily though birth, and secondly through the symbolic initiation" represented by the circumcision of eight-day-old boys.[20] In contrast, members of the Essene

---

[18] Elisha Qimron, *Megilot Midvar Yehudah: Hahiburim Ha'ivriim*, 2 vols. (Jerusalem, Israel: Yad Itzhak Ben Tzvi, 2010); Geza Vermes, *The Dead Sea Scrolls in English*, 4th edn. (London: Penguin, 1996).

[19] The influence of Hellenism on second-century-BCE Palestinian Judaism – with elements of the gymnasium, contests, sports, baths, and many other dimensions of the material life – attested by archeological evidence, Josephus and other sources have been very widely covered. This includes even the culture of the priestly sacrifices. There is no space, or need, to belabor the comparison with the austerity of Qumran. See, for example, Lawrence H. Schiffman, *From Text to Tradition: A History of Second Temple and Rabbinic Judaism* (Hoboken, NJ: Ktav Publishing House, 1991); Martin Hengel, *Judaism and Hellenism: Studies in Their Encounter in Palestine during the Early Hellenistic Period*, trans., John Bowden (Eugene, OR: Wipf and Stock Publishers, 1974).

[20] Vermes, *The Dead Sea*, 48.

or Qumran groups joined through a deliberate choice and a display of tested commitment.

The "Community Rule" document records the excoriation of sins that were linked to pleasure seeking and sensual desires and, along with these, the failure of character leading to misery: "[G]reed, slackness in the spirit of righteousness, wickedness, lies, haughtiness, pride . . . abominable deeds in a spirit of lust, ways of lewdness" (4.9–4.10) are some of the vices. The sensory terms are strong: "maasei toa'va be-ruah zenut" points directly to sexual acts driven by unbridled desire, linked in connotation with prostitution.[21] In "Commentary on Psalms" (4Q171.10), the author identifies the evil ones (*bnei bliya'l*) as those who derive pleasure from all the delights of the earth and satisfy themselves in all the pleasures of the flesh ("yita'ngu be-chol ma'dnei ha-aretz ve-hitdashnu be-chol ta'nugei basar").[22]

The result is symmetrical because the punishment for sins is also in the flesh: "The Wicked and the Holy" ("Pesher a'l Ha-kitzim" 4Q181) states that those who wallow in sins will receive "great judgments and evil diseases in the flesh" ("mehilim ra'im ba-bashar") according to the mighty deeds of God. In other words, where the sin is sensual, so is the consequence. However, since the sinner pursues pleasure, what he gets is misery: "The Community Rule" states: "The times of their generations shall be spent in sorrowful mourning and bitter misery" ("evel, yagon, da't merurim").

In contrast, the elect, the righteous ones, will know pleasures of a different sort: "The Testament of Qahat" (4Q542), which is in Aramaic rather than Hebrew promises (1.1–1.10): "And He will make for you rejoicing and for your sons joy for the generations of truth for ever . . . And be holy and pure of all fornication in the community. And hold the truth and walk straight, and not with a double heart." Similarly, "The meek shall inherit the earth and will enjoy great peace," (Psalms 37:8–37:19) means that ascetics who undertake the hardships (*ta'nit*) will know great joy.[23] The Qumran documents are just as rich with promise of certain sorts of pleasure as they are with condemnation of others. A brief sample includes the following statements:

[21] Qimron, *Megilot*, vol. 1, 216 (1.216).
[22] See also *Kohelet* 2:8–14, where accumulating wealth and pleasure is judged as empty vanity.
[23] "Commentary on Psalms" 4Q171 3.8, 10 (Qimron, *Megilot*, 2. 301); in this text, *hita'ngu* and *yita'ngu* are past and future tense of the verb "to enjoy." Note that in verse 8, the subject is positive and, in verse 10, negative; the pleasure vocabulary does not reveal the evaluated quality of the pleasure.

He will enlighten with joy the children of Israel (*le-hair be-simha brit Israel*);
Righteousness shall rejoice on high, and all the children of His truth shall
jubilate (*yagilu*) in eternal knowledge. ("The War Rule" 17.7–17.8)

The "Thanksgiving Hymns" (*Megilat Ha-Hodayot*) 4QH, lines 20.4–20.6,
state: "My spirit will expand in happiness and exultation and I shall reside
securely in the domicile of His Holiness; Quietly and calmly in peace and
blessing in the tent of honor and salvation."[24] In the absence of joy – that
is, in the face of the depression that may have accompanied the hardships
of life in the desert – we see in "Second Ezekiel" (4Q385) the author
beseeching God: "Instead of my grief [give me joy, and] rejoice my soul.
And the days will hasten quick" ("ten li sason tahat doni ve-sameah
et nafshi").

Alongside the literary condemnation of sensual pleasures as sins and the
proclamation of loftier types of pleasure such as joy, jubilation, *simha*, and
sason, there are the ascetic practices that scholars have noted in reference to
life in Qumran such as fasting, hard labor in the heat, purifications, and
others.

The historical data does not prove empirically the precise connection
between suppression of sensual (novelty) pleasures and the emergence of
mastery pleasure – those described as joy, jubilation, and others. The
hypothesis that such a causal relationship exists will receive some support
by looking at further examples that support the church-sect theory. The
fact that novelty sensual pleasures are condemned while mastery pleasure is
prized shows, at the very least, that sect-based ideology seeks to promote
such a connection. However, only experimental work can offer actual
validation. This will be discussed in the last section of this chapter,
following the description of Hindu material and the Bruderhoff.

Pashupata and Aghori

The Pashupata ascetic group dates roughly to the second century CE and
was established by a man called Nakulisha or Lakulisha. As the sect name
indicates, it represents a renunciatory group that is associated with the god
Shiva (Pashupati), the union with whom serves as the highest goal of
spiritual practice. The evidence for the group's existence is based on direct
textual sources, the *Pashupata Sutra* and the commentary of Kaundiya, and
indirect references in ancient texts such as the *Mahabharata*, several

---

[24] Qimron, *Megilot* 1.88, my translation.

Puranas, a number of later Upanishads, and, later on, Madhava's encyclo-
pedic *Sarvadarshanasamgraha* (fourteenth century).[25]

Broadly speaking, the Hindu religious culture of the second century
CE, shortly before the rise of the Gupta Empire, consisted of the social
world of dharma, as prescribed by Dharmashastra texts such as *The Laws of
Manu* (*Manava Dharmashastra*). According to such texts, the social and
religious world was divided by social classification – the four varnas – and
by stages of life – the four ashramas – that applied to members of the upper
varnas.[26] The stages guided the male individual from childhood to old age,
consisting of the student, the householder, the forest dweller or retiree, and
the renouncer. The four stations support four normative values: kama
(love), *artha* (material means), dharma (morality), and moksha (liberation). The final stage sees the man who has left his family and property
to pursue the highest religious idea, moksha, or liberation from the cycle of
rebirth and permanent suffering. The dharma texts describe this ideal path
in individual terms, but, like many contemporary texts, they were aware of
the existence of many ascetic and monastic groups – Hindu, Jain, and
Buddhist – that drew young adherents who had not completed the full
course of the four ashramas.[27] These groups consisted of *samnyasis*
(renouncers) who were often united only by having been initiated by the
same guru or by gurus who belong to the same philosophical-monastic
tradition known as *sampradaya*. Many of these group "members" were
individually wandering ascetics with markings that aided the initiate to
identify their group affiliation.

The Pashupatas were both similar to these groups and markedly different as well.[28] They were individual ascetics who pursued forms of conduct
that were sharply at odds with mainline dharma culture but also differed

---

[25] *Pashupatasutram with the Commentary of Bhagavatpad Shri Kaundinya* (Varanasi, India: Acharya
Krishnananda Sagar, 1987); *Pāśupata Sūtram with Panchārtha-Bhāṣya of Kauṇḍinya*, Haripada
Chakraborti (Calcutta, India: Academic Publishers, 1970); Madhava Acharya, *Sarva-Darśana-
Samgraha*, trans., E. B. Cowell and A. E. Gough (Varanasi, India: Chowkamba Sanskrit Series
Office, 1961).

[26] Historians take Manu's prescriptions with a grain of salt as an idealized vision, not proper
sociohistorical data. See Romila Thapar, *Ancient Indian Social History: Some Interpretations* (New
Delhi, India: Orient Langman, 1978).

[27] Patrick Olivelle, *Ascetics and Brahmins: Studies in Ideologies and Institutions* (London: Anthem
Press, 2011).

[28] J. Van Troy and J. Von Troy, "Ayatana in the Pāśupata Tradition," *Proceedings of the Indian History
Congress* 33, no. 1 (1971): 164–179; Minoru Hara, "Pāśupata Studies II," *Vienna Journal of South
Asia Studies* 38 (1994): 323–335; Minoru Hara, "Nakulīśa Pāśupata Darśanam," *Indo-Iranian
Journal* 2, no. 1 (1957–1958): 8–32; Peter Bisschop and Arlo Griffith, "The Pāśupata
Observance (Atharvavedapariśiṣta 40)," *Indo-Iranian Journal* 46, no. 4 (2003): 315–348.

from the ascetic or disciplinary practices – that is, yoga, mantra chanting, or sacrifices of more highly regarded groups. The Pashupata practices, as we shall see shortly, demonstrated a profoundly anhedonic worldview. They are described in the third chapter of the *Pashupata Sutra* with the commentary of Kaundiya, which was written about two centuries after the sutra text. Following the description of the practices, I shall briefly survey the affective philosophy that underlies these practices and which promotes a far more elevated type of positive affect. This can be seen in the second chapter of the text.

A few words about sutra texts may be helpful to the reader. These are ancient texts that constitute the foundation of Hindu philosophy and other areas of knowledge. They consist of extremely brief aphorisms that extend at times to a single word such as "Harṣāpramādī" in 2.12. Without the aid of the commentary (*bhashya*), written by an adept in the tradition associated with the sutra text, the meaning of these aphorisms would elude the modern reader. But even with such commentary, the Sanskrit text is difficult to follow – even in translation. The following brief overview of practice and belief attempts to trace the fine line between oversimplification and an overly technical presentation.

The *Pashupata Sutra* indicates that the practices of the Pashupatas consist both of manifest and hidden forms. What is meant by hidden or unmanifest in this context is that the true meaning of the observable practice is hidden (3.1). The text ("Pretavaccharet") commands the Pashupati practitioner to wander like a *preta*, or the ghost of a departed person (3.11). His body is to be smeared with ashes and soiled with dirt like a poor man and a lunatic. He should grow a beard and allow his nails and body hair to grow long. He thus presents an appearance of someone who violates the norms of dharma. Furthermore, he should pretend to be asleep at inappropriate times and places (3.12). Whether lying down or seating, he should nod and yawn like a sleepy man and then suddenly awake and sharply tremble with his head and the rest of his body as though he had just suffered a frightening dream. Sometimes the ascetic even snores ("krāthanādī")in order to draw attention to his pretend sleep. He is an actor intent on inducing insult ("avamāna").

And the insults do come (3.3). People insult the Pashupati because everything external about him is "contrary to the injunctions" ("viparīta pravṛttim") offered by the dharma texts. They call him a lunatic, an idiot, an ignorant and evil man who flaunts the rules of good conduct (3.7). In the face of such insults, the ascetic lies happily ("sukham hi avamataḥ") while remaining disengaged from it all. However, there are more than verbal insults to contend with. The text actually instructs the Pashupati, as he wanders, to induce assault (3.5). The assault is physical ("kāyika"), involving "sticks and fists." According to the commentary, this painful assault is, for the practitioner, equivalent to the coronation of a king ("rājābhiṣeka").

The tolerance of abuse by those who mistake the Pashupati's behavior destroys all his sins (3.6). These sins are of two kinds, those derived from pleasure (*sukha*) and those derived from pain (*duhkha*). The former are listed as madness, pride, illusion, sleep, idleness, experiencing rheumatism, the absence of social marks ("aliṅga"), constant lying, or enjoying huge meals. Those sins that relate to pain are headaches, toothaches, eye disease, and similar ailments. All of these sins and their manifestations are eliminated by the assault that the Pashupati suffers. The religious mechanism is familiar to scholars of Hinduism: the ascetic takes the good merit of those who assault or insult him and thereby increases his level of purity. The argument is that sin purifies ("pāvaka") by causing the fall or the suffering of the sinner.[29] It follows that the suffering that the ascetic brings on himself by means of his abusers adds to his purity – that is, purifies his sins. The sutras reveal a negative attitude toward sensory pleasures and seek to eliminate the negative consequences of those sins caused by attachment to such pleasures. Nonetheless, the text is affective in promising the practitioner a high level of another sort of pleasure.

The pretenses of Pashupata ascetic conduct are predicated on the notion of reality as a game or play. The second chapter (sutra 2) analyzes the root of the word for God ("Devasya") as deriving from the root "divu" in the sense of playing. God is a player at play and playing is understood in this context as the production of endless effects at one's own sweet will – it is a realm of perfect autonomy ("krīḍāyāma").[30] The ascetic gains access to this realm in his own pretenses. The result is "Harṣapramādī" – that is, delight, satisfaction and excessive joy attained by following the Pashupata course (2.12). According to 2.13, the Pashupati acquires this level of joy ("harṣa") by bathing in the temple, laughing inappropriately, pretending to sleep, jerking his limbs like a paralytic – he also attains miraculous powers about which he never boasts. The obstacles to attaining this level of joy and this greatness ("māhātmyam avāpnoti") include the body, its senses, and so forth ("dehendriyādi") acting like a chariot with wicked horses (2.14).

[29] *Sarva-Darśana-Saṃgraha*, trans., Cowell, 104.
[30] "The characteristic of playing is the production of endless effects, etc., at one's sweet will. Devata means the quality of such playing." *Pashupata Sutra*, 116, fn. 6.

A mental obstacle is inability to concentrate on one's behavior due to impiety (*adharma*). Additionally, material goods such as the gifts of cows, land, and gold are obstacles to the attainment of heaven (2.15). In contrast, the gift of the self (*ātmā pradāna*) is what leads to unity with Rudra – that is, heaven. In other words, from the virtue that is attained by the supreme asceticism (*tapas*), the highest good is attained – but not from attachment to the body and its senses or to the acquisition of sense objects (material goods).

The text (2.16–2.17) is careful to point out that the practices of Pashupata, such as lying on ash ("*śayana*"), are distinct not only from ordinary conduct but also from the religious practices of performing sacrifices or those of the Yoga and Samkhya schools, which are also ascetic to an extent. It is only the Pashupati who attains union with Rudra, which is like a union with thousands of Brahman – far greater than the goals of other spiritual practices. Rudra is the source of the highest level of happiness, *samasta sukha*, and the ascetic who attains union with God is cautioned not to become attached to this joy or the feeling of acquiring supernatural powers leading to pride, for he would then need to perform further penance (2.19–2.20).

Due to the relatively sparse quantity of historical data on the Pashupata group, it is impossible to say how the pressure to conform to mainstream dharma might have impacted it in practice and theory. However, the case of the Aghor group in contemporary Varanasi (India) may be instructive.[31] And this group has been studied with plenty of documentary evidence. Although the Aghor Shaivite tradition ascribes Vedic origins to itself, the actual group that Baba Bhagavan Ram belongs to traces itself to the lineage started by Baba Kinaram in the seventeenth century. The old Aghor tradition was turned by Baba Bhagavan Ram into a society "dedicated to social service."[32] Previously, the *aughars* (Aghor renouncers) were "itinerant mendicants roaming in the wilderness and cremation grounds," following transgressive practices.[33] Because the *aughar* ascetic models his behavior on the horrific aspect of Shiva, he spends his days and nights on the cremation grounds; he wanders almost naked and covered from ashes of cremated bodies. The *aughar* ascetic uses drugs and intoxicants, ignores

---

[31] Jishu Shankar, "From Liminal to Social in the Modern Age," in *Lines in the Water: Religious Boundaries in South Asia*, eds., Eliza Kent and Tazim Kassam (Syracuse, NY: Syracuse University Press, 2013), 330–355; Ron Barrett, *Aghor Medicine: Pollution, Death, and Healing in Northern India* (Berkeley: University of California Press, 2008); Jonathan P. Parry, *Death in Banaras* (Cambridge, UK: Cambridge University Press, 1994).
[32] Shankar, "From Liminal," 330.   [33] Ibid., 331.

the rules of purity, often uses a human skull as a feeding bowl, and ignores gender and caste distinctions and boundaries, which are based on the rules of purity. He eats polluted foods and cultivates a "frightening demeanor."[34] All of this isolates the *aughar* from society although *aughars* were said to cultivate supernatural powers, which drew social attention.

Like the Pashupati ascetic, the *aughar* moves about individually (with the exception of those who join a monastic location), but he receives initiation by a guru who belongs to the Aghor tradition. In the popular imagination of Varanasi residents, it is precisely the transgressive nature of the *aughar*, ignoring rules of pollution and so forth, that allows him to act in a socially reforming manner – unlike other ascetics who are careful about maintaining the rules of dharma, especially ritual purity. But Shankar presents this as a dilemma: "How to maintain their social persona and continue their social work while either defending or negating the very same practices that are said to accord special powers to them and make them especially suitable for social work."[35]

This dilemma, or paradox, shows a sect dealing with the pressure to soften its more radical departures from the mainstream in order to open its social boundaries and function in the broader social setting in Varanasi. Ron Barrett analyzes this dynamic in great detail. Describing the social reforms of Sarkar Baba, Barrett notes that he elevated the status of women in the household and society in general, insisted that the renouncers in the ashram make regular visits to their parents, eliminated dowries among his followers and simplified weddings, eliminated or reduced caste distinctions in marriages, and increased the literacy among girls.[36] These reforms went hand in hand with his own insistence on immersion in freezing water during winter meditation, maintaining long fasts, and still consuming intoxicants – albeit in a limited manner. Barrett notes that "the worldly reorientation of Aghor posed significant challenges to its membership. Chief among them was the threat that Aghori would develop an attachment to money and power, the new intoxicants of the tradition."[37]

And indeed, as these worldly factors penetrated the tradition, so did ordinary dharma distinctions. For example, Barrett records the difficulties that Doms (low-caste cremation operators) and fishermen now have, needing to register as they enter the ashram in Varanasi: "The ashram residents explained that they were reluctant to host some of these Doms and fishermen because their history of drinking and rude behavior."[38]

---

[34] Ibid., 334; Parry, *Death in Banaras*, 252, 256–257.   [35] Shankar, "From Liminal," 331.
[36] Barrett, *Aghor Medicine*, 96.   [37] Ibid.   [38] Ibid., 97.

Thus, ironically, as the group opens up in the service of social reform, which is consistent with their own austerity and with their counter-dharma transgressive ethos, it loses those same values on behalf of mainstream norms, where caste and manners still count.

While it is impossible to say that the same would have happened with the Pashupata groups, these developments are certainly consistent with the statistical data provided by Stark and his colleagues in reference to North American groups. One such group is the topic of the next section.

The Bruderhof Groups

The Bruderhof religious community is a recent phenomenon of about the past one hundred years. It is closely associated with the Hutterite Church in the United States – a relationship that places the Bruderhof in the midst of the Hutterite crisis known as the "Schmiedeleut Schism."[39] The Hutterites are an Anabaptist offshoot established by Jakob Hutter in 1527 and currently spread in hundreds of communities around the world. In North America in the 1980s, they underwent a crisis, long in the making, of dealing with technological, economic, and social changes that challenged their long-standing conservatism. The Bruderhof represented a reformist opening of the more austere Hutterite despite the fact that they are far more exacting than mainstream Protestant denominations in North America.

The Bruderhof group emerged in the 1920s in post–World War I Germany in response to the horrific violence and without any initial relation to the Hutterites. The founder was Eberhard Arnold, and the driving values were pacifism and international socialism. In that sense, the idea resembled the early Israeli kibbutz movement, but the Bruderhof also promoted a strong theological ideal that grew and became more focused as Arnold moved closer to the North American Hutterites. Early colonies were founded in Paraguay and in the 1940s the groups moved to North America. The increasing proximity to the Hutterites in the 1970s drew numerous members of Hutterite communities who were attracted to "the childlike submission and unreserved obedience by the common people to a hierarchy-type government."[40]

---

[39] Yossi Katz and John Lehr, *Inside the Ark: The Hutterites in Canada and the United States* (Regina, Canada: University of Regina Press, 2012), 179; Alvin J. Esau, *The Courts and the Colonies: The Litigation of Hutterites Church Disputes* (Vancouver, Canada: University of British Columbia Press, 2004), ch. 8.

[40] Katz and Lehr, *Inside the Ark*, 181.

Possibly the strongest feature of the Bruderhof life was the combination of austerity and joy, even exuberance. This began with the poverty and hardship that characterized the early years as they moved to the farm in England, which lacked even the most basic furnishings.[41] But that hardship was not merely circumstantial as a beginning struggle: it was central to their chosen way of life. The Mennonite scholar Harold Bender wrote in *The Christian Monitor* in 1931: "It was from this fact of the Brotherhood's poverty that I received my strongest impressions, namely of the devotion of these people to their faith and principles. Many of the members had formerly held good positions ... but they had given up everything and were willing to suffer and sacrifice and bear hardship for the sake of their cause."[42] Thus, the community adopted a permanent way of life that was characterized by simple clothing and housing and austerity in every kind of implement and furniture. Work was ongoing and demanding, but the difficulties and struggles of life and even death were taken as an instrument for finding meaning and joy.[43]

These very difficulties, and additional ones were erected as barriers that had to be dealt with by individuals who wished to join. The new applicant was not subject to "initiatory" rituals in the manner of esoteric mystical groups, but joining was both a physical and social-psychological ordeal. Benjamin Zablocki, who has analyzed the Bruderhof groups from a sociological and psychological point of view in *The Joyful Community*, uses Robert Lifton's psychiatric resocialization scheme to understand the process that the applicant undergoes.[44] This consists of three primary steps: the stripping process, identification, and death and rebirth of self. The first element consists of assaults on identity, establishment of guilt, self-betrayal, and pursuit of a breaking point. All of this leads to a constructive process that culminates in the birth of a new self. Scholars of religion can easily identify in this scheme elements of initiatory rituals and language from around the world. And they can correlate this scheme with the symbolic or structural analysis of religion scholars like Mircea Eliade,

[41] Yaacov Oved, *The Witness of the Brothers: A History of the Bruderhof* (New Brunswick, Canada: Transaction Publishers, 1996), 113.

[42] Oved, *The Witness*, 45; Esau, *The Courts*, 15.

[43] Emmy Arnold, *A Joyful Pilgrimage: My Life in Community* (Rifton, NY: Plough Publishing House, 2011), 108.

[44] Benjamin Zablocki, *The Joyful Community* (Chicago: University of Chicago Press, 1980), 248. See Robert Lifton, *Thought Reform and the Psychology of Totalism* (New York: W. W. Norton, 1963).

anthropologists like Victor Turner, and others who have sought to explain the process of initiation.[45]

The Bruderhof groups do not apply physically coercive tests or degrading initiatory ordeals. However, the hard physical labor and the long hours of work represent a trial for the urban applicant. Furthermore, along with comforts, the novice must learn to renounce individual choice and learn to delay every form of gratification in a manner that depends on the will of others, who now make decisions for him. Most difficult of all, the novice is subject to a painful process of socialization, experiencing isolation and what feels like ostracism, before full acceptance to the group.[46] The novice does not become a proper member of the close-knit community until he has experienced what Zablocki, following Lifton, calls "ego loss" – that is, a socially reconstructed self that follows the systematic disassembly of his previous self by means of hardships and social isolation.[47]

The hardships that characterized the life of Bruderhof communities were both circumstances of harsh countryside conditions and a chosen path. In either case, the austere life took on a moral dimension in juxtaposing the virtues of austerity with the moral laxity of plenty and pleasure. This is how Eberhard Arnold himself put it in *Warum wir in Gemeinscaft Leben*: "Such a common life is no place to look for the idyllic existence of human comforts and pleasures. It in no way provides satisfaction for romantic desires or selfish cravings for personal happiness."[48] The training that the novice undergoes in accepting hardships is thus also tied to a moral program and a moral discourse with which he reflects during his trial period: "It is my sinfulness, and not their injustice, which causes me to suffer." The novice gradually joins the group as his "pride" or sense of self-importance diminishes in physical hardship and moral self-blame. Arnold argued that it is only by leading a blameless life – the rejection of gratification and self-importance – that one finds the way "to change the world, to make it pleasant to live in."[49]

It is interesting to note that in this quote, Arnold links austerity to a pleasant life and, indeed, Zablocki has recorded and analyzed the central role of joy in the life of the Bruderhof. The connection between austerity, discipline, and the delay of gratification in the life of the community and

---

[45] Mircea Eliade, *Rites and Symbols of Initiation* (New York: Harper & Row, 1965); Victor Turner, *The Forest of Symbols: Aspects of Ndembu Ritual* (Ithaca, NY: Cornell University Press, 1967).
[46] Zablocki, *The Joyful*, 246–247; Oved, *The Witness*, 311–312.
[47] Zablocki, *The Joyful*, 265; Donald C. Pennington, *The Social Psychology of Behavior in Small Groups* (East Sussex: Psychology Press, 2002), 77.
[48] Oved, *The Witness*, 32   [49] Ibid., 50.

the emergence of joy as a key feature of such life points to mastery
pleasure. For example, Emmy Arnold writes in her memoir (*A Joyful
Pilgrimage*): "Good discipline is kept by speaking openly, not behind a
person's back. Joy and cheerfulness are constantly expressed in good-
natured joking, and on a deeper level in quoting words of faith from the
Bible."[50] If Zablocki's study is reliable, there may be no better case for
studying the role of mastery pleasure, in the form of joy, the strengthening
of a community's internal bond, and serving as a unifier in the face of
disintegrative forces. Indeed, joy appears to be the dominant religious
emotion associated both with communal living and especially with the
faith in God: "The Spirit of joy in the Living One, in God as the only real
life; The Spirit drives us to all people and brings us joy in working and
working for one another."[51] The communal and religious, the love and the
joy, are described as that which "God's Kingdom" alone can bring.

Zablocki analyzes this joy as a socially integrative force. The initiatory
hardships and ego loss that the applicant suffers are not sufficient to
produce communal experience – some positive collective affect is also
required. Joy helps "in harnessing the collective behavior experience" –
that is, "transforming it into enthusiasm for and commitment to the
group."[52] The use of a term such as joy is problematic for a sociologist
who admits that "there is no exact word to describe the phenomenon" that
he is calling joy or euphoria.[53] Zablocki proposes "exaltation" as perhaps a
more accurate term. Clearly, this is some elevated and highly positive affect
that an observer may perceive, and there is no reason why selecting this or
that word – for example, joy, exaltation, euphoria, or exuberance – would
actually aid in a precise analysis of the actual feel. However, there is a
pattern to the emergence of that affect, and that pattern links it to the
pattern of mastery pleasure. Zablocki describes this pattern: "Bruderhof
members speak of patterns of joy. They recognize a certain indissoluble
relationship between joy and struggle:

> The euphoria has to be regained again and again. The Holy Spirit is always
> a visitor, never a possession. God doesn't need us, but if we are worthy, His
> spirit comes to us.[54]

In other words, the joy comes after a crisis and it depends on the way that
the crisis is overcome by means of faith and discipline. The entire way of

[50] Arnold, *A Joyful*, 157.
[51] Ibid., 256. Compare this to Philo's description of the Therapeutae in *De Vita Contemplativa* in
Chapter 4.
[52] Zablocki, *The Joyful*, 166.   [53] Ibid., 159.   [54] Ibid., 160.

life in the Bruderhof community – the austerity, discipline, and faith – prepares the members to overcome the crisis and experience the benefit of self-conquest, which is joy.

And just as the evolutionary theory of group solidarity and religious motivation predicts in regards to mastery pleasure, the Bruderhof joy is a unifier, motivator, and energizing affect. As a member put it in Zablocki's study: "The real euphoria of community living comes from the continual fulfillment you feel, that you're at peace with yourself, and you're at peace with your neighbors, and you're doing what you really think you should be doing."[55] The joy helps "in harmonizing the collective behavior experience" – that is, "transforming it into enthusiasm for and commitment to the group."[56]

These two primary dimensions of Bruderhof joy, its relation to struggle and its unifying and energizing effect toward communal goals, help us situate the Bruderhof in the general scheme of church-sect theory along with the Qumran sect and the Pashupata ascetics. The three cases share several common features: formal or informal initiation and initiatory hardships, ongoing austerities, a theory of sin and emphasis on the sensory nature of sin, depersonalization, insistence on discipline and self-control, a distinct and powerful relationship of individual to God, prominent discourse, and display of joy. One other feature – in-group socialization – is shared by two of the three groups, excluding the Pashupatas, who tend to move about the countryside as individuals.

All three cases show a correlation between affect regulation and self-awareness, as well as self-identity of the individual in relationship to the group or to the social world. What the cases demonstrate is the loss of individuality, immersion in the group in the case of Qumran and Bruderhoff or in Shiva-identity in the case of Pashupata. Extreme affect regulation in the form of endurance of hardship in pursuit of higher pleasure (joy) played a role in the way that individuals were socialized into the sectarian world to which they belong. So the primary fact that emerges from the comparison is not necessarily group cohesiveness but depersonalization and new identity formation. This appears to be a more essential feature of the sect category, perhaps a condition for others, such as group cohesiveness and altruism.[57]

---

[55] Ibid., 160.   [56] Ibid., 166.

[57] The subject of depersonalization usually appears in research that focuses on the psychological or psychiatric dimensions of cult and cult trauma. See for example, James L. Griffin, *Religion That Heals, Religion That Harms: A Guide for Clinical Practice* (New York: Guilford Press, 2010), 134.

Note on Reduction

A question that arises is to what extent can we explain the pattern that has emerged in comparing three unrelated communities in terms of evolutionary theory – even cultural evolution. Could the behavioral dynamics not have developed from a certain ideological or philosophical realization of what is good and right – or meaningful – and thus be explained as a purely cultural response to intellectual agendas?[58] One effective way of illustrating such a possibility would be to trace the ideological influence of a sect such as the Qumran community – using perhaps its practices related to sex and food – through New Testament Christianity and through the two or three first centuries of the common era until we arrive at the moral sermonizing about sex and food by figures such as Origen and Clement and perhaps as far forward as Augustine.[59] There is no leaning in such a theorizing toward biological explanations of any kind. Whether married or celibate, in the case of the *yahad* group, the members of the Qumran community exhibited a particular social ethos in regard to sexuality and food – fasting, simplicity, and purity of food – that stood in contrast to mainline Jewish-Hellenistic culture. This clearly had an effect on the early Christian communities in Palestine and the Eastern Mediterranean. Would it be fair to draw the conclusion that the social-sectarian nature of Qumran and the social structure of early Christian communities, rather than some ethical or theological idea about chastity, was the decisive factor? As we consider that the Greco-Roman world was finding out about Qumran via the writings of Josephus, Philo and Pliny the Elder, we need to remember that the ideology of such writers – and the examples they chose to highlight – was already deeply influenced by Neoplatonism and Stoicism. Philo, for example, saw in Qumran an example of what he had already reported in reference to the Egyptian Therapeutae, whom he contrasted with Greek culture in the areas of sex and food.

While the precise relationship between philosophical ideas and social factors cannot be sorted out in the single case of pleasure, Clement of

The Bruderhof group is not considered a cult, and perhaps "depersonalization" is too strong a term for this case.

[58] The topic of causality versus interpretation in historical and comparative research is enormous and cannot be broached in this limited space. In more recent times, it involves Karl Lamprecht's "New History," Max Weber's *Verstehen*, Heidegger and Gadamer's hermeneutics, feminist theory, postmodernism, and other approaches.

[59] This is what Peter Brown does with reference to sex in *The Body and Society: Men, Women, and Sexual Renunciation in Early Christianity* (New York: Columbia University Press, 1988), 37 ff.

Alexandria (ca 150–225) can be used as a case study against the overly reductive sociobiological argument. He was a resident of the cosmopolitan Alexandria and was familiar with the great gastronomic offerings of that city. In *Christ the Educator*, he lists a dazzling array of food offerings available to residents of that city – eels, mussels, oysters, and scallops, to name just some of the seafood offerings – and describes the variety of ways such foods are cooked and served. But the survey leads him to this conclusion: "We must restrain the belly." The purpose of life should not be pleasure, and food should be "plain and restrained."[60]

As far as sex was concerned, Clement was even stricter. He regarded any practice of making the sexual act more pleasurable as "vulgar and plebeian." He applauded Moses for prohibiting the eating of hyena meat due to the animal's sexual behavior.[61] Clement was just one example of a church father whose views on food and sex contrasted with his Greco-Roman milieu and then hardened into the much broader Christian ethos of medieval and later times. And yet he was a sophisticated urban dweller, widely read in philosophical and aesthetic Greek literature as well as Jewish and Stoic sources, which are on display in his evaluation of sexual and dining conduct. He was fascinated by an ethic that comported with his philosophical and scientific worldview rather than acting based on his implicit situation in a particular social organization.

The church-sect theory forces us to isolate variables that may be at work in explaining both religious views and practices. The social-organizational dimension is the variable that appears to be most consistent with evolutionary theory where the formation of groups and their success in competitive environments are driving forces. Clearly, the gap between such a theory and the work of religious historians such as Peter Brown and others is decisive.[62] If the methodological gap is unbridgeable, then the exercise of discussing Qumran, Pashupata, and Bruderhof in a single context may have been interesting but theoretically insufficient. Is there any experimental method of narrowing the gap between anhedonic practices and ideologies and reductive theorizing?

Field researchers like Harvey Whitehouse, Richard Sosis, and others have examined the evolutionary role of religious beliefs and rituals in the formation and strengthening of groups. For example, Sosis has argued,

---

[60] Clement of Alexandria, *Christ the Educator*, trans., Simon P. Wood (New York: Fathers of the Church Publication, 1954), 2:1:3–4.

[61] Brown, *The Body*, 132–133.

[62] Robert Bellah's *Religion in Human Evolution* is probably the most prominent example of such theorizing in recent years, but he is not a historian.

based on field studies, that rituals such as initiation "promote group cohesion by requiring members to engage in behavior that is too costly to fake."[63] The cost is the pain or discomfort applied to the initiate, and ritual success is the display of a stoic tolerance of these trials. The reward is admission into the group, which also benefits by the display of solidarity – a sign of prosocial behavior.

While this anthropological work is useful, it leaves untouched the matter of evolutionary fitness in relation to specific religious groups. Group fitness can be viewed in the context of reproductive success, both the group's and that of the individual members. Individual submission to the authority of elders, especially in social and religious matters – accepting norms that regulate individual gratification – would contribute to both individual and group fitness, at least up to a point. This appears to resolve the dilemma Darwin had pointed out of the conflict between group and individual fitness. But the smaller intentional groups – like the Pashupata, Aghori, and Qumran (*yahad*) – are more like monastic groups that tend to reject reproductive success and depend on voluntary joiners rather than demographic continuity and growth. In such groups, there is more than submission to religious hierarchy; there is actually a loss of individuality – that is, complete immersion in the group identity or in God. Therefore, the initiatory ordeals should not be evaluated in the same way as tribal initiation where group solidarity is directly linked to group and individual fitness in an evolutionary sense. Furthermore, inasmuch as the groups studied by anthropologists articulate religious worldviews as a factor in the justification of the rituals, we have not properly situated the religious in relationship to the biopsychological factors.[64]

Methodologically speaking, to understand the function of uncomfortable or painful practices like initiation, one should look at examples taken from nonreproductive and nonreligious groups that also insist on initiation as a condition of membership.[65] These can include academic groups,

[63] Richard Sosis, "The Adaptive Value of Religious Ritual: Rituals Promote Group Cohesion by Requiring Members to Engage in Behavior That Is Too Costly to Fake," *American Scientist* 92, no. 1 (2004): 166–172; Harvey Whitehouse and Jonathan A. Lanman, "The Ties That Bind Us: Ritual, Fusion, and Identification," *Current Anthropology* 55, no. 6 (2014): 674–695.

[64] Other factors – such emotional arousal, group identification, or identity fusion – have been more precisely investigated. Whitehouse and Lanman, "The Ties." See Jose M. Marques, Dominic Abrams, and Rui G. Serodio, "Being Better by Being Right: Subjective Groups Dynamics and Derogation of In-Group Deviants When Generic Norms Are Undermined," in *Small Groups*, eds., John M. Levine and Richard Moreland (New York: Routledge, 2006), 157–176.

[65] Donald C. Pennington, *The Social Psychology of Behavior in Small Groups* (East Sussex: Psychology Press, 2002), 1–26.

military groups, professional groups, social clubs, and others. One example is the "crucible" initiation rite – a "physically and mentally grueling final test before being recognized formally as a member" of the marines.[66] The rite is classical initiation inasmuch as it involves separation (humiliation), transition (hand-to-hand wrestling in "the bear pit"), and reincorporation (mock jump, baptism by drinking noxious liquids). Another example – in this case, in an experimental setting – is the study of student groups. Naturally, a large proportion of experimental studies take place on university campuses. The study of initiation rituals on campuses is international in scope – suggesting that the phenomenon is not merely an aspect of American campus life.[67]

The most famous and still highly cited study was published in 1959 by Aronson and Mills, and it is particularly salient to the present discussion because it focuses on the hedonic dimension of group initiation: "The Effect of Severity of Initiation on Liking of a Group."[68] In brief, students were divided into three groups, which had to read aloud passages to students in a sex education group. The first sample had to read out loud highly embarrassing (obscene) words, the second sample read milder passages with sexual terms, and the third read neutral material. Members of the three sample groups were given headphones with which they listened to a long and dull discussion related to the psychology of sex and were asked to rate their level of enjoyment of the discussion. Those students who went through the most difficult experience related the highest level of enjoyment, and those who had read neutral material reported the lowest levels of enjoyment. Aronson and Mill accounted for this by means of the recently published theory of Festinger on cognitive dissonance.[69] The satisfaction comes from reducing the highly displeasing mental incoherence between the embarrassment of the obscene readings and one's self-image as a decent person. This theory is still influential in explaining the hedonic results of Aronson and Mill's experiment.[70]

---

[66] Kirsten M. Keller, Kimberly Curry Hall, William Marcellino, and Jacqueline A. Mauro, *Hazing in the U.S. Armed Forces: Recommendations for Hazing Prevention Policy and Practice* (Santa Monica, CA: Rand Corporation, 2015).

[67] Diana Dias and Maria Jose Sa, "Initiation Rituals in University as Lever for Group Cohesion," *Journal of Further and Higher Education* 38, no. 4 (2014): 447–464.

[68] Eliot Aronson and Judson Mills, "The Effect of Severity of Initiation on Liking of a Group," *The Journal of Abnormal and Social Psychology* 59, no. 1 (1959): 177–181. See also Susan T. Fisk, Daniel T. Gilbert, and Gardner Lindzey, *Handbook of Social Psychology*, vol. 1 (Hoboken, NJ: John Wiley and Sons, 2010), 61.

[69] Leon F. Festinger, *A Theory of Cognitive Dissonance* (Evanston, IL: Row, Peterson, 1957).

[70] Donald Pennington, *The Social Psychology of Behavior in Small Groups* (East Sussex: Psychology Press, 2002), 78. Over the decades, the theory has spawned multiple subsidiary paradigms: belief

Such a theory may indeed explain reports by students or even soldiers who emerge from initiatory ordeals with a highly favorable impression of those who humiliated them and include positive affect in their assessment of the overall experience. However, a number of problems persist: (1) Cognitive dissonance theory implies certain judgments related to one's world and one's self-image that may be based on a culture of individuality that is characteristic of the modern West. It may be impossible to universalize the theory. (2) The experiment conducted by Aronson and Mills is not fine-grained enough to eliminate other possibilities. For example, it is possible that the reported enjoyment is due to the subjects' display of a capacity to overcome the displeasure of embarrassment or that the pleasure is a sort of mastery pleasure (achievement) as observed and approved by the listeners of the readings. For example, the experiment could be repeated, but this time, before putting on the headphones, the subjects should read reports of assessments of their reading. Half of each group – obscene, mildly sexual, neutral – should read positive assessments and the other half should read negative assessments of their readings. It is possible to predict that those students who read mildly sexual material but saw positive assessments would actually report a higher level of enjoyment of the material they have to listen to than those who read obscene material but received negative assessments.[71]

This revised experimental approach may link signaling theories such as that of Richard Sosis with experimental results involving nonreligious groups. In the absence of any religious factor, however indirect, subjects who demonstrate ability to overcome unpleasant or painful experiences may be enjoying the approval of others.[72] Because I do not know if such an experiment has been conducted, it is not possible to evaluate such a theory in contrast with cognitive dissonance theory. The two theories can work in tandem – social approval of mastery display may actually help the reduction of cognitive dissonance.

disconfirmation, effort justification, induced compliance, and others. The theory has largely morphed into attribution theory. For a critical review, see Eddie Harmon-Jones and Judson Mills, "An Introduction to Cognitive Dissonance Theory and an Overview of Current Perspectives on the Theory," *Science Confluence Series* (Washington, DC: American Psychological Association, 1999): 3–21, and more recently, Joel Cooper, *Cognitive Dissonance: 50 Years of a Classic Theory* (Los Angeles: Sage Publishers, 2007).

[71] Joel Cooper, *Cognitive Dissonance: 50 Years of a Classic Theory* (Los Angeles: Sage Publishers, 2007), 101; J. Aronson, H. Blanton, and J. Cooper, "From Dissonance to Disidentification: Selectivity in the Self-Affirmation Process," *Journal of Personality and Social Psychology* 68, no. 6 (1995): 986–996.

[72] See Robert Merrihew Adams, *A Theory of Virtue: Excellence in Being for the Good* (Clarendon: Oxford University Press, 2006), 219; Theodore Millon and Melvin J. Lerner, *Handbook of Psychology, Personality and Social Psychology* (Hoboken, NJ: Wiley and Sons, 2003), 13.

In religious contexts, it would be extremely difficult to conduct such experiments. Historical data on martyrs such as Al Hallaj, Perpetua, and Rabbi Akiva – if it can be trusted, which is highly questionable – shows martyrs who not only defy their torturers and mocking mobs but also declare their joy in the face of both pain and social rejection.[73] If nothing else, such literature highlights an ideology that promotes a mastery pleasure that does not depend on social approval – although there is a sense of positive affirmation that is based on the presumed surveillance of an approving God. It is safe to say that in three cases discussed in this chapter, the role of God as such an approving entity is real. God is not merely a source of authority represented by the group but a living presence in the consciousness and self-identity of the novice who joins the group. God is also implicated, along with the group, in impressing on the subject an awareness of his sinfulness, which is linked to sensory objects or sensual desires. Finally, while the reported satisfaction, the joy, would emerge from the mastery that is displayed to both God and the group, the religious theory at work is that such joy is a gift from God, not a product of some internal psychological process.

A cognitive-evolutionary theory that accounts for prosocial behavior in terms of the conception of a being who observes and punishes cheaters needs to account for the joy that is so prominent in such situations. It must also account for the consciousness that the source of joy is that being, the same one who can be so punitive. Finally, the theorist needs to account for the fact that this type of joy – in psychological terms, the mastery pleasure developed through cultural learning – is a fairly recent development in human evolutionary history. This is a tall order, and the work needs to continue.

---

[73] A. Glucklich, *Dying for Heaven* (New York: Harper Collins, 2009), 251–286.

CHAPTER 7

Narratives and Rituals of Pleasure

Introduction

This chapter looks in some detail at two narratives that deal with the subject of pleasure: The "Rasa Lila" narrative embedded in the *Bhagavata Purana* (*BhP*), book 10, and Paul Ricoeur's chapter 4 ("The Fragility of Affect") in *Fallible Man*.[1] This may appear to be a strange choice – given the vast difference in time, style, purpose, and sensibility – but both do, in fact, deal with the subject of pleasure in a way that invites such a juxtaposition. The chapter will then look at a third narrative whose treatment of pleasure is obscure: Nahman of Bratslav's "The King's Daughter Who Went Missing."[2] The argument of this chapter is that the mutual illumination obtained through the first two narratives helps us understand the third. The chapter also looks at two rituals – the first is the annual performance of the Rasa Lila during the Holi spring festival and the second is the General Rectification – the penitential ritual invented by Nahman.[3] The rituals will demonstrate the prescriptive value of the religious narratives in actual practice. They will allow us to evaluate whether Ricoeur's abstract, perhaps introspectively devised phenomenology has legs to stand on in practice and whether religious practices can ameliorate the fragility in our human condition where it comes to feeling and affect.

---

[1] Edwin F. Bryant, *Krishna: The Beautiful Legend of God* (London: Penguin, 2003); Graham M. Schweig, *Dance of Divine Love: The Rasa Lila of Krishna from the Bhagavata Purana* (Princeton, NJ: Princeton University Press, 2005); Paul Ricoeur, *Fallible Man* (New York: Fordham University Press, 1986).

[2] Marianne Schleicher, *Intertextuality in the Tales of Rabbi Nahman of Bratslav: A Close Reading of Sippurey Ma'asiyot* (Leiden, the Netherlands: E. J. Brill, 2007).

[3] McKim Marriott, "Holi: The Feast of Love," in *Krishna: Myths, Rites and Attitudes,* ed., Milton B. Singer, 99–112; Zvi Mark, *The Revealed and Hidden Writings of Rabbi Nahman of Bratslav* (Berlin, Germany: Walter de Gruyter, 2015); Arthur Green, *Tormented Master: A Life of Rabbi Nahman of Bratslav* (Tuscaloosa, AL: University of Alabama Press, 1979).

In this chapter, I avoid calling the "Rasa Lila" a myth and "The King's Daughter" a fairy tale. I do not believe doing so would contribute to the argument I am making about pleasure in religious narrative and ritual. Ricoeur agreed with Mircea Eliade that myth always dealt with origins; this could be the origin of the whole of reality or a fragment of reality such as an ethical rule, a political institution, "or even the mode of human existence according to this or that condition, innocent or fallen."[4] The Krishna narrative, on this theory, perhaps explains the origins of Krishna devotionalism in Mathura (or all of Vraj), along with the social practices and institutions that owe their existence to such devotionalism.[5] "The King's Daughter" relates the origins of humanity's present day fallen condition – that is, our estrangement from God and our sinfulness.

But contemporary scholarship on the subject of mythology is far less clear and straightforward. Bruce Lincoln, for example, begins his historical study of the uses of the concept of "myth" by admitting that myth cannot be defined. For example, he situates Eliade's theory of mythical origins as a single moment in a long history of ideas, which itself is a sort of "mythos" – a reflection of social and cultural power relations and agendas.[6] Indeed, as Laurie Patton and Wendy Doniger noted twenty years ago, "the hope for elegant master theory has atrophied."[7] The theories of Frazer, Jung, Freud, Levi-Strauss, Eliade, and others "have lost their power of persuasion."

My own agenda here does not require definitional clarity in regards to the narrative practice that scholars call "myth." It is clear that the *Bhagavata Purana*'s "Rasa Lila" and Nahman of Bratslav's "The King's Daughter" are both narratives or stories that play a significant role in the religious lives of two recognized religious communities, and that this role includes descriptive and prescriptive dimensions that are linked to religious action – a festival and a penitential rite.[8] Both narratives, finally, bear directly on the subject of pleasure and its relationship to joy or happiness.

---

[4] Paul Ricoeur, *Philosophical Anthropology* (Cambridge, UK: Polity, 2013), 161.

[5] Thomas J. Hopkins, "The Social Teachings of the Bhagavata Purana," in *Krishna: Myths, Rites, Attitudes*, ed., Milton B. Singer, 3–22; Ravi M. Gupta and Kenneth R. Valpey, *The Bhagavata Purana: Sacred Text and Living Tradition* (New York: Columbia University Press, 2013).

[6] Bruce Lincoln, *Theorizing Myth: Narrative, Ideology, and Scholarship* (Chicago: University of Chicago Press, 1999); see also his "Mythic Narrative and Cultural Diversity in American Society," in *Myth and Method*, eds., Laurie Patton and Wendy Doniger (Charlottesville: University of Virginia Press, 1996), 163–176.

[7] Laurie Patton and Wendy Doniger, eds., *Myth and Method*, 2.

[8] The Nahman story is prescriptive even when not explicitly referred to by penitents. See Schleicher, *Intertextuality*, 104–105; See also Ora Wisking-Elper, *Tradition and Fantasy in the Tales of Reb Nahman of Bratslav* (Albany: State University of New York Press, 1998), 58–59.

What may be far more controversial about this chapter is the juxtaposition of such examples of programmatic religious narratives with what is usually regarded as academic and therefore dispassionate and objective discourse: Paul Ricoeur's phenomenology of pleasure in *Fallible Man*. My argument is that Ricoeur's precise rendering of affective "fragility" and the "disproportion" of feeling does not explain the other two narratives but belongs with them as a distinct – but mutually illuminating – account of positive affect as a matter of spiritual interest. As it turns out, there is actually something obscure in Ricoeur that the two older narratives help us understand: namely, the role of play (the religious ritual) in the resolution of our affective fragility. There is a hint in *Fallible Man* that the outward action of feeling, its intentional orientation, gives the world its affective qualities – as lovable or hateful –   and this is a sort of "game" of objectification or the "game of objects" colored by affect.[9] But this is not precisely the same game as the one played in the ritual of Holi in India and the General Rectification (*ha-tikkun ha-kelali*) in Nahman's system.

Bhagavata Purana: Krishna and the *Gopis*

The overall narrative of Krishna, as told in the *Bhagavata Purana, Harivamsa, Mahabharata*, and *Bhagavad Gita*, is familiar. In brief, Krishna was born as the eighth child of Vasudeva and Devaki. His uncle, King Kamsa, was determined to kill the infant due to a prophesy that Devaki's eighth child would kill him. The infant was saved by Vishnu, who placed him with Nanda and Yashoda to be raised in the village of Vrindavana. Krishna grew up in that idyllic environment but had to overcome the many assaults against him instigated by demonic forces on behalf of his evil uncle – whom he finally killed.

Krishna's life as a youngster in the village has been the focus of literature, stage performances, rituals, films, music, and every other artistic medium. It was a colorful, playful, and often mischievous life with the villagers, especially the *gopis*, the shepherd girls. At the heart of the long *Bhagavata Purana* – in book 10, that covers the narrative of Krishna's life in Vrindavana – is an inserted literary gem that occupies chapters 29–33. This is the Rasa Lila text about Krishna and the *gopis* – a vividly erotic but equally theological and even philosophical rumination about pleasure, devotion ,and social life. The Rasa Lila presents a sustained treatment of

---

[9] Ricoeur, *Falllible*, 89.

the situation of humans between the love of God and the constraints of social existence.

The basic narrative facts of chapters 29–33 are few and simple: The women of the village – the *gopis* – give up their domestic chores and leave home in order to frolic with Krishna. Due to his amorous attentions, they become proud, and so he disappears. The *gopis* seek him out desperately, interrogating all of nature concerning his whereabouts – to no avail. In his absence, the women imitate the play (*lila*) they had previously engaged in with Krishna, each young woman alternately assuming a different role in the play. However, one favored *gopi* has been allowed to join Krishna when he disappeared, but she, too, was finally abandoned due to her pride. Eventually, Krishna reappears and after a pointed verbal exchange in which he emphasizes a non-sensory approach to devotion and tells the *gopis* to resume their social obligations, the Rasa Lila begins between Krishna and the women.

The text has been analyzed and interpreted in a variety of ways by early commentators and contemporary scholars.[10] However, in order to understand the text's description and conception of pleasure, it is necessary to provide specific details touching on that theme. The following are some of the key moments from the narrative.

The Rasa Lila narrative, narrated by Shri Shuka, opens with Krishna, with his powers of becoming manifest (*yogamaya*) "turned his thoughts toward enjoying love (*vīkṣya rantum*)" as the jasmine flowers bloomed, under moon rising in the east.[11] Krishna played his flute, "capturing the hearts of the beautiful-eyed women and arousing Kama – the God of love."[12] The women came to Krishna, some abandoning the milking of cows, others leaving the milk on the fire and the cakes in the oven. Other chores were also abandoned as the women rushed to be with Krishna. They ignored the pleas of their husbands, fathers, and brothers: "they were in a state of rapture."[13]

---

[10] G. Schweig links the narrative to the progress of the devotee in yoga and devotion, away from death, rebirth, and karma (in a word, suffering) to the supreme joy of freedom. See, for instance, *Dance*, 155. For a non-theological analysis, see Tracy Coleman, "Viraha-Bhakti and Strīdharma – Rereading the Story of Kṛṣṇa and the Gopīs in the Harivaṃśa and the Bhāgavata Purāṇa," *Journal of the American Oriental Society* 130, no. 3 (2010): 385–412. Coleman argues against the notion that the Rasa Lila is socially liberating for women.
[11] *Bhagavata Purana* (*BhP*), 29.1.   [12] Ibid., 29.3–29.4.
[13] Ibid., 29.8; *mohitaḥ* means beguiled, according to Apte's dictionary, and Schweig translates it as "entranced" rather than being in a state of rapture.

Those who could not physically leave "thought of Kṛṣṇa with eyes closed, completely absorbed in meditation (*dhyāna*)."[14] These women's bad karma was destroyed by the pain of separation – they left their body and united with the "supreme soul" they considered as their lover.[15] In the forest, Krishna addressed the women, imploring them to return to their families and responsibilities: "hurry now to the cow-pen and serve your husbands."[16] That, Krishna stated, is the highest dharma for a woman. In fact, there was no conflict between that dharma and loving God: "Love for me comes from learning about me, seeing me, meditating on me and reciting my glories – not in this way, by physical proximity."[17]

The women responded by rejecting their social dharma: "Renouncing all enjoyments of the senses (*viṣaya*), we are devoted to the soles of your feet."[18] "Let this be our *dharma* when it comes to you, the source of this advice, O Lord – after all, you are the soul within all relatives."[19] "Our hearts, which were absorbed in our households, have been stolen away with ease by you, as have our hands from domestic chores."[20] "It is clear that you have accepted birth to remove the tribulations and fears of Vraj just as the Lord, the Primeval Person protects the denizens of heaven."[21]

Having heard this appeal, the narrator reports, Krishna "laughed and enjoyed in amorous pleasures (*arīramat*) from compassion, even though his satisfaction is self-contained (*ātmā rāmo*)."[22] "Arousing Kama in the young women of Vraj with jokes, smiles and glances, playfully scratching their breasts, girdles, thighs, hair and hands with his nails, and embracing them with outstretched arms, he gave them pleasure (*ramayāṃ cakāra*)."[23]

All of this pleasurable attention made the women proud, and Krishna disappeared "out of kindness." Chapter 30 thus begins with the search for Krishna and culminates with the play of the *gopīs*: "The *gopīs* [uttering] these crazed words, became perplexed in their search for Kṛṣṇa. With their hearts [dedicated] to him, each of them initiated the *līlā* of Bhagavān."[24] Then, on the banks of the Kalinidi River, the *gopīs* sang to Krishna, the remover of fear and pain, praising the sweetness of his words, which are life-giving for those who are suffering.

---

[14] Ibid., 29.9.

[15] Ibid., 29.10–2.9.11. This narrative is based on Bryant's translation. However, the pertinent line reads: "dhyānaparāpatācyutāśāleṣanarivṛtayā kaśīṇamaṅgalāḥ," which translates, "because of the joy of embracing with Acyuta (Krishna) that was achieved by means of meditation, the pleasures of ordinary life were diminished." This translation is closer to that of Schweig than Bryant.

[16] Ibid., 29.22.   [17] Ibid., 29.27.   [18] Ibid., 29.31.   [19] Ibid., 29.32.   [20] Ibid., 29.34.

[21] Ibid., 29.41.   [22] Ibid., 29.42.   [23] Ibid., 29.46.   [24] Ibid., 30.14.

Krishna then appeared, and the pleasure giving resumed. One *gopi* was "burning with love" while another trembled with the fury of love.[25] Another drew Krishna into her heart through her eyes. All of them massaged his hands and feet. Krishna then assured them that he had disappeared in order to increase their devotion to God – as a service to them. It is at that point (chapter 33) that the celebration of Rasa Lila began with a dancing circle of *gopis*. Although they were many, each thought she was alone with Krishna. "They were intent on amorous pleasure (*ratipriyā*) and overjoyed (*muditā*) by Kṛṣṇa's touch."[26] "Kṛṣṇa placed his arm on the shoulder of one of the *gopīs*. Smelling it, fragrant as a blue lotus and smeared with sandalwood, she kissed it, the hair of her body tingling with rapture (*hṛṣṭa romā*)."[27] The women were delighted as they danced and sang.

"Although content within himself, the Lord became manifest in as many forms as there were *gopī* women, and enjoyed himself with them in *līlā* pastimes."[28] "Kṛṣṇa's desires are always fulfilled, and his propensity for enjoyment is fulfilled within himself, but during all those nights he participated in this way in the company of throngs of young women. Such nights, brilliant with the rays of the moon, are the setting for *rāsa* in both poetry and prose that describes autumn."[29]

This profoundly hedonic narrative may be the best-loved religious work in India. And it is also one of the most thoroughly analyzed. Surprisingly, the sophisticated and extensive treatment of pleasure – in a variety of forms – has escaped focused scholarly attention. I shall return to this pleasure following a reading of Ricoeur's own text on pleasure.

Paul Ricoeur's *Fallible Man*

Paul Ricoeur wrote *Fallible Man* (1960) before his turn to hermeneutics, and the book stands as the author's move away from existential phenomenology.[30] The agenda of the book – the origins and implications of human evil as rooted in "disproportion" – are quite broad. However, in the process of examining the full range of this fallibility, Ricoeur devoted a superb section (chapter 4) to affect. This opens up a nuanced

---

[25] Ibid., 32.5–32.6.   [26] Ibid., 33.8.   [27] Ibid., 33.11.   [28] Ibid., 33.19.
[29] Ibid., 33.25.
[30] Don Ihde, *Hermeneutic Phenomenology: The Philosophy of Paul Ricoeur* (Evanston, IL: Northwestern University Press, 1971). David Pellauer and Bernard Dauenhauer, "Paul Ricoeur," *The Standford Encyclopedia of Philosophy*, 2016, https://plato.stanford.edu/archives/win2016/entries/ricoeur/ (accessed November 22, 2018).

phenomenology of pleasure that I am hijacking as a descriptive narrative
that can stand on its own in order to be contrasted with other, "mythical"
narratives of pleasure.

Ricoeur's narrative is a phenomenology of human pleasure and happiness and, thus, is not meant to serve as an explanatory tool, a key for
unlocking the meaning of symbolic narratives such as myths. It is a precise
description offered via introspection.[31] Though fine-grained, it may be
either accurate in its description of pleasure or entirely off point. In either
case, it is a narrative about pleasure and thus presents the opportunity of
juxtaposition in relation to the Purana's own narrative about pleasure. Due
to our own contemporary situation, we naturally wonder whether
Ricoeur's narrative can somehow illuminate the older one and not vice
versa. By "illuminate," which is not the same thing as explain, I mean that
it helps us see that whatever the mythical discourse about Krishna and *gopis*
means – what the characters stand for in some meta-narrative frame of
reference – they clearly and explicitly appeal to feelings, affects, and
subject–object relations. And they share this focus with the work of
Ricoeur. It is important to note that juxtaposition is not an explanation
and may never be so, however suggestive the exercise may seem.[32] A third
item – a broader frame of reference – may have to be added before a true
explanation for the meaning of the myth can emerge.[33] That will potentially be the ritual use of narratives.

The following material comes directly out of chapter 4 of *Fallible Man*,
an early text in which Ricoeur examines the emergence of evil beyond pure
reflection – that is, the domain of image, symbol, or myth. He presupposes
a split or "disproportion" between the discursive and objective, and
affective "ante-predicative" domain of experience. In chapter 4, the
broader examination narrows down to the domain of pleasure and happiness and offers a very precise phenomenological narrative about "feeling,"
which can be defined as a combination of intention and affection. "Feeling, for instance love or hate, is without any doubt intentional: it is a
feeling of 'something' – the lovable, the hateful." Intentionality "designates

---

[31] The analysis reveals Ricoeur's indebtedness to Maurice Merleau-Ponty – specifically, *The Phenomenology of Perception*, trans., Colin Smith (London: Routledge, 2003).

[32] Ricoeur reflected on this point – the tension between structuralism and phenomenology as an explanatory tool – in *The Conflict of Interpretations: Essays in Hermeneutics* (London: Continuum Press, 2005), 33.

[33] Ricoeur sometimes offered a functionalist understanding of pleasure that was indebted to Freudian theory – at least in the analysis of art appreciation: *The Conflict*, 196–198.

qualities felt on things, on persons, on the world." Intentionality also "manifests and reveals the way in which the self is inwardly affected."[34]

The affective aspect of feeling corresponds to that which I have earlier described as its hedonic tone and as ineffable: "The affect aspect of feeling vanishes as soon as its intentional aspect fades away, or at least sinks into an inexpressible obscurity."[35] "Since the whole of our language has been worked out in the dimension of objectivity, in which the subject and the object are distinct and opposed, feeling can be described only paradoxically as the unity of intention and an affection, of an intention toward the world and an affection of the self."[36] Recall that in a previous chapter, in Thomas Mann's description of clouds and music, an entire evening scene was described as pointing indirectly to the obscure inner affect that assigned qualities to these objects, and such descriptions were therefore offered as the public face of an inner state that must remain ineffable.[37] Ricoeur's description would thus apply to the author's technical difficulty with affect: "It is only thanks to its aim, overspilling itself into a felt quality, into an affective 'correlate,' that feeling can be expressed, said, communicated."[38]

Ricoeur regards this dual aspect of feeling as a paradox: "How can the same experience designate a thing-quality and, through this thing-quality, manifest, express, and reveal the inwardness of an I?" The answer is that this is due to the "reciprocity of feeling and knowing."[39] Knowing is the exteriorizing and posing of the object in "being," which sets up a "cleavage" between the object and the subject. Feeling, in contrast, is "the manifestation of a relation to the world that constantly restores our complicity with it, our inherence and belonging in it." This is more profound than polarity and duality. That relation to the world is "pre-reflective and pre-objective," and due to the duality of language, it can only be approached indirectly.

The paradox of object and inner I is the product of the knowing function. Ricoeur notes that "We can see why feeling, thus intermingled

---

[34] Ricoeur, *Fallible*, 84.
[35] Ibid., 84. See Maurice Merleau-Ponty's schematic description of this phenomenon in *Phenomenology of Perception*, trans., Colin Smith (London: Routledge, 2003), 179: "Simple representations can replace the natural stimuli of pleasure and pain according to the laws governing the association of ideas ... these substitutions superimpose pleasure and pain to circumstances which are naturally speaking, matters of indifference to us."
[36] Ricoeur, *Fallible*, 88.
[37] "Only this one spot enchanted him, relaxed his willpower, made him happy." Thomas Mann, *Death in Venice*, trans., Stanley Appelbaum (New York: Dover Publications, 1995), 34.
[38] Ricoeur, *Fallible*, 84.   [39] Ibid., 85.

with the adventure of knowledge and objectivity, must present to reflection the paradoxical intentional texture that we described. For it is on the things elaborated by the work of objectification that feeling project its affective correlates, its felt qualities: the lovable and the hateful, the desirable and the loathsome, the sad and the joyous; thus it seems to play the game of the object." The feeling appears as "a coloring of the soul: it is this landscape which is cheerful, and it is I who am elated."[40]

Feeling itself is also cleaved by a "disproportion" in Ricoeur's terms. An objective account, such as biology, would explain the division of feeling on the basis of the harm or help that designates the value of a feeling. But Ricoeur emphasizes the distinct, nonobjective way that feeling exhibits its inner conflict, one that is not based on function or objective analysis. This points to the distinction, in feeling, between pleasure and happiness. "Thus our whole reflection on disproportion comes to center itself on one point that is somehow the locus and the node of disproportion. It is this affective node which Plato called *thumos* and tried to situate between *epithymia*, sensuous desire, and reason, whose specific desire is *eros*."[41] "The inner conflict of human desire reaches its climax in *thumos*," which is the human feeling par excellence.

The affective (non-intentional) already represents human fallibility in that it diverges toward *epithymia* and eros or the animalistic and fully human. Methodologically this means that "By whatever name this primordial duality is called – opinion and science, intuition and understanding . . . presence and sense –it forbids us to formulate a philosophy of perception prior to a philosophy of discourse and forces us to work them out together, one with the other, one by the other."[42] And, "If one does not take into consideration the primordial disproportion of vital desire and intellectual love (or spiritual joy), one entirely misses the specific nature of human affectivity."[43] Clearly a biologically reductive theory of pleasure, as adaptation, would crash in such a failure.

Affect is, at its root, both pleasure and happiness, where the primordial *thumos* is more basic than either of these. "There are two kinds of *terminations* of affective movement: one of them completes and perfects isolated, partial, finite acts, or process. This is pleasure."[44] Furthermore, "The perfection of pleasure is finite. It dwells only in the instant, precarious and perishable like the very goods whose possession pleasure manifests in enjoyment."[45] The other is happiness: "It falls on the other one to be

[40] Ibid., 88.   [41] Ibid., 91–92.   [42] Ibid., 92.   [43] Ibid.   [44] Ibid., 93.   [45] Ibid., 94.

the perfection of the total work of man; this would be the termination of a destiny, of a destination, or an existential project. This would be happiness . . . the fullness of happiness or beatitude."[46]

In this formulation, happiness is not a negation of pleasure but the turning, so to speak, of the basic affect toward eros, which allows us to evaluate the other as mere pleasure. "There is a doubling or second degree feelings that allows us to critique the affectivity. This is a felt critique like a discontentment in mere pleasure." It is too easy to turn this into a moral judgment that pleasure is evil but we must avoid this trap and allow the critique to remain affective – a manifestation of the "eclipse of pleasure by happiness." Happiness does not transcend the would-be evil of pleasure but is the very perfection of pleasure. As Ricoeur understands it, pleasure is more primordial than any adventitious evil. Human experience is broader than a moral split between pleasure and happiness might imply. Action "aims both at a self-sufficient totality, which would give, which would be beatitude, the enjoyment of happiness, at a finite realization in discrete acts, in "results" sanctioned by a consciousness of success or pleasure."[47]

But, unlike happiness, pleasure "puts the seal of its perfection on bodily life . . . pleasure punctuates and ratifies my organic rootedness in the world."[48] Pleasure binds one to life. And yet, "pleasure is total as is happiness; it represents happiness in the instant; but it is precisely this compression of happiness into the instant that threatens to arrest the dynamism of acting in the celebration of *living*."[49]

In the domain of sexuality, exemplified plentifully in the narrative of the Purana, or in the domain of sexual pleasure, the connection between the vital or instinctual and "the human" becomes fully manifest. Sexuality becomes human sexuality when "sexual satisfaction can no longer be simply a physical pleasure. The human being, through pleasure, beyond pleasure, and sometimes by sacrificing pleasure, pursues the satisfaction of the quest with which 'instinct' becomes overlaid; a certain indefiniteness thus enters into it while it is being humanized."[50]

In sum, describing affectivity as "feeling," Ricoeur writes, "The universal function of feeling is to bind together. It connects what knowledge divides; it binds me to things, to beings, to being."[51] But feeling also, as a result, "stretches the self between two fundamental projects, that of the organic life that reaches its term in the instantaneous perfection of pleasure, and that of the spiritual life that aspires to totality, to the perfection of

[46] Ibid., 93.   [47] Ibid., 94.   [48] Ibid.   [49] Ibid.   [50] Ibid., 128.   [51] Ibid., 131–132.

happiness."[52] "It seems, then, that *conflict* is a function of man's most primordial constitutions; the object is synthesis; the self is conflict."[53] This is a latent inner conflict that makes it possible to internalize the external conflict between our efforts and affirmations and the forces of nature and the forces of familial, social, and cultural environments.

Analysis of Narrative and Phenomenology

Applying Ricouer's phenomenology to our reading of the "Rasa Lila" is very suggestive and tempting. And there are also points of similarity between Ricoeur's phenomenology and Samkhya-Yoga philosophy, which is the theoretical background of the Purana where the text is embedded, and certainly many of its Indian commentaries.[54] But this would assume that the mythical figures such as Krishna, *gopis*, and male relatives some-how represent – stand for – entities in Ricoeur's narrative like feeling, pleasure, happiness, or in Samkhya (*purusha, prakriti*, etc.).[55] This is not only highly speculative but brings to mind Jonathan Smith's warning about construing similarity as explanatory, in an act of magical thinking.[56] We can't ignore the essential difference in the context from which each narrative emerges and the function it fulfills in the practices of different worlds. But if magic is the flaw in comparing narratives, there are other ways of thinking about similarity – and, indeed, about magic – as Stanley Tambiah showed in his analysis of the Araka creeper magic.[57] The ana-logical similarity that Tambiah regarded as relevant to analysis is not between discrete objects in one context resembling discrete objects in another context but in the role of the object in a system of relationships within two contexts.

In our case, one does not speak of Krishna as primordial affectivity, the *gopis* as vital desire, and their male relatives as intellectual love, however

---

[52] Ibid., 132.   [53] Ibid.

[54] Gerald James Larsen, *Classical Samkhya: An Interpretation of Its History and Meaning* (Delhi, India: Motilal Banarsidass, 1998), 171–175; Edwin F. Bryant, *The Yoga Sutras of Patanjali* (New York: North Point Press, 2009), 189–190; Swami Āraṇya Hariharānanda, *Yoga Philosophy of Patañjali* (Albany: State University of New York Press, 1983), 157 and passim.

[55] The common denominator until Levi-Strauss's structuralism was the semiotic function of mythical characters, objects, and actions. See Sigmund Freud (*Totem and Taboo, The Interpretation of Dreams*), Carl Jung (*Essays on the Science of Mythology*), Ernst Cassirer (*Symbol, Myth and Culture*), and many others.

[56] Jonathan Z. Smith, *Imagining Religion: From Babylon to Jonestown* (Chicago: University of Chicago Press, 1982), 19–35.

[57] Stanley J. Tambiah, "The Form and Meaning of Magical Acts: A Point of View," *HAU: Journal of Ethnographic Theory* 7, no. 3 (2017): 451–473.

tempting it may be to do so. In fact, I would even hesitate to use Samkhya metaphysics and isolate Krishna as *purusha* (spirit) and the *gopis* as *prakriti* (materiality), as some may be tempted to do. Instead, the useful correspondence is in the dynamic relationship that applies between the key figures in two narratives that focus on pleasure. In order to see how such an analysis might work, some areas of narrative intersection should be pointed out:

In Ricoeur's narrative feeling exhibits an intentional dimension, which is sensory and verbal, and an affective dimension, which is ineffable and obscure. In the "Rasa Lila" narrative, Krishna – "whose joy is perfect" – becomes manifest and subject to sensory interaction, or disappears and can only be reached through profound introspection.

That same split applies to the affective dimension in Ricoeur, which suffers from a "disproportion" in the dual forms of vital desire (*epithymia*) and reason (eros) or pleasure and intellectual love or spiritual joy. This disproportion is what Ricoeur called "affective fragility." The two – desire and reason – do not exist in opposition, but the latter completes the former. There can be a spilling into the momentary pleasure by the totality of happiness: Action "aims both at a self-sufficient totality, which would give, which would be beatitude, the enjoyment of happiness, at a finite realization in discrete acts, in "results" sanctioned by a consciousness of success or pleasure."[58] In relational systemic terms, just as experience is bifurcated between feeling and knowing, affectivity is split between the momentary object-aiming pleasure and the infinity of intellectual love or spiritual joy – happiness. The latter is free of constraints that attention imposes on affect by tying itself to objects in the world.[59] The solution to the split between pleasure and happiness is not the labeling of pleasure as evil, and it takes place by means of the saturation of the momentary by means of the eternal: even pragmatic relations between desire, intention, action, objects in the world and success, and the characteristics of pleasure can be instruments for spiritual joy.[60] Ricoeur's narrative describes the systemic relationship of his "actors" as a split and leads to a potential resolution.

This is the case for the actors in the "Rasa Lila" narrative as well. The essentially affective attitude that Krishna arouses is clear, but it manifests in

---

[58] Ricoeur, *Fallible*, 94.
[59] This could be the simple view of episodic pleasure vs. the dispositional view.
[60] For an influential contemporary application of this philosophy, see Chade-Meng Tan, *Search Inside Yourself: The Unexpected Path to Achieving Success, Happiness (and World Peace)* (San Francisco, CA: HarperOne, 2012).

both a sensory and externalizing impulse and a contemplative, inward-looking manner. But there are other actors in this narrative: the male relatives and the social obligations that the *gopis* neglect in order to be with Krishna: in short, the context in which affective consciousness exists. The initial narrative "crisis" – the mythical bifurcation, if you will – is the departure of the women from their social world. This is a parallel to the first "disproportion" – the disproportion in experience, in Ricoeur's terms, between knowing one's obligations and feeling – that is, the intentional and the affective. The second narrative "crisis" is the disappearance of Krishna rending the consciousness of the *gopis* between sensory delight in the physical Krishna and loving Krishna through contemplative introspection. This bifurcation corresponds, as a relationship, to the second dispro-portion – a bifurcation within feeling itself between vital desire and spiritual joy.

Krishna applauds spiritual joy – that is, love for the absent God – but finally does offer himself in a sort of physical way to the *gopis* in the Rasa Lila. He urges the women to return to their relatives and their duties. He does not reject social relationships and dharma in favor of either sensory or meditative pleasure but offers a synthesis between the obligations of society and the love that is *bhakti*. The key ingredient in the Purana narrative, one that Ricoeur does not explore in his own, is the play: the realization that a game must be set up in order to saturate the momentary and the external with the eternal. The play is the circular dance in which every woman feels that Krishna is exclusively with her, and which serves as the model for the Holi festival. In the Rasa Lila play, Krishna is both sensory and internal. He is literally fantastic.[61]

It may be most appropriate to argue that both narratives describe the relationship in feeling, between sensory pleasure and a higher level of pleasure that can be termed joy or happiness. Both touch on religious themes to illustrate this point: the Purana explicitly and Ricoeur implicitly. Both descriptions contain a comprehensive human theory: positive affect is intrinsic to human consciousness, and in thought and action such affect can take two directions: sensory-animalistic (pleasure) or fully human (joy). These two do not negate but complete one another – as long as a method is in place. So the truly interesting question in regard to pleasure is not "what does the Krishna narrative mean?" Instead, one can dare to ask:

---

[61] The logical paradoxes and dynamic play between irreconcilable poles of thought and perceptions have been explored by G. Bateson, H. G. Gadamer, and A. Droogers and in Hinduism by D. Handelman and D. Shulman. For details, see Chapter 4.

Is the theory of the Krishna myth – and that of Ricoeur – true? Do they offer a valid description of pleasure in religious contexts? It is essential that we find a religious context where descriptive-phenomenological work provides evidence for both the details of Rasa Lila and the "fragility of feeling," and discover whether such a context supports the theory that underlies both narratives. Such a context may be the play of Rasa Lila in the festival of Holi.

Holi Festival

The Holi festival is India's most globally familiar festival – just ahead, perhaps, of Divali.[62] As a spring festival, it is celebrated on the full moon night and day of the lunar month of Phalgun, celebrating the new crop and, of course, the Rasa Lila of Krishna and the *gopis*. Around the world, the festival is largely associated with the colorful powders and dyes that are tossed[63] into the air and on the celebrants who choose to "play Holi."[63] But there is a great deal more to the festival, and an absorbingly vivid description was penned by McKim Marriott – "Holi: The Feast of Love," which was based on field work in the 1950s in the village of Kishan Garhi, which is located across the Yamuna River from Mathura: the land of Krishna in myth, pilgrimage, and ritual practice. The following details of the festival are taken from Marriott's experiences as a participant-observer.

The event began on a full moon evening in early March with a large bonfire into which stolen combustible items were tossed. The fire was described as the burning of the evil demoness Holika. The American researcher was then invited: "Saheb will play Holi with us?" and a description was provided with suggestions of some playful violence. But he received reassurance: "It is a *lila* – a divine sport of Lord Krishna!"[64] Marriott then observed young men handing out and tossing grains of the new crop and others pelting villagers with mud and cow-dung water as boys were heaving dust into the air and at adults. One young man was

---

[62] On the lesser-known agonistic nature of ancient Indian rituals, see George Thompson, "Ahaṃkāra and Ātmastuti: Self Assertion and Impersonation in the Ṛgveda," *History of Religions* 37, no. 1 (1997): 141–171. See also the horse sacrifice ritual in *Shatapatha Brahmana* 13.5.2.1–13.5.2.2.

[63] "Khelna," to play, is suggestive of the game that the festival performance represents. John Stratton Hawley, *At Play with Krishna: Pilgrimage Dramas from Brindavan* (Princeton, NJ: Princeton University Press, 1981), 15. The festival has changed considerably since the 1950s, but Marriott's description continues to be cited along with more recent descriptions. C. J. Fuller, *The Camphor Flame: Popular Hinduism and Society* (Princeton, NJ: Princeton University Press, 2012), 131, 144.

[64] Marriott, "Holi," 100.

seized and placed on a donkey facing backwards and was thus ridiculed.
A "male dancer with padded crotch" was writhing in solitary states of
fevered passion, miming sexual activities.[65] Everywhere in the village,
women were beating men on the shins with canes as the men barely
protected themselves and smiled. Liquid dyes and powder were tossed
into the air and at each other. The researcher heard rumors of adultery
taking place on that day and sexual innuendo was heard everywhere, such
as "Do you want some seed from me?" An informant told him: "Yes! All
greet each other with affection and feeling. Lord Krishna taught us the
ways of love, and so we celebrate Holi in this manner."[66] Marriott was
given liquid *bhang* (cannabis) to drink, which he claimed undermined his
ability to report further details, or understand what he had seen.

The following year, refusing the intoxicant, he was able to identify the
pattern that underlies the violence and erotic behavior he was witnessing.
The women who were caning men were from the low castes of laborers
and craft workers and their victims were Brahmins and landowner
men – village leaders. The young man sitting backwards on the donkey
was the "king of Holi" – a Brahmin as well. The individuals, dressed as
gopis, who were tossing mud and dirt on the leading men of the village
were those who were normally responsible for maintaining purity – including two young priests. The sexual innuendo often came from religious
figures, such as the ascetic who was singing sexual songs in front of the
moneylender's home.

Marriott offers two types of explanation for the Holi festival behavior.
The first type is functionalist, linked to the anthropologists Radcliffe-
Brown and Malinowski, and it concerns the perpetuation and mainten-
ance of social structure by the periodical ritual reversal.[67] The second falls
in the domain of the history of religions and looks at the sectarian influence of devotional Vaishnavism of Sri Caitanya that had arrived to this
region by means of Bengali missionaries, the Gosvami priests, in the
sixteenth century.[68] An older spring fertility ritual was overlaid with
elements of Krishna mythology and Vaishnava theology – not unlike the

---

[65] Ibid., 103.   [66] Ibid., 104.

[67] Functionalists analyze society as a system, and the role of individuals cannot be discerned from the
stories they tell or the meanings they ascribe to situations. Radcliffe-Brown and Malinowski (or
better yet, even Talcott Parsons) would not serve Marriott very well in his task if the *meaning* of
Holi were the object of research. See George E. Marcus and Michael M. J. Fischer, *Anthropology as
Cultural Critique: An Experimental Moment in the Human Sciences* (Chicago: University of Chicago
Press, 2014), 199.

[68] Marriott, "Holi," 107; Lavanya Vemsani, *Krishna in History, Thought, and Culture: An Encyclopedia
of the Hindu Lord* (Santa Barbara, CA: ABC-CLIO, 2016), 248–250.

way that the Hebrew exodus from slavery narrative overlays the spring ritual of Passover.[69]

The functionalist and the history of religion approaches are difficult to reconcile, but this is not the agenda here. If, in the minds of participants, the Holi festival is about Rasa Lila, the Puranic narrative about the play of Krishna, and if that Rasa Lila narrative had been largely about affective consciousness and its bifurcation in human thought and action into pleasure and joy, which is the theory explored here, how does the Holi festival contribute to this analysis? What does the Holi festival teach us about the actual experience of affective consciousness? As far as we know, the participants were not given questionnaires or even asked about their feelings – including what and how they enjoy in the elements of the Holi celebration. Such data must remain conjectural because it is based on observation of behavior and speech. Can we assume that the young man miming sex was enjoying this and that his laughing audience was as well? Can we also assume that the low-caste women caning high-ranking men were pleased to do so and that the smiles and laughter of the "victims" also reveal enjoyment? Finally, does the constantly repeated discourse about love and about emulating Krishna also reveal some sort of joy? If the answer to all of these is affirmative, which is hardly controversial, it may be possible to offer a hedonic theory of the Holi festival.

As Marriott has noted, the festival is both a fertility-thanksgiving bacchanalia and a devotional celebration of Rasa Lila. One could almost make the case that the Puranic text was itself born of such an agricultural-fertility context, but in the village of Kishan Garhi the two elements are clear. The obvious elements of the agricultural celebration include the distribution of new crops; the tossing of seeds, cow dung, and mud; the drinking of intoxicants; and others. According to comparative studies of agricultural rituals in other cultures, the bacchanalian elements of erotic displays are also related to fertility and, interestingly, so are the beatings with canes, and violence in general, which are associated with fertility magic.[70]

---

[69] The subject of spring fertility magic was amply covered by James Frazer in *The Golden Bough* and by Mircea Eliade in his *Rites and Symbols of Initiation* (and elsewhere). A much more recent collection of studies that align with my own approach to ritual as play is Renfrew et al., eds., *Ritual, Play, and Belief*, 292.

[70] An extreme example of this regenerative symbolism is discussed by David Carrasco, "Sacrifice/Human Sacrifice in Religious Traditions," in *The Oxford Handbook of Religion and Violence*, eds., Mark Juergensmeyer, Margo Kitts, and Michael Jerryson (New York: Oxford University Press, 2013), 222.

However, it is easy to see how a Vaishnava- and Krishna-worshiping theologian would find in such a ritual a fitting match for the ritual performance of Rasa Lila. After all, while there is none of the violence in the Purana, there is a good deal of erotica in the relationship between Krishna and the *gopis*. Furthermore, the *gopis*, who are women, violate their social obligations – *stri-dharma* – as they seek Krishna and ignore the demands of their social superiors – their husbands, fathers, and brothers – that they return home. The Rasa Lila then combines two of the key elements seen in the Holi: erotic conduct and violation of dharma. However, from the hedonic or affective perspective, the text explored the bifurcation of affect into pleasure (erotic play) and spiritual joy (meditative focus), which the narrative sought to blend

That same bifurcation – or "disproportion," in Ricoeur's term – can be seen in the Holi displays of sensory pleasure, which are violent and sexual at once, and the villagers' discourse about the love of Krishna. This is the very split that characterizes the "fragility of affect" as two distinct but related forces pull affective consciousness in two directions – the material and the spiritual. What makes the Holi festival special is the "play " – that is, the make-believe enactment of *lila*. *Lila* in the narrative of the Purana was both divine and human play: It was divine because Krishna, though perfect in his own pleasure, made himself enjoy the *gopis*. It was human when the *gopis* imitated the play of Krishna in the forest. The Holi ritual is a game played by humans as modeled on the play in which the *gopis* engaged. It is modeled on a mythic model. The game of Holi is intentional fantasy, like a stage play in which opposing concepts such as erotics and violence or embodiment and spirit can coexist with a wiggle room between the opposites. The play is bounded in time, it is counterfactual (fantastic), it has rules for how to play, and the players choose to play and obey those rules. In other words, the game of Holi combines the absolute freedom of fantasy with the self-control that is self-imposed by the decision to obey the rules of the game. The pleasure of play, which was discussed in a previous chapter, comes from this combination of freedom and control in a domain that is not entirely real but is saturated with meaning due to the ideas that it imitates.[71]

The game of Holi combines narrative elements from the mythology of Krishna along with what Ricoeur would describe as the "vital desire" associated with fertility bacchanalia. The mythical elements are love – sensual,

[71] Colin Renfrew, "Introduction: Play as the Precursor of Ritual in Early Human Societies," in *Ritual, Play*, eds., Renfrew et al., 15.

emotional, and devotional – and *lila* – the legitimization of the temporary suspension, indeed reversal, of dharma. Due to the saturation of the celebration play with *bhakti*, that is, love for Krishna, such a suspension is not a violation of dharma or social order, but its saturation with vitality. In the Purana, Krishna did not urge the *gopis* to violate dharma but to enhance their daily social lives with his love. From the perspective of affect, he was inviting them to permeate the momentary pleasure with the infinite joy and their embodied existence with eternal meaning.

In the ritual of Holi, which is Rasa Lila with agricultural elements, one finds the solution to the fragility of affect for a short duration. The key is the play and the hedonic mechanism is play pleasure. Play pleasure is what the barber's wife feels as she is empowered to smack the landowner on his shins, but she also understands exactly how hard to hit. Play is also the pleasure that the landowner feels by being targeted and being allowed to respond with a crude sexual comment while taking his punishment passively. Play pleasure is informed by the novelty pleasure of spontaneity and by the mastery pleasure of self-control, both of which it frames by means of a religious imagery. Hence, once we take the play of Holi into account as the place where the Puranic Rasa Lila actually takes shape, it becomes clear that the narratives of Ricoeur and the myth are indeed mutually illuminating. The village actors playfully exhibit the bifurcation of feeling because the play grants them the freedom and the space to do so. The social benefits of the ritualized play are enormous: it takes a great deal of trust to hit a superior on the shins and for the superior to allow an inferior to do so. This act of trust is predicated on the need of both actors to belong to the village society writ large, and a great deal of satisfaction derives from the affirmation of this need in the play of the ritual.[72] One could argue that the smearing of paint on other people's faces situates the Holi performance in the category of masking, as a means of depersonalization or loss of social and hierarchical identity – a source of liberating joy.[73]

The question that must be addressed is whether the lesson of Ricoeur, the Rasa Lila and the Holi festival, can be generalized to other narratives and to other rituals, perhaps other religious traditions. The three contexts I have been discussing focus explicitly, though not exclusively, on positive

[72] Ellen Dissanayake, "From Play and Ritualisation to Ritual and Its Arts: Sources of Upper Pleistocene Ritual Practices in Lower Middle Pleistocene Ritualised and Play Behaviors in Ancestral Hominins," in *Ritual, Play*, eds., Renfrew et al., 87–100.

[73] Yosef Garfinkel, "Dancing with Masks in the Proto-Historic Near East," in *Ritual, Play*, eds., Renfrew et al., 162–164.

affect and most religious narratives and rituals do not. Therefore, what can we take from this exercise, and how might we apply it elsewhere? In order to answer this question, I shall look at a Jewish narrative and ritual that, on the surface, appear to share nothing at all with the *Bhagavata Purana* and Holi.

Nahman of Bratslav (1772–1810): Story and Rituals

The first story in Nahman's collection is called "The King's Daughter Who Went Missing."[74] In this section, I shall summarize and discuss the story with reference to rituals that were also created by Nahman: *Hatikkun ha-kelali*, which means universal or general rectification. The analysis will demonstrate the usefulness of Ricoeur's phenomenology of pleasure in helping us understand the fundamental, if not always explicit, similarity in the relationship between narrative and ritual in regard to human affectivity in religious contexts.

The story begins by telling us that the king had six sons and one daughter, his favorite. However, the king cursed his daughter that the "Not Good" should take her, and she disappeared. The so-called Second to the Kingdom, along with a servant, went to find her, which constitutes the rest of the tale. He located a castle in a desert where the princess was being held captive by the "Not Good." The palace was a place of sensual pleasures where music was played to entertain those in attendance. The princess told him of the tests he had to overcome if he was to liberate and return her to her father: He had to seclude himself for a whole year in which he needed to fast and remain awake. However, on the last day of his trial, the Second ate an apple and fell asleep. After this sad failure, another test was set up – he was permitted to eat this time but not sleep. That meant he could not drink wine, which would send him to sleep. Again, on the last day, the Second drank wine and fell asleep. The princess then disappeared to a golden mountain, on top of which was a castle made of pearls. However, she left behind clues that sent the Second to the desert, where he encountered three giants who denied knowing about the palace on the mountain. In the end they did help him, the third giant delivering him to the mountain in a storm. The narrator informs us that the Second

---

[74] Nahman of Bratslav, *Likutey Moharan*, vol. 5, ed., Chaim Kramer (Jerusalem, Israel: Breslov Research Institute, 1993); Nahman of Bratslav, *Likutey Moharan ha-Menukad* (Jerusalem, Israel: Moharanat Institute, 1994); Nahman of Bratslav, *The Lost Princess & Other Kabbalistic Tales of Rebbe Nahman of Bratslav* (Woodstock, VT: Jewish Lights Publications, 2005), 1–24; Arnold J. Band, *Nahman of Bratslav: The Tales* (New York: Paulist Press, 1978), 51–62.

to the Kingdom would have to be wise and intelligent in order to return the princess to her father, although that has not yet happened and will take a long time. The story ends unresolved at that point.

According to most commentators, the story was told in such a way that listeners had to begin thinking about repentance or spiritual awakening.[75] In other words, the story serves a performative function, both describing in a symbolical way why repentance is necessary and urging the listeners to repent their sins.[76] The story hints at a sin, injustice, and impurity that require rectification of individual wrongs for the benefit of all mankind. The initial event – the expelling curse – is not the sin; after all, the king in the tale represents God.[77] Instead, there is a primordial metaphysical event, a fracture that takes place between the divine transcendent and immanent, in the manner of Lurianic Kabbalah on the crisis of creation and as Nahman depicts it in narrative.[78] In the struggle to repair the fracture, via repentance, humanity needs to overcome the temptations of sensual objects and desire – represented in the story by means of the apple, wine, sleep, and so forth.[79] In the religious world that Nahman occupied – he was the grandson of the Besht (Baal Shem Tov), founder of the Hasidic movement – there was a special individual who acted on behalf of humanity and that was "Zaddik ha-Dor" (the righteous leader of his generation): Nahman himself or other Hasidic leaders to come.

This leader "will have to ascend from *Yesh* (existence) to *Ayin* (emptiness). *Ayin* constitutes the transcendent realm of reality, and to arrive there the *Zaddik ha-Dor* must be in contact with the transcendent essence of God, he must rectify the divine sparks from within the confines of Yesh." When he accomplishes this astonishing act of repair, Israel – all of mankind – will "live in the Edenic closeness to God."[80] Fully aware of

---

[75] Band, "Introduction," in *Nahman of Bratslav: The Tales*, 34; Marianne Schleicher, *Intertextuality*, 95.

[76] Schleicher, *Intertextuality*, 136–137; Yehudah Liebes, *Studies in Jewish Myth and Messianism* (Albany: State University of New York Press, 1993), 145.

[77] But Schleicher notes that there is also a hidden subtext of possible incest (between the king and the princess), *Intertextuality*, 106, fn. 39. On the theme of creation and incest, see Wendy Doniger O'Flaherty, *The Origins of Evil in Hindu Mythology* (Berkeley: University of California Press, 1976), 51–55.

[78] According to Yehudah Liebes (citing traditional sources), the princess represents the soul rather than the Shekhina (divine immanence); hence, this is a psychological and not cosmological narrative. *Studies*, 206, fn. 123; See also Aryeh Kaplan and Chaim Kramer, *The Seven Beggars & Other Kabbalistic Tales of Rebbe Nahman of Breslov* (Woodstock, VT: Breslov Research Institute, 2005), 68.

[79] Gershom Scholem, *On the Kabbalah and Its Symbolism* (New York: Random House, 1996), 119 and passim.

[80] Schleicher, *Intertextuality*, 137.

the catastrophe of the false messiah Shabbetai Zvi (1626–1676), Nahman
had a collective agenda in telling the stories – that is, to conceptualize the
role of the *zaddik* (righteous one) on behalf of his people, indeed humanity
as a whole.[81] However, the stories also served as inspiration for individual
acts of repentance, which is what *tikkun* (repair or rectification) means. In
the Jewish year 5566 (1805–1806), Nahman insisted on a three-step
rectification consisting of *tikkun hazot* (midnight prayer), *ha-tikkun
ha-kelali,* and private fast days due to some inkling of a messianic event
and an expectation of redemption. The assumption was that human
sinfulness was delaying redemption but that external action like the
movement Shabbetai Zvi initiated was dangerous.[82]

Nahman devised a variety of rituals – rectifications or *tikkunim* – that
included very specific ones such as for nocturnal emission and transgres-
sions in business and in speech – and, finally, also a universal rectification
or *kelali,* meant for the pervasive (licentious) desire to which all humans
are vulnerable. The following discussion is limited to *ha-tikkun ha-kelali,*
which Nahman argued was critical because a person who could overcome
such a desire can overcome every other type of desire. According to Zvi
Mark, it is important to draw a distinction between the specific rectification for nocturnal emission and the general rectification, although both
utilize the reading of ten chapters from Psalms.[83] The *tikkun kelali*
identifies sexuality at the core of human desire, but the rectification does
not relate to a particular sexual sin but to a more general condition called
niuf that literally means adultery but, in this case, sexual desire in general.

The *tikkun* has a number of elements: "When a person recites the first
verse of the Shema, he must close his eyes tightly, corresponding to the
'beautiful maiden who has no eyes.' [That is] because when lewd thoughts
come to a person, the rectification is that he recite [the first verse of] *Shema*
[('Hear O Israel, the Lord our God, the Lord is one')] and [then] *Barukh
shem* [(the non-biblical verse, *Barukh shem* . . . – 'Blessed be the name of
His glorious sovereignty for ever and ever')]."[84] The assumption here is
that the licentious desires are caused by sight and that shutting the eyes

---

[81] Liebes, *Studies,* 115.   [82] Green, *Tormented Master,* 207.

[83] Liebes, *Studies,* 136–138, comments on the significance of the ten chapters. See Psalms 16, 32, 41,
42, 59, 77, 90, 105, 137, and 150.

[84] Mark, *The Revealed,* 145; *Likutei Moharan,* I. 36:3, www.sefaria.org/Likutei_Moharan?lang=bi
(accessed March 4, 2019); the shutting of the eyes in repentant prayer, or the visual
inaccessibility of Krishna to his devotees, is an invitation to turn inward in the relationship
between perception and affect. It is an opening rather than a closing of relatedness. See Merleau-
Ponty, *Phenomenology,* 167.

ritually, at the very least, expresses if not causes, the nullification of desire.[85] In graver instances, where desire is powerful, another component of the rectification is induced weeping and tears. In such cases, when "he cannot tear himself away from it, then he must also shed tears when he accepts the sovereignty of heaven [i.e., while reciting the *Shema*]."[86]

According to Nahman, both tears and licentious desires originate from excess that gathers in the spleen – that is, turbidity in a person's blood. The spleen is polluted by Lilith, which is the wicked sovereignty, representing "mixed multitudes" rather than the twelve tribes of Israel.[87] When a person shuts his eyes tightly he integrates himself into the level of the "beautiful maiden who has no eyes" – a reference to the Zohar symbol of holy sovereignty.[88] When a person sheds tears, "then the excess – i.e., the licentious desires ... are pushed out and emerge outside."[89] The combined action of weeping while reciting the Shema is not merely the saving of the individual sinner from the sin of desire, "but rather it serves as a vital stage as the revelation of the Torah."[90] In other words, the sin is not annihilated as if it had never taken place – it served a useful purpose. There is a familiar Kabbalistic idea that underlies this assumption: that is, the breaking of the husk before the eating of the fruit. The soul goes into exile, into various evil aspects of a person's character in order to break them as a sort of test that purifies the soul. The fruit in this Kabbalistic imagery is the revelation of Torah or the words of the *zaddik*.

The link here to the narrative of the Second to the Kingdom, as he wanders and repeatedly fails, is clear. Key to the rectification is the test to break the husk (*klipa*) and "know that the essence of complete repentance [is achieved] when a person goes through those places literally where he had been before [his] repentance ... but he now turns his back on them."[91] The tests of breaking the husks, the change of attitude – elevating the spirit in positive action, the praise of the *zaddik* – all of this is a gateway to joy, represented by the beautiful maiden who has no eyes. The reading of the ten Psalms chapters, which are songs of praise to God and joy (*simhah*), enhance this sense of supreme well-being that follows repentance. Even the weeping is saturated with joy:

---

[85] Mark, *The Revealed*, 145.   [86] *Likutei Moharan*, I. 36.4.   [87] Mark, *The Revealed*, 148.
[88] Scholem, *On the Kabbalah*, 141.   [89] Mark, *The Revealed*, 149.   [90] Ibid., 149.
[91] *Likutei Moharan*, II. 49; Mark, *The Revealed*, 165; Mark has devoted a great deal of attention to the hedonic/affective dimension of Nahman's work, including play pleasure as jesting: Zvi Mark, *Mysticism and Madness: The Religious Thought of Rabbi Nahman of Bratslav* (New York: Continuum, 2009), 264–265 and passim.

The essence of the high level of weeping is [attained] when it results from joy and gladness. And even regret is very good when it is due to joy – when it, due to a person's great amount of joy in the Lord, be He blessed, he regrets and languishes greatly, because he had rebelled against Him in earlier days. And weeping is aroused in [this person] out of a great deal of joy.[92]

Nahman links this joy (*simhah*) to the *shofar* (horn) blowing during Rosh Hashanah (New Year) service introduced by Psalm 89:17: "In your name they rejoice all the day," forming the acronym for weeping (*bekhiah*) according to the calculation of *gematria* (biblical numerology). The blowing of the *shofar*, the sound of weeping, regret, and repentance must originate from joy and it produces joy. In both the words and actions of Nahman, joy and sadness interact in a dialectical process: "simple joy confronts sadness and brings it to itself, thus creating a new and more complex sort of joy."[93] A parable in *Likutei Moharan* describes this:

> Sometimes when people are joyous and dancing, they grab a man from outside their dancing circle, one who is sad and melancholy, and force him to join with them in their dance. Thus it is with joy: when a person is happy, his own sadness and suffering stand off on the side. But it is a higher achievement to struggle and pursue that sadness, bringing it too into the joy, until it is transformed.[94]

In the work of Nahman, as in other Hasidic writers, one clearly sees the tension between sensual desire and joy. But there is also a recognition, based on Kabbalah, that although desire must be transcended, the path to supreme joy leads through the realm of matter, which includes both pleasure and sadness. This can only take place by means of a ritual in which a character from the Zohar is emulated or in which one pretends to cry but then shed real tears.

Obviously, the distinct cultural idiom of eighteenth- and nineteenth-century Hasidism does not resemble the poetic discourse of the *Bhagavata Purana*, and neither one of these two reads like the nuanced abstractions of Ricoeur's phenomenology. But on the subject of pleasure, some systemic observations are worth pointing out.

[92] *Likutei Moharan*, I. 175.1 (Joy is *simha* and gladness is *chedva* in the text.); Mark, *The Revealed*, 188.
[93] *Likutei Moharan*, I. 175.2; Green, *Tormented Master*, 142.
[94] *Likutei Moharan*, II. 32.2 (Sadness is *a'tzvut* and melancholy is *mara shchora* in the text.); Green, *Tormented Master*, 142.

Conclusion

The theme explored in this chapter is central to many religious traditions; there are many other narratives (myths, folk tales, stories) and rituals that deal with the subject of pleasure and even with the "fragility" or bifurcation between sensory pleasure/desire and spiritual joy. To give one example of each – story and ritual: the libretto of *Tannhauser* in the Wagner opera explores the hero's rejection of sensual pleasures in Venusburg in favor of the spiritual joys and suffering above ground. Similarly, the Day of the Dead (Día de los Muertos) in Mexico celebrates the juxtaposition between the sadness of loss and the celebration of life. This chapter was not intended as a survey of a religious genre but a closer examination, with few examples, of a process that requires focus.

However, it's important that we don't attempt to take away too much from the reading of three distinct cultural narratives. The difference between the three must be maintained. Still, there is a broad framework encompassing the three narratives indicating that positive affect is fundamental to human consciousness and that, at its root, it is singular. That is, pleasure that attaches itself to objects in the fleeting moment and joy that transcends objects and time originate from that single basic source and represent a split of one movement. In Hasidism, the one is sinful and the other is sacred, while Ricoeur has pointed out the problem with such a judgment. Meanwhile, Krishna *bhakti* is closer to Ricoeur's narrative – and it is important to retain these differences. Nonetheless, all three contexts identify a fissure ("disproportion") in the basic affectivity, and it is the role of religion, or specifically rituals, to overcome the consequences of such a rift by either transforming pleasure into joy or saturating one with the other.

Rituals do so by turning the narrative into a summons and then a score or a script with which to engage the two dimensions of affectivity in the play of the rite. Ritual is the place where the two types of affectivity – the sensory and the spiritual – pleasure and joy – can share a single context; it has to be a ritual. That is because it is inconceivable that social life (dharma) be truly eroticized in the mode of loving Krishna beyond all distinctions.[95] And it is also inconceivable that sensual desire be permanently squelched by means of a legal commandment, let alone a mere story. A play has to take place where the participants choose to play, and in that

---

[95] Again, according to Tracy Coleman, this is not what the Rasa Lila seeks to do. See "Viraha-Bhakti," 385.

space, they enjoy the freedom to experiment with the repair of fragility. It is only in the ritual response to the narrative that living individuals can potentially attain the simultaneous realization of our embedded existence in nature – the subservience to sensual pleasure – and, at the same time, realize human potential to achieve freedom and attain lasting joy.

CHAPTER 8

A Scholar's Shabbat in Central Virginia

Introduction

Since the publication of William James's *Varieties of Religious Experience*, the concept of religious experience has been defined, analyzed, and argued over extensively. It has also become perhaps unnecessarily complex, both in terms of how "religion" is understood and in the way that "experience" needs to be understood in the context of religion.[1] Certainly, sometimes the question of religious experience is highly unclear in a way that justified the scholarly efforts: if one reports a dream in which a long-since-dead grandfather appears out of a cloud and cautions the dreamer about the urgency of avoiding sin, it is fair to ask whether this constitutes a religious experience – or merely a psychological event. James gave several striking examples along these lines. For example, in his chapter on conversion (lecture 9) James describes an "unlettered" man, Stephen H. Bradley, who was not sure he "had religion," but during one Sabbath in 1829, he went to hear the "Methodist at the Academy."[2] The sermon concerned the Day of Judgment and was delivered in a solemn and "terrible" manner, which Bradley had never heard before. "I trembled involuntarily on the bench where I was sitting though I did not feel anything at heart."[3] The following day, the same thing happened. However, on the night of the second day, Bradley reported, "my heart increased in its beating, which soon convinced me that it was the Holy Spirit from the effect it had on me. I began to feel exceedingly happy and humble."[4]

Such cases, and William James's lectures, split the field into two main directions of inquiry. On the one hand, Bradley, after some delay, began to exhibit distinct physiological symptoms such as rapid pulse, mental

---

[1] Talal Assad, *The Geneologies of Religion: Disciplines and Reasons of Power in Christianity and Islam* (Baltimore: Johns Hopkins University Press, 1993), 29.
[2] William James, *The Varieties of Religious Experience* (New York: Collier Books, 1961).
[3] Ibid., 161.   [4] Ibid.

arousal, and elevated mood, which we are invited to consider as the characteristics of a distinct and sui generis occurrence in his mind – a true religious experience. On the other hand, James tells us that Bradley judged the symptoms to be a visitation by the Holy Spirit, which means that he already possessed a frame of reference with which he interpreted the physiological event as religious.

In her analysis of the work of William James in *The Varieties*, Anne Taves explains the agenda that guided this sort of split analysis and the overall design of James's scientific study of religion.[5] The broad framework was evolutionary, and the explanatory goal was to account for the psychological and social function of religion, and religious experience, without discounting the sense of religious believers that their experience is real. The resolution to what seems a contradiction is James's adherence to the theory of the subconscious, as quoted by Taves from James: "the subconscious self is nowadays a well accredited psychological entity; and I believe that in it we have exactly the mediating term required."[6] James, then, was a functionalist, like Durkheim, who accepted the distinctiveness of religious experience but accounted for it in a ground-up naturalistic manner – that is, based on the psychological science of his day, without discounting the extraordinary feel of religion.

However, the case of Stephen Bradley comes up again in Wayne Proudfoot's *Religious Experience* as illustrative of a different way of understanding religious experience – namely, top down. According to Proudfoot, what must be explained is not what caused the increased heart rate but why someone like Bradley and others like him "understood what happened to them or what they witnessed in religious terms."[7] The answer to this question comes from understanding the "concepts and beliefs" they held, their commitments, and the "contextual conditions" in which they operated. People who report "religious experiences" are actually providing explanations – making attributions and ascriptions – for phenomena that others may deem as merely psychological, physical, or perhaps even medical. Proudfoot asserts a position that is widely held in academic circles that "Religious experience cannot be identified without reference to concepts, beliefs, grammatical rules, and practices."[8]

[5] Taves, *Fits, Trances & Visions*.
[6] Taves, *Fits*, 280. A detailed evaluation of the influence of this theory is recounted in 219–299.
[7] Wayne Proudfoot, *Religious Experience* (Berkeley: University of California Press, 1995), 226.
[8] Ibid., 228.

In general, the field of religious scholarship is split between those who seek to understand how some physiological–psychological events can function as, contribute to, or altogether constitute religious experiences, while other scholars (like Proudfoot) focus on the conventional and culturally defined notion of what "religious experience" means and, thus, how the overall event is deemed to be religious, setting aside any explanatory force of the physiological event.[9]

These sorts of discussions tend to focus on rather unusual occurrences. I propose that it is possible to keep the discussion on far less rarefied grounds and demonstrate that if you spend three hours at a Conservative synagogue on a Shabbat morning, then, conventionally speaking, a great deal of what transpires there is indeed a religious experience. This is no different from going to a concert at the Kennedy Center and undergoing a musical experience – even if it is punctuated by episodes of micro-sleep. Neither musical nor religious experience is controversial in such circumstances, and nothing spectacular needs to take place physiologically or psychologically. In short, this is Wayne Proudfoot's position. However, up to now, the discussion has focused on "religious," and not much has been said about experience – a more diffuse and difficult concept.

The subject of experience received its most notable recent treatment in Thomas Nagel's "What Is It Like to Be a Bat?"[10] The question of first-person vs. third-person description of consciousness certainly applies to the matter of reported enjoyment of any activity or situation and certainly a religious context. For example, recent Western usage looks at experience as a personal, subjective, and internally localized phenomenon aligned with a modernist conception of the conscious self.[11] An archaic or non-Western conception of experience can be public and situational, describable only in collective terms.[12] This fact already sets up a barrier between an

---

[9] Both approaches have been immensely fecund. For example, see V. S. Ramachandran and S. Blakelee, *Phantoms in the Brain* (New York: William Morrow, 1999); A. Newberg and E. d'Aquili, *Why God Won't Go Away* (New York: Ballantine, 2001); Paolo Nencini, "Psychobiology of Drug-Induced Religious Experience: From the Brain 'Locus of Religion' to Cognitive Unbinding," *Substance Use and Misuse* 45, no. 13 (2010): 2130–2151. On the cultural–linguistic side, there is S. T. Katz, *Mysticism and Language* (New York: Oxford University Press, 1992). Ralph Hood calls the latter "diversity theorists," which would include Proudfoot. They assign to culture and specifically to language a preeminent role in defining – indeed, constituting – the religious experience. Hood et al., *The Psychology*, 359–360.

[10] Thomas Nagel, "What Is It Like to Be a Bat?" *The Philosophical Review* 83, no. 4 (1974): 435–450.

[11] Charles Taylor, *Sources of the Self: The Making of the Modern Identity* (Cambridge, UK: Cambridge University Press, 2006), 185–198.

[12] Alan Roland, *In Search of Self in India and Japan: Toward a Cross-Cultural Psychology* (Princeton, NJ: Princeton University Press, 1989), ch. 7.

eighteenth-century Hindu and a twenty-first century Presbyterian – both of them describing the enjoyment of some experience. However, in a nonphilosophical treatment of conventionally understood religious experience, it may be adequate to quote John Dewey, whose definition of experiences touches on some of the issues but allows us to gloss over them for the sake of brevity. Experience, he writes,

> includes what men do and suffer, what they strive for, love, believe and endure, and also how men act and are acted upon, the ways in which they do and suffer, desire and enjoy, see, believe, imagine – in short, processes of experiencing ... It is "double barreled" in that it recognizes in its primary integrity no division between act and material, subject and object, but contains them both in an unanalyzed totality.[13]

The goal of this book has been to describe and explain the prevalence of pleasure in the religious life. And, indeed, much of the discussion in early chapters took shape by means of the evolutionary framework: the three types of pleasure are based on behavioral adaptation, and the regulation of pleasure has been discussed in the context of cultural evolution and as a factor in the formation of religious groups. So the question for discussion here arises in a different manner: Inasmuch as pleasure is a physio-psychological product, does its function in evolutionary history, including the evolution of social processes, actually explain anything meaningful in reported religious experiences, which are conventional and combine subjective with objective facts? Does the cross-cultural, cross-traditional prevalence of pleasure – positive affect – in reports of religious experience indicate that the top-down theory is not exclusive? Is there a genuine physiological or psychological fact that transcends the frame of reference with which Proudfoot and others account for religious attribution? After all, if a Christian attributes his pleasure to the Holy Spirit and a Vedantist Hindu to *atman*, these are radically distinct frames of reference, and yet both reports connect their elevated affect to the fact of having some religious experience at a bare minimum and to the noetic contents of the religious experience at a maximum.

This chapter needs to look in some detail at a non-controversial religious experience. It must then address the question of pleasure raised earlier. The report must show a precise awareness of the events that constitute the religious experience – however mundane – as well as the

---

[13] John Dewey, *Experience and Nature* (LaSalle, IL: Open Court, 1925), 10–11.

conceptual frame of reference and the psychological responses to the overall situation, which include elevated positive affect.

Shabbat Service

The question of religious experience becomes more interesting when we ask whose religious experience and what sort of religious experience is under consideration. A bar mitzvah boy, the rabbi, an insurance agent, his wife, a college physics professor, and a feminist theologian – all at the same synagogue at the same time – can hardly be said to undergo the same identical experience. In undertaking the task of describing religious experience and explaining the role of pleasure, it is necessary to stipulate which single subject is undergoing the Shabbat services. Furthermore, it is obvious that the best subject is the one whose inner perceptions, feelings, and thoughts are accessible to description and analysis. The best choice, naturally, is the author of this text, a scholar of religion who has participated in these (Conservative) services over several years. The impetus for going to Shabbat services was my wife – I am not a practicing Jew and lack faith in metaphysical realities that can be characterized as Jewish. For these reasons, I have opted over the years to enrich my understanding of the Shabbat services by reading some of the philosophical and theological works that helped shape Conservative Judaism in America, as gleaned from the syllabi of Jewish Theological Seminary and from conversations with the learned rabbi of the central Virginia synagogue. The readings included obvious sources, such as Abraham Joshua Heschel and Louis Finkelstein, but also less obvious – and more foundational – writers like Franz Rosenzweig and Emmanuel Levinas.[14] I read these not as a philosopher or historian of ideas but as a skeptical, perhaps even cynical, congregant looking to make sense of a surprisingly pleasant experience. The result is a complicated picture with moving parts – some in focus, others fuzzy.

The service begins at 10:00 a.m. and the liturgy comes from *Siddur Sim Shalom* and the Torah with commentary of *Etz Hayim*.[15] Most of the service is in Hebrew, although the liturgy is available in both Hebrew and

---

[14] These are just some of the most prominent and relevant for this discussion:
　　Abraham Joshua Heschel, *The Shabbat: Its Meaning for Modern Man* (New York: Farrar, Strauss, Giroux, 2005); Franz Rosenzweig, *The Star of Redemption*, trans., Barbara E. Galli (Madison: University of Wisconsin Press, 2005); Emmanuel Levinas, *Totality and Infinity: An Essay on Exteriority* (Pittsburgh, PA: Duquesne University Press, 2004).

[15] David L. Lieber, ed., *Etz Hayim: Torah and Commentary* (New York: The Rabbinical Assembly, 2001); *Siddur Sim Shalom for Shabbat and Festivals* (New York: The Rabbinical Assembly, 1998).

English. The synagogue is not very large, and a typical Shabbat service, excluding bar or bat mitzvah events, will include about thirty congregants, split evenly between men and women. The service, including the kiddush – that is, blessing of the wine and bread before lunch – lasts about two and a half hours and consists of readings and singing from the siddur, an interpretive talk (*dvar Torah*), the reading of the Torah portion (*parashat ha-shavua*) – all of these conducted by the rabbi, a *hazan* (cantor), and lay leaders from the congregation. The following is a very cursory glance at some of the elements taken from the siddur.

The service is not a narrative, properly speaking, but a celebration of God's holiness and compassion on this holy day – a prolonged gesture of gratitude, praise, and reciprocated love. Nonetheless, a discernable temporal theme of creation, revelation, and redemption runs through the liturgy: "You are eternal before creation and since creation, in this world and in the world to come."[16] Creation is more than the making of a physical world: "The soul that You, my God, have given to me is pure. You created it. You breathed it into me."[17] This accounts for our gratitude: "I am grateful to You, living, enduring Sovereign, for restoring my soul to me in compassion."[18]

The reciprocal gratitude in the form of the prayer is freely given, although our freedom is tenuous, as we are vulnerable to forces that are not always easy to control: "Keep us from error, from sin and transgression ... let no evil impulse (*yetzer ra*') control us."[19] But this is not a request for policing because God's supervision is predicated on love: "Deep is your love for us. Adonai our God, boundless Your tender compassion."[20] The congregation declares its own love of God in that most paradigmatic of all love statements: "Shema Israel Adonai Eloheinu Adonai Ehad ... You shall love Adonai your God with all your heart, with all your soul, with all your might."[21]

The siddur praises song: "Halleluyah! Sing a new song to Adonai where the faithful gather,"[22] and the congregation sings often: "Ha-oseh shalom bi-meromav, hu ya'seh shalom a'leinu," and many other songs. The siddur also praises dance: "Praise God with drum and dance, with flute and spring."[23] And the service is rich with bodily gestures such as the rising on toes and bowing as everyone declares: "Kadosh kadosh kadosh Adonai Tz'va-ot m'lo khol ha-aretz kvodo."[24] And when the Torah scroll is taken out of the *aron ha-kodesh* and carried through the aisles of the synagogue,

---

[16] *Siddur*, 67.   [17] Ibid., 63.   [18] Ibid., 61.   [19] Ibid., 65.   [20] Ibid., 110.
[21] Ibid., 112.   [22] Ibid., 100.   [23] Ibid.   [24] Ibid., 110.

as members touch the Torah with the tip of their prayer shawl or siddur and then kiss these, the entire congregation sings: "Yours Adonai is the greatness, the power, and the splendor."[25]

After the service proper ends, the members of the congregation fold their prayer shawls, return the siddur and *Etz Hayim* Torah to the bookshelf, and gather in the large dining hall. Each takes a cup with wine or grape juice, and before the blessings of the wine and bread commence, the congregants face the eastern wall on which the biblical verse from *Exodus* forms the words to the song in which everyone joins: "Ve-shamru benei Israel et ha-Shabbat, la-a'sot et ha-Shabbat le-dorotam, berit olam." ("And the children of Israel observed the Shabbat in order to make the Shabbat a covenant for ever.") The blessings on the wine and the bread that is distributed among the congregants are the final verbal exchange with God. A line forms in front of the buffet, rich with food that different families take turn providing, and the members of the congregation load their plates and find a sitting spot around one of the many round tables. The mood is joyful and animated with the sound of boisterous conversation rising in the hall.

The service has a rhythm: it moves between reading and standing or rocking back and forth, and the prayers proceed in singsong cadence. The liturgical contents move in time between past and future and then back to the past. There are recursive and repeated readings, blessings, and hallelujahs. The overall impression in me is of a dynamic movement forward – then back and forward again – defying the straight arrow of time.

Like everyone else – as far as I can tell – I find all of this highly enjoyable in a variety of ways. Unless one is Marcel Proust, it is virtually impossible to accurately describe even a single moment of impression, let alone the entire duration. My feelings and thoughts move in and out of focus, and I have no idea how to describe my experience as religious in any but a most conventional manner. There are clear prescriptions telling us how one ought to enjoy Shabbat. The siddur states – quoting Psalms 29, 98, and others – that we shall break out in joyful song for Adonai or that one would be happy to uphold the Torah of Adonai. And Heschel, following a well-known Kabbalistic tradition tells us we welcome the Shabbat like a bride at her wedding.[26] Like the other congregants, I know this, but my experience is different because I do not feel like breaking out in song, and the bride metaphor does not speak to me after a ninety mile commute to the synagogue.

[25] Ibid., 141.   [26] Ibid., 18, 154; Heschel, *The Shabbat*, 54–55.

Because I read *The Star of Redemption* and *Totality and Infinity* hand in hand with *Siddur Sim Shalom* – visiting the two phenomenology works periodically, setting them aside, and then revisiting them – it is safe to say that I not only constructed a frame of reference for something that existed outside of such readings. The synagogue experience was a practicum, or – to be honest – a play, in which phenomenological readings, liturgical sentiments, and embodied movements in the company of others came together. There was little else.

Franz Rosenzweig on Time and Love

Rosenzweig distinguishes God as a mythical entity from the transcendental God and the mystery of what he calls "no" and "yes" – that is, how nothingness becomes the world: "The figure of God, until now hidden in the metaphysical beyond of myth, steps into the visible and begins to light up."[27] The creation is a primordial event that human thought places in a primordial past. But in revelation, which takes place in the present, creation bursts into the immediate present, not as a fated effect but as love – which is ever new and unconditioned. It is in this momentary – ever-present – quality of love that God becomes manifest. Revelation is thus the giving as gift of love by God and the receiving of love by the beloved soul that offers love as a return gift. By virtue of this offering back of a return gift, the soul "becomes complete serenity and a blissful soul in itself."[28]

But I do not interpret this as indicating that the Shabbat service is a mystical event. In fact, Rosenzweig makes a statement that flies in the face of the long history of mystical theology. The mystic, Rosenzweig writes, is "scarcely half a man, he is only the vessel of the raptures he feels."[29] The soul cannot remain in this bliss, in merely its being loved by God. "In the bliss of love received from God, the soul that had merely surrendered has no feeling for the world, or rather for anything outside of God."[30] Indeed, "Man defined only as an object of divine love is cut off from the whole world and closed in himself." The comment Jean-Luc Marion made in reference to Levinas's discussion of love as "amorous autism" applies here as well: there is something "autistic" about such an existence – steeped merely in the bliss of divine love – as the world outside beckons.[31]

---

[27] Rosenzweig, *The Star*, 124.   [28] Ibid., 175.   [29] Ibid., 224.   [30] Ibid., 222.
[31] Jean-Luc Marion, "The Intentionality of Love," in *Prolegomena to Charity*, trans., Stephen D. Lewis (New York: Fordham University Press, 2002), 77.

But even that state of bliss is ultimately frustrating because, as Rosenzweig puts it, to the cry of the soul, "no answer comes echoing from the mouth of the lover."[32] The condition of the soul in this state remains beloved but mute. The soul aspires to form an astonishing supernatural community with God, which cannot be sustained. Hence, the beloved soul must "step out of love's magic circle," and instead of answering God's love, it must speak in its own name.[33] In other words, it must translate what it received in the magic circle of love into the love that it offers in the real world, and it is from this love (not the love of God) that redemption will ultimately come. The soul now must take the moral stance because the mystical unity, the isolation, is immoral.[34]

Now, as leading to redemption, the individual becomes fully human and heroic in a new way: deeply human, trembling "in all his limbs at knowing he is simply mortal – out of this earth his joy springs and upon his sorrows this sun shines."[35] The beloved who knows how to return love as a gift turns that love to the neighbor – as a commandment. This commandment implies freedom – the will to give love freely, despite it being a commandment. There is a direct connection between a decree or intervention from God and human freedom. As Rosenzweig tells it, man has the freedom to decide to pray to God, but he prays, as we have seen: "Lead us not into temptation." The freedom is only meaningful inasmuch as man is subject to the possibility of temptation – that is, to forces outside our control. For "God wants only those who are free for his own," and thus, God has to tempt man.[36]

The commandment to love the neighbor draws on that same love that man freely offers as a reciprocated gift for God. "Love for God must be externalized in love for the neighbor."[37] That love is instantaneous – always and entirely in the present moment, ever renewed. This love is at the root of redemption, which is anticipated in the present but will be fulfilled in the future. Such a love is set up, prepared, by the prayers that came before, voiced or mumbled in a group. Just as creation is past and revelation present, so redemption is future, but a future anticipated now.

The temporal quality of human experience of God in creation, revelation and redemption resonate with the experience of standing as a group – wine cup in hand – and singing "ve-shamru." The moment of

[32] Rosenzweig, *The Star*, 219.   [33] Ibid., 219–220.   [34] Ibid., 223.   [35] Ibid., 225.
[36] Ibid., 284. In this vein, see Hugo Rahner on joy and tragedy in connection with human freedom facing God: *Man at Play*, trans., Brian Bettershaw and Edward Quinn (New York: Herder and Herder, 1967), 39–40.
[37] Ibid., 230.

singing enfolds in conscious awareness recollection, presence, and anticipation. The eye contact reveals a mutuality of "I and you" that is even
stronger than the "we," while theology is pushed to the background before
the power of the moment and its gestures.

In Rosenzweig's conception of time, a recursiveness predominated.[38]
The eternal is present within the momentary now, tomorrow is today, but
today also includes yesterday and vice versa. In prayer, all of this plays in
the mind of the congregant. It is much like dancing in a circle while
singing a repeating refrain.

Rosenzweig had a great deal to say about music, singing, and gesture in
a way that informs my understanding of the present experience in the
dining hall. He writes, "For it is music which raises that first intimate
connection that is founded in the mutual space and the mutual hearing of
the word to the conscious and active intimate connection of all who are
assembled ... That space first created by architecture is now really filled
with the sound of music."[39]

Just as Heschel famously wrote that the Shabbat builds a structure in
time, Rosenzweig also contrasts space and time, where music is the
aesthetic embodiment of time that now fills our space. And, "to this
mutuality of life, as it is realized in the sacrament, the music now first
tunes the soul."[40] The Jewish philosopher was writing about Christian
sacrament and choral music, but not in order to contrast this with Jewish
prayer and song. I believe he would have written the same about Hindu
bhajans (devotional songs). Beyond even the music are, for instance, the
gesture, the dance, and the glance and then, ultimately, silence. But these
are not occasions for the soul to withdraw into itself – to seek that divine
embrace again – but, on the contrary, to come out to mutual encounter
with others.

All of this phenomenological reflection in *The Star of Redemption* speaks
to me in the dining hall, cup in hand. Nowhere do I see a soul enraptured
by submersion in God's love. Instead, there is a joy that resonates in the
mutual interactions within this small gathering and shaped in a temporal
aesthetic by the consciousness of singing together. The two – community
and song – are intertwined as enjoyment. How does that work?

Rosenzweig reflected in detail on music and on the way singing creates
community. A careful reading of *The Star of Redemption* might even
suggest that Rosenzweig's theological phenomenology is structured like a
musical score: past, present, future (creation, revelation, redemption) with

[38] Ibid., 306–310.   [39] Ibid., 383.   [40] Ibid.

tripartite units dominating the book (three parts, each consisting of three books). True, the connection to the geometric form of the six-point star is at the forefront, but the book is essentially temporal in conception. Furthermore, the existential human response to God resembles the structure of psychological response to music. This includes, for example, the role of memory and anticipation shaping the ever-shifting contours of the conscious present. But Rosenzweig, an eclectic and erudite writer, was no music psychologist. If we introduce a scientific analysis of music appreciation to his own reflections, we may get a glimpse of his sharp intuition regarding the emotional and affective response to the process of creation–revelation–redemption that underlies his story of the soul's experience in the present moment. Such a review might also help me understand my own enjoyment of singing "ve-shamru" in the dining hall before lunch.

Music

A number of psychological principles underlie the enjoyment that listeners derive from music. To begin with, music "allows expression and regulation of emotion" at the same time that it evokes pleasure."[41] Such regulation includes enhancement and control of one's own emotions as well as communication of emotion among others who may or may not be experiencing the same music. On a deeper psychological level, tonal patterns are encoded and stored in neurological structures that allow storage and memory of structural regularities, which lead to expectancies. In his autobiography from 1887, Darwin wrote that he should have listened to more music than he had, "for perhaps the parts of my brain now atrophied would thus have been kept active through use. The loss of these tastes is a loss of happiness, and may possibly be injurious to the intellect, and more probably to the moral character, by enfeebling the emotional part of our nature."[42]

Indeed, the same brain centers associated with reward, motivation and pleasure are involved in the processing of musical information – which is experienced as the joy of listening to music. "Pleasure in music arises from interactions between cortical loops that enable predictions and

---

[41] Robert J. Zatorre and Valorie N. Salimpoore, "From Perception to Pleasure: Music and Its Neural Substrate," *Proceedings of the National Academy of Sciences* 110, supplement 2 (2013): 225–241, 227.

[42] Quoted in ibid., "From Perception," 226–227.

expectancies to emerge from sound patterns and subcortical systems responsible for reward and valuation."[43] From an experiential point of view, the neurological dynamics that process tonal information in time can be profoundly evocative without any reference to "material" or representational facts in the world. For example, acceleration, retardation, pause, and syncopation in a particular passage (the Adagio in Beethoven's Piano Concerto No. 5 versus the opening of Vivaldi's Gloria in D Major, RV 589) create an emotional narrative without any referential reality. If accompanied by a rising or descending pitch, the effect is more complicated yet – and with lyrics, a whole new way of thinking emerges.

In sum, the final experience is thus a product of sound, perception and neural processing, cultural learning, memory, evaluation, psychological expectation including tension and release, and social bonding. The association of music pleasure with social consequences is a complex and ambiguous matter. Some researchers have offered a social cohesion hypothesis of music pleasure, which would be consistent with the intuitive observations of Rosenzweig – namely, that singing increases communal bonding. This is an adaptationist theory, and there are others, such as those associated with the function of music in courtship and mating.[44] Walter Freeman argues that music and dance in tribal societies "give great pleasure and catharsis to those caught up in the communal spirit of the events."[45] The "feeling of bonding" and the "formation of a neural basis for social cooperation" are produced by the mechanism that evolved to support sexual reproduction.[46]

Others have rejected this theorizing.[47] However, there is strong empirical evidence linking music to group identity and behavior as a cultural fact.[48] For example, the French show a measurable preference for French music above German music, and people can be induced to make

[43] Ibid., 225.
[44] Wallin, *Biomusicology*; N. Wallin, B. Merker, and S. Brown, *The Origins of Music* (Cambridge, MA: MIT Press, 2000).
[45] Walter Freeman, "A Neurobiological Role of Music in Social Bonding," in *The Origins*, ed., N. Wallin, 419–420.
[46] Ibid., 420.
[47] Aniruddh D. Patel, *Music, Language and the Brain* (New York: Oxford University Press, 2008), 375.
[48] Charles Areni and David Kim, "The Influence of Background Music on Shopping Behavior: Classical versus Top-Forty Music in a Wine Shop," http://acrwebsite.org/volumes/7467/volumes/v20/NA-20, 1993 (accessed January 28, 2019);
    Martin Stokes, *Ethnicity, Identity and Music: The Musical Construction of Place* (New York: Bloomsbury Academic, 1997).

measurably more expensive purchases by hearing more culturally elevated music. Such evidence suggests that the cultural dimension of musical enjoyment involves acquired taste and learned, rather than biologically given, emotional regulation. There is a strong suggestion that in addition to the hardwired cortical sources of musical pleasure, there is a process more closely akin to mastery pleasure, which – though learned – is highly functional in the bonding that takes place in groups of strangers.

Thus, to return to the event that takes place during the singing of "ve-shamru" with people who are almost strangers to me, this is how Rosenzweig might put it if he were to combine biological knowledge with his phenomenological reflections: As I sing, I am present, the tune and the words demand this of me, and so I pay attention to the song. Knowing the tune – the lyrics are on the wall – is based on my memory, but the tempo has been decided by someone else, and I conform. My enjoyment then is not entirely my own, just as the structure and speed of the song are not my own. My assent to sing and enjoy the song is an opening of my inner self, an acceptance of the others who are there. If the "love" that Rosezweig attributes to the soul in such a situation is too strong to describe my mood (and perhaps what I see in others), I can draw on others to account for this. I choose then to reflect on Levinas, who – I believe – is very useful for understanding not only the mood but the entire ethos of the synagogue and the religious experience it induces in me and possibly others.

The fixed nature of the liturgy, its weekly repetition, and its appeal to the Absolute are comforting, but also put me in a paradoxical state. These aspects seem to deprive me of spontaneity, even freedom, but we are told that God only wants the free. The day is patterned, but I desire freedom that goes beyond structure. And so, while the affective and emotional dimension of Shabbat is enriched by the service, what about the moral dimension and, at its core, my freedom?

The resolution to this inner conflict is a powerful sense of being at play, participating in a sacred play. For example, assume that there was a God and he possessed this or that character and required of us humans one thing or the other. How might one conduct himself under these circumstances? The play reminds me that my relationship to the Other, as play, always leads me beyond myself, not to some reality that the play represents but to the flow of play itself. Because it is play, it does not impose an ontological structure on my reality and situates me in some theoretical space. But because I choose freely to participate in the pattern of the play, I am able to move beyond the reality that I had previously defined as binding on myself.

It is important to note that the notion of play underlying these impressions overlaps but is not identical with game. The Shabbat service is not a game, though some anthropologists following in the broad trail left by Huizinga's *Homo Ludens* may regard it as such. I experience the service as play in the sense that Gadamer uses as *Spielraum*, which means something like leeway or wiggle room.[49] Here, this means the space between what an activity like a ritual stands for and what it literally embodies. Also, and related to that, it is the space between believing and not believing and the space between total constraint – obedience to law – and absolute freedom. The space is not static but dynamic – that is, I vacillate back and forth between the poles that define the *Spielraum* and get a thrill from that. The vacillation itself is pleasurable in the manner that attention disengages from one thing and engages elsewhere and back again.[50] And above all of that, the pleasure I get from playing, the play pleasure, is a reminder that enjoyment is in my very nature as an experiencing self even when the playing ends. I recognize in these thoughts my reading of Emmanuel Levinas.

Levinas and the Pleasure of Existence

In his phenomenological mode of expression and programmatic rejection of Husserl and Heidegger, Levinas is interested in the same thing that the men and women around me – as members of a Conservative congregation – are interested in: the ethics of mutual responsibility and good works.[51] The transcendence of a divine Creator that dominates the liturgy is, to my reckoning, the face of the transcendent other person, bridged here through religious action and language.

Levinas shows a significant debt to Rosenzweig (among others). However, while for Rosenzweig, "revelation" was the divine command to redeem the world through love of the neighbor, Levinas's emphasis was more ethical in relation to the other than spiritual-emotional. And, unlike

[49] Gadamer, *Truth and Method*, 108; See also David L. Miller, *Gods and Games: Toward a Theology of Play* (New York: The World Publishing, 1970), 74–76; Handelman and Shulman, *God*, 42.

[50] According to Richard Schechner (*The Future*, 25) there are six parameters for the space in which the vacillation occurs: structure, process, experience, function, ideology, and frame. See Chapters 4 and 5. See also Philip A. Gable and Eddie Harmon-Jones, "Approach-Motivated Positive Affect," *Psychological Science* 19, no. 5 (2008): 476–482.

[51] Thomas G. Casey, "Levinas' Idea of the Infinite and the Priority of the Other," *Gregorianum* 84, no. 2 (2003): 383–417; Scott Davidson and Diane Perpich, *Totality and Infinity at 50* (Pittsburgh, PA: Duquesne University Press, 2012), 105–126.

Rosenzweig (and Buber), the relation to the other was not symmetrical, and this relationship, characterized by separation, is mediated through responsibility above love.[52]

However, the task of bridging, or the pursuit of what Levinas calls "Infinity," is not simple or self-evident because of the obstacle of systems – that is, "Totality." The basic difference is the non-representational nature of Infinity that cannot be grasped by the theoretical and representational intentionality of Totality.[53] Levinas opens his great work *Totality and Infinity* with the metaphors of war (totality) and peace (infinity) – painting the ontological and axiological concepts with judgment. He rejects totalizing systems of thought and promotes in their place non-representational individual existence. Here natural needs are faced and overcome, but not suppressed, as they constitute the basis of the self's encounter with life as affectivity: both pain and enjoyment. Infinity is freedom where "Desire" above response to needs is the reigning motivation (toward Infinity) and where speech as a form of interrelatedness is more important than one's role in the scheme of things. Infinity lends itself to religious axiology but only as long as it is not mistaken for the fulfillment of history. The focus remains on experience, which means "relationship with the absolute other," and on the ethical obligation of mutual responsibility to the other human, who is the face of the Infinite Other.[54] In the Conservative synagogue in Virginia, as in others, this often translates to the promotion of the twin values of *tikkun olam* (global activism) and *gmilut hasadim* (mutual support).

What, finally, should I make of the elevated affect that runs throughout the Shabbat morning services of the skeptic that I am? Should I go back to evolutionary psychology and talk about the motivation that underlies social bonding? Or should I discuss the joy of mastering the details of a liturgy and ritual actions and the satisfaction of displaying such mastery in public? If religious experience is taken as a conventional designation, then it is safe to do so. But it is also uninteresting: after all, the same sort of pleasure can be found in mastering the lyrics of several songs and singing in a college a capella choir. By the standards of that very same liturgy I have mastered (*Sim Shalom*), this is a social and aesthetic joy, not entirely what I am told the Shabbat means. I believe it is necessary to be more precise

[52] Nigel Zimmermann, *Facing the Other: John Paul II, Levinas, and the Body* (Eugene, OR: Cascade Books, 2015), 140–142.

[53] Casey, "Levinas' Idea," 385.

[54] C. Fred Alford, "Levinas and Winnicott: Motherhood and Responsibility," *American Imago* 57, no. 3 (2000): 235–259.

and examine the satisfaction I have experienced in the synagogue as it is
before looking at how it functions. Levinas has been useful in this regard.

Levinas's discussion of pleasure, or what he calls "enjoyment" and
"happiness," is closely bound in his distinction between being and existence. Existence, to repeat, is the living engagement with things we need in
time while being is the ontological situatedness in a system of ideas, in a
theory. The engagement with needs (breathing, looking, eating) provides
the content of an enjoyment that defines living, but the relationship is not
of cause–effect. Levinas calls this relationship "nourishment," which is the
"transmutation of the other into the same."[55] Specifically, "an energy that
is other, recognized as other … becomes in enjoyment, my own energy,
my strength, me."[56] To sum this up, Levinas declares that all enjoyment is
"alimentation." A lived life, in existence, is to nourish on the objects of
need and, beyond that, to enjoy being aware of such nourishment. It is to
enjoy enjoyment. In this sense, enjoyment is "the ultimate consciousness
of all contents that fill my life – it embraces them."[57]

Levinas's understanding of pleasure thus transcends the biology of needs
fulfilled in the bare sense of homeostasis. It is an awareness of the
relationship with the things we need and a valuing of this enjoyable
dependence and, in that relationship, finding happiness, which is independent of these needs. Happiness is the independence within dependence. The biological understanding, in contrast, is Aristotelian in looking
to cause–effect (such as novelty pleasure) and ends–means (mastery pleasure): the way we have discussed pleasure in earlier chapters of this book.
A phenomenologist like Levinas (or Ricoeur) would say that pleasure is not
the qualitative or evaluating response to objects in the world or in awareness. Both Levinas and Ricoeur state that enjoyment is "the very pulsation
of the I." Enjoyment or happiness is beyond objects, beyond being, "in
which things are hewn."[58]

However, it is important to keep in mind that the I exists dynamically;
it moves in time with expectation and memory. Happiness, therefore, is an
accomplishment in the self's movement beyond being. Happiness implies

[55] Levinas, *Totality*, 111.   [56] Ibid.
[57] Ibid. Edna Langenthal calls this foundational notion "structure of life," which is not hedonic
pleasure: "Welcoming the Other: Hospitality, Subjectivity and Otherness in the Thought of
Emmanuel Levinas and the Biblical Story of the Hospitality of Abraham," in *Levinas Faces
Biblical Figures*, ed., Yael Lin (Lanham, MD: Lexington Books, 2014), 35–60.
[58] Levinas, *Totality*, 113. This differs from Husserl, for whom pleasure is intentional, and from a
theologian like Paul Tillich, who distinguished pleasure (as intentional) from bliss. See, *Systematic
Theology*, vol. I (Chicago: University of Chicago Press, 1951), 280.

the memory of what one aspired to beyond being situated in a system of concepts. Happiness is the mastery of one's needs: "That man could be happy for his needs indicates that in human need the physiological plane is transcended."[59] It is not the body that is transcended but the physiological. The body itself is the instrument of mastery with which one enjoys the other.

This notion of pleasure is both subtle and paradoxical, but the paradox is resolved when we realize that Levinas is distinguishing between our conception of reality as a system of ideas and existence itself. In the system, objects cause pleasure. In existence, in "living from," enjoyment is object-less – that is, it is not an effect but the very nature of the self as awareness. So, the prayer, the companionship, and the singing are modes of being conscious of being conscious in a particular way. They define the happiness of enjoying the metaphysical other – which itself is no object or concept at all, certainly not for a skeptical atheist. These rituals are not ontological but relational events – they are the way that enjoyment takes in the other. Happiness is awareness of such enjoyment.

Levinas's analysis of happiness as a meta-psychological state of awareness speaks to religious experience in a Shabbat service better than a biological theory. It describes the experience, if by that term one means the conscious observation of and participation in those happenings that take place for approximately three hours in the synagogue. During that time, I give myself over to the play that relates to "real life" in the same way that "existence" in Levinas relates to "being." Within this space that I play, the other is transmuted into my playing self. This is what Levinas writes:

> The inversion of the instincts of nutrition, which have lost their biological finality, marks the very disinterestedness of man. The suspension or absence of the ultimate finality has a positive face – the disinterested joy of play. To live is to play, despite the finality and tension of instinct to live from something without this something having the sense of a goal or an onto-logical means – simply play or enjoyment of life.[60]

Because I do not deny the force of purposive activity in my life, I am narrowing this all-embracing observation and limiting it to Shabbat services for a reason. The long commute from home to the synagogue and the drive back are not part of the sacred play of Shabbat services. Neither is my work on Monday and the rest of the week. In short, I find Levinas's phenomenology of pleasure (with its denial of biology) useful for

---

[59] Levinas, *Totality*, 115.   [60] Ibid., 134.

understanding my enjoyment of the Shabbat services but not my practical life outside the walls of the synagogue. It may be that for others in the synagogue, the services are no play or game at all. Moreover, for me, other modes of play, like singing in an a capella choir would have been, are not like the Shabbat. This is because, though lacking "purpose," they are not objectless in the same way. Their object, such as singing well or performing before an audience, does constitute an ends–means relationship in which the accomplishment pleasure is implicated. The religious play, for me, is unique, not in that God is beyond sight or even that the Shabbat service is played only as if there is a God. The play unfolds in the utter unimaginability of God as an object of consciousness or the incommensurability of God with the play, and yet the pleasure emerges in relationship to an "other," the not I, which behaves dynamically as I wiggle between belief and utter disbelief.[61]

None of what I have described necessarily applies to any other participant in a religious event. My observations would not work for those in the synagogue for whom God is some sort of true object – including Person or Creator. It would also not apply to the congregants who have not read Levinas or Rosenzweig, or have understood them in a different manner, or have not connected them to the Shabbat service. Outside of the Conservative synagogue, religious individuals whose conventional religious worldview sanctifies objects in the world (forests, mountain, holy persons) will enjoy entirely different religious experiences as well. In short, religious experience varies with cultural and doctrinal frameworks along with individual circumstances. Hence, the variety of religious experience is nearly infinite. As a result, the role that pleasure plays as a dimension of religious experience is also infinitely variable. For example, in the absence of the hyper-self-awareness induced by phenomenological reflections, the pleasure may more clearly reveal the work of psychological adaptation: the strengthening of communal ties, regulation of mate selection, the promotion or enhancement of self-regulation, the refinement of affirmative motivation, altruism, and so forth.

In the case of the skeptical, perhaps somewhat standoffish subject who is aware of the religious service as a play, the pleasure may be compared to the *rasa* of Hindu *bhakti* theorists, or the metaphorical theorizing about pleasure that originates in the *Song of Songs* and becomes disembodied in Origen and other Christian thinkers. Both Hindu and Christian theorists refuse to attribute the devotee's bliss to a "cause," properly speaking.[62]

---

[61] See Huizinga, *Homo Ludens*, 139, on St. Francis.   [62] See Chapter 2 of this book.

However, in the absence of God within the synagogue play, the similarity is only partial: On the one hand, the pleasure is not experienced as the effect of concrete causes like food and sex, or even singing and companionship. But, on the other hand, the pleasure is not attributed to God. In terms of the adaptive categories I have been using, this has been a complex sort of play pleasure, which leads me back to Gadamer and my free play in the wiggle room.[63]

The Wiggle Room Pleasure

In this section, I step out of the first-person perspective on the religious experience to adopt a more objective point of view in order to analyze the role of pleasure in all of this. It is no easy task to link the pleasure obtained by a hyper-self-aware religion scholar during a twenty-first-century religious service to evolutionary psychology. To be sure, there are moments of novelty pleasure – that first bite into the bagel with the cream cheese and lox. And there are moments of mastery pleasure as well, such as the feeling of accomplishment at having memorized portions of the siddur along with the timing and cadence of prayers and songs. Other congregants may share these sorts of pleasure, which may serve some of the social functions discussed in previous chapters. There is nothing uniquely religious about such examples. The pleasure that accompanies my perception of Shabbat service as play is more interesting and hard to describe and account for in any functional manner.

Several chapters in this book have discussed the subject of play. It figured in the discussion of mysticism (Chapter 5), magic (Chapter 6), and the biology of pleasure (Chapter 2). The most detailed treatment of play and its relationship to pleasure featured in the discussion of mystical joy as play pleasure, in connection with the writings of Plotinus and C. S. Lewis.

My own experience during Shabbat service is neither mystical nor magical. As already noted, the pleasure I identify as attendant on the participation in the service is also – to a great extent – novelty and mastery. But play pleasure colors my overall experience in more subtle and interesting ways. The science underlying such a hedonic experience is complex and often controversial. According to some researchers, there are as many

---

[63] There is no clear evidence to decide whether play is beneficial in human development as a bio-evolutionary or merely as cultural-developmental function. Peter K. Smith, "Social and Pretend Play in Children," in *The Nature of Play*, ed., Pellegrini, 173–212.

as thirteen categories that constitute a framework for analyzing such play pleasure.[64] These include creation, exploration, discovery, difficulty, competition, danger, captivation, sensation, sympathy, simulation, fantasy, comradery, and subversion. One example – difficulty – shows that shooting at a target that is too big reduces the enjoyment of the play.[65] All of these do not figure in every play situation, naturally. Bungee jumping includes danger but not necessarily sympathy. My own experience in the synagogue lacked danger and competition, but I can identify all the other categories in my experience.

James A. Russell, as we have seen in the Introduction to this book, speaks of "core affect" with two underlying dimensions: good–bad and activation–deactivation. Thus, good and activation combine to form the single feeling of ecstasy.[66] But core affect, simple in principle, is experienced in complex ways. Due to the modular brain circuitry that underlies it, it possesses "fast, mandatory, unique output," which both influences and is influenced by perceptions thoughts and emotions. The overall effect – the "psychological construction" of the experience – consists of facial and vocal expressions, autonomic nervous system, emotional behavior, the conscious experience of having an emotion, appraisal, attribution, and emotion regulation.[67] It is important to recall that the concept of core affect is more basic than both "pleasure" and "emotion," which are often contrasted as distinct phenomena.

An example of Russell's approach can be offered: The appraisal yielded by observation of a highly monotonous stimulus, such as twenty-five consecutive exposures to Ravel's Bolero, will lead to deactivation and a reduction of pleasure, resulting in boredom. The experience can also lead to displeasure and activation, resulting in frustration and annoyance. However, children derive great pleasure – in Russell's terms, "activation" and "good" – from repeated exposure to the same show, say, an episode of "Blue's Clues," which may be due to their discovery of new elements in each showing.[68]

---

[64] Brigid Costello and Ernst Edmonds, "A Study in Play, Pleasure and Interaction Design," *Proceedings of the 2007 Conference on Designing Pleasurable Products and Interfaces* (Helsinki, Finland, 2007), 76–91.

[65] Costello and Edmonds, "A Study," 80.   [66] Russell, "Emotion," 1264.

[67] Ibid., 1268–1271.

[68] Daniel Anderson, Jennings Bryant, Alice Wilder, Angela Santomero, Marsha Williams, and Alisha M. Crawley, "Researching Blue's Clues: Viewing Behavior and Impact," *Media Psychology* 2, no. 2 (2000): 179–194.

It should be obvious that a detailed description of a three-hour experience of enjoyment would have to touch the conscious surface of all these factors that drive the hedonic flow. Furthermore, because "experience" itself is a densely constituted reality that includes, at the very least, beliefs, desires, hopes, and the search for meaning, following Dewey's definition, the description of the experience of play enjoyment would now become a Tolstoy-level challenge.

As noted, I recognize in my Saturday morning most of Costello's categories, excluding danger and competition, and all of Russell's elements of psychological construction. There is even subversion, which operates in two directions: Outward subversion is my awareness that my skepticism subverts the intent of the service. Inward subversion is the awareness of how the service and the other participants subvert my skepticism. In play, both take place simultaneously, which I experience as humorous, worthy of laughter. It may be similar to what years ago one of my professors, Harvey Cox, called the approach of the jester, which is a "theology of juxtaposition." This "celebrates the collision of symbol and situation as the occasion of new experience and unprecedented perception."[69] I would laugh about it, but I must control that desire, which is also satisfying in a distinct but closely related way.[70]

The complexity of the situation disinvites simple reduction to psychological and certainly biological causes. Biology and psychology are certainly at work, but a description of the experience as play pleasure remains, in principle, an exercise in descriptive discourse. If kittens could speak and write, if kittens looked for the meaning of their life, their own play pleasure would perhaps be similar.

---

[69] Harvey Cox, *The Feast of Fools: A Theological Essay on Festivity and Fantasy* (Cambridge, MA: Harvard University Press, 1969), 132.
[70] Kerrie P. Lewis, "Social Play in the Great Apes," in *The Nature*, ed., Pellegrini, 32.

Conclusion
What about Joy?

Because this book was written in English, the two words that dominated were pleasure and joy. Joy was the interesting word, the one that can presumably teach us about religion and positive feelings. But joy is a fairly vague word, and besides, a great deal of the material comes from other languages. Can we learn something new about joy, even here, at the tail end of the book? Would it pay to look at the word in the languages of religious documents – Italian, French, Spanish, German, Hebrew, Sanskrit? Translation is messy business, but it may be possible to pick *gioia, joie, alegria, Freude, simha,* or *sukha.* But this dictionary exercise is not very interesting and certainly not revealing. A better idea is going back to the sources.

In St. Francis's *I Fioretti* we read: "questa poverta-umilita, vuota di tutto, e pienezza di gioia, perche è esperienza di Dio."[1] The text states that this poverty-humility, empty of all things, is the fullness of joy because it is the experience of God. So, for St. Francis, joy is a pleasure that does not derive from external objects. Is this reliable? A non-Latin example may enlighten us further and I choose Yehudah Ha-Levy, the great Jewish poet from Spain, whose poetry mourned the exile and longed for the distant holy land: "hem ha-smehim le-shalvatech, ve-hakoavim a'l shomamutech." The poet remarks that "they, your friends, who are joyful [from *simha*] due to your peace and are pained, due to your abandonment."[2] This second example complicates matters for us because the joy in Ha-Levy is directed at the wellbeing of Zion. There is no point even trying this same exercise with Sanskrit texts. To give a brief example, where Olivelle's superb translation of the Upanishads uses Joy, one finds not just *sukha* or *harsha* but *ananda* (*Brihadaranyaka Upanishad* 4.3.9), *rama* (*Taittiriya Upanishad* 1.6.2) and other terms.

---

[1] B. Bughetti, *I Fioretti di San Fracesco* (Roma, Italy: Citta Nuova Editrice, 1999), 109.

[2] Yehudah Ha-Levy, "Zion, Ha-lo Tishali Li-Shlom Asiraich," http://nextbookpress.com/download/ The_Selected_Poems_of_Yehuda_Halevi.pdf (accessed January 25, 2019).

Is there a clearly bounded semantic field that allows us to understand "joy" in a meaningful way? Is there a significant distinction between joy and pleasure, on the one hand, and bliss on the other? For example, when a team wins a game do the fans cheer in joy? In contrast, when the star of the opposing team is injured and carted off the field, do the fans also cheer in joy, or is it some other sort of pleasure? Is there such a thing as censorable joy? The language of positive affect is a mess of semantic confusion as the following map demonstrates.

Informally, it may be fine to say that you were glad Messi left the game due to injury, but it would be strange to say that this caused you joy. This compares poorly with the many terms for pain that you are asked to sort out on the clipboard at the waiting room for the pain clinic. It also compares poorly with the precision of words an expert might use to describe the qualities of a good or bad wine.

The reader may recall the suggestion of James Russell that there are two axes (good–bad and energized–depleted) that help us identify ecstasy as very pleasurable and energized, whereas pleasurable but not so energized may be contentment. But this, too, is fairly impoverished.

While joy semantics frustrates us, religions around the world and throughout history have manufactured in practice an impressive range and flavors of positive states. I suggested, then, that a basic framework that does not discriminate among such states based on semantic nuances would be useful. This is a functional framework, which is based on human decision making in response to external–internal and environmental–social circumstances. The framework consisted of three fundamental hedonic consequences that emerge from the decision-making, the adaptive, process. These were

1. Novelty-replenishment
2. Mastery
3. Play

You can feel joy from drinking water in the desert (1), from conquering a high peak in the Himalayas (2), or from blowing soap bubbles (3). It is not the word that tells us where the positive feeling belongs: where it came from, what sort of social role it fulfills, and even – to some extent – how it feels.

And so, in religious literature, we have reasonably clear evidence of such useful functional discrimination in relationship to the positive feelings that go by a variety of names. If the positive feeling is associated with the senses or objects of sensory desire, it is probably (1) and then often excoriated. In such cases, a word like pleasure is more common than joy or gladness, but this is not an ironclad rule. In contrast, if the positive feeling is associated with self-control, obedience to internal authority, extreme effort, modesty, or humility, this is probably a case of (2). In such cases, the positive feeling receives praise and is rarely described as "pleasure." Instead, joy and gladness are more common.

Finally, if the positive feeling is associated with events or states that are divorced from commonplace reality – either a ritual setting or an individual pursuit that is imaginative, counterfactual, and entirely voluntary – but that requires a certain level of mastery, this is a case of (3). The terminology that describes such a feeling includes – in addition to joy – words like thrill, ecstasy, bliss, and rapture. None of this is precise in a mathematical or grammatical level of accuracy. But there is an underlying order, a "law" perhaps – in the scientific sense of the word.

The argument that supports this idea of an order is as follows. Some pleasures pose a threat to the well-being of a group – religious or otherwise.

Such pleasures need to be controlled for the sake of the collective. Other pleasures actually benefit the group. But these can be difficult and must be learned. For example, if one learns to enjoy patience and charity, not to mention empathy, as gratifying skills, the group benefits. Groups with more altruistic individuals fare better than groups with too many selfish and lazy individuals. This is persuasive but still too basic. It turns out that culture – and religions – offer a great deal more in life than just the enjoyment of altruism for moral rewards. Hence, play is the context where one enters freely into the life of the mind, the imagination and utilizing the tools of mastery, can move in the realm of play this way or that – like a surfer cutting through the wave and not just clinging to the board. At the most rarefied levels play is masterpiece art, Bach's *St. Matthew Passion* – beautiful and enjoyable far beyond what the story of the gospel requires. It is also St. Francis's *Little Flowers*: an enjoyable journey into the experiences that inspired him to write. The consolations and meaning-inspiring joys of the religious life manifest in play – but only for those who have already learned mastery.

It would be useless to connect that highest of good feelings to evolution in some biosociological reduction. It's true that play has a role in the psychology of other mammals. It is also true that in the field of neuro-esthetics, beauty has been linked to evolutionary biology. Finally, it is true that the field of religious studies is not privileged in the sense that it lies beyond psychological or even biological theories. After all, the focus of this book has been pleasure in a variety of forms, and pleasure is a biological fact. But the extent of the reduction I was willing to pursue was behavioral adaptation: human decision to approach or avoid. As it turns out, such a mechanism has enormous consequences that can be utilized and manipulated to produce the most rarefied and meaningful affects.

The most elevated hedonic affect is play, and while the fact of playing is rooted in biological psychology, the rules of play reach – via culture – upward and beyond the simple biological theory. The experience of play, discernable by means of careful introspection, is as free and unpredictable as the pattern of paint splatter on the canvas of Jackson Pollock. It feels this way, and that is why we refuse to acknowledge the biological and even the psychological roots of our religious experiences. However, it turns out, there is a pattern in Pollock's splattered paint, and I believe there is also a pattern to the nature of pleasure in religious life and religious experience. If we exclude religious doctrines, ideas, and the broad spectrum of actions, this pattern certainly appears to apply to the pleasure we get from all of these.

Bibliography

Abrutyn, Seth. "Religious Autonomy and Religious Entrepreneurship: An Evolutionary-Institutionalist's Take on the Axial Age." *Comparative Sociology* 13, no. 2 (2014). 105–134.

Acharya, Madhava. *Sarva-Darśana-Saṃgraha.* Translated by E. B. Cowell and A. E. Gough. Varanasi, India: Chowkamba Sanskrit Series Office, 1961.

Adams, Robert Merrihew. *A Theory of Virtue: Excellence in Being for the Good.* Clarendon: Oxford University Press, 2006.

Adamson, Melitta Weiss. *Food in Medieval Times.* Westport, CT: Greenwood Press, 2004.

Alcaro, Antonio, and Jaak Panksepp. "The SEEKING Mind: Primal Neuro-Affective Substrates for Appetitive Incentive States and Their Pathological Dynamics in Addiction and Depression." *Neuroscience and Behavioral Reviews* 35, no. 9 (2011). 1805–1820.

Alford, C. Fred. "Levinas and Winnicott: Motherhood and Responsibility." *American Imago* 57, no. 3 (2000). 235–259.

Alles, Gregory D. *The Iliad, Ramayana, and the Work of Religion: Failed Persuasion and Religious Mystification.* University Park: The Pennsylvania State University Press, 1994.

Anderson, Daniel, Jennings Bryant, Alice Wilder, Angela Santomero, Marsha Williams, and Alisha M. Crawley. "Researching Blue's Clues: Viewing Behavior and Impact." *Media Psychology* 2, no. 2 (2000). 179–194.

Aquinas, Thomas. *Summa Theologiae.* www.newadvent.org/summa/4041.htm.
Summa Theologica. Ontario, Canada: Devoted Publishing, 2018.

Arbel, Keren. *Early Buddhist Meditation: The Four Jhanas as the Actualization of Insight.* Oxon: Routledge, 2016.

Ardley, Gavin. "The Role of Play in the Philosophy of Plato." *Philosophy* 42, no. 161 (1967). 226–244.

Areni, Charles, and David Kim. "The Influence of Background Music on Shopping Behavior: Classical versus Top-Forty Music in a Wine Shop." http://acrwebsite.org/volumes/7467/volumes/v20/NA-20, 1993.

Arnason, Johann P., S. N. Eisenstadt, and Bjorn Wittrock. "Introduction: Archaic Backgrounds and Axial Breakthroughs." In *Axial Civilization and World History*, edited by Johann P. Arnason et al., 15–18. Leiden, the Netherlands: E. J. Brill, 2005.

Arnold, Emmy. *A Joyful Pilgrimage: My Life in Community.* Rifton, NY: Plough Publishing House, 2011.

Aronson, Eliot, and Judson Mills. "The Effect of Severity of Initiation on Liking of a Group." *The Journal of Abnormal and Social Psychology* 59, no. 1 (1959). 177–181.

Aronson, J., H. Blanton, and J. Cooper. "From Dissonance to Disidentification: Selectivity in the Self-Affirmation Process." *Journal of Personality and Social Psychology* 68, no. 6 (1995). 986–996.

Assad, Talal. *The Geneologies of Religion: Disciplines and Reasons of Power in Christianity and Islam.* Baltimore: Johns Hopkins University Press, 1993.

Assmann, Jan. "Axial 'Breakthroughs' and Semantic 'Relocations' in Ancient Egypt and Israel." In *Axial Civilization and World History,* edited by Johann P. Arnason et al., 133–156. Leiden, the Netherlands: E. J. Brill, 2005.

The Search for God in Ancient Egypt. Ithaca, NY: Cornell University Press, 2001.

Atran, Scott. *In God We Trust: The Evolutionary Landscape of Religion.* New York: Oxford University Press, 2004.

Aydede, Murat. "An Analysis of Pleasure Vis-à-Vis Pain." *Philosophy and Phenomenological Research* 61, no. 3 (2000). 537–570.

Bainbridge, William Sims, and Rodney Stark. "Sectarian Tension." *Review of Religious Research* 22, no. 1 (1980). 105–124.

Band, Arnold J. *Nahman of Bratslav: The Tales.* New York: Paulist Press, 1978.

Bardo, M. T., R. L. Donohew, and N. G. Harrington. "Psychobiology of Novelty Seeking and Drug Seeking Behavior." *Behavioral Brain Research* 77, no. 1 (1996). 23–43.

Barkley, Russell A. "The Executive Functions and Self-Regulation: An Evolutionary Neuropsychological Perspective." *Neuropsychology Review* 11, no. 1 (2001). 1–29.

Barrett, Ron. *Aghor Medicine: Pollution, Death, and Healing in Northern India.* Berkeley: University of California Press, 2008.

Barthes, Roland. *The Pleasure of the Text.* Translated by R. Miller. New York: Farrar, Strauss, Giroux, 1975.

Bastian, Brock, Jolanda Jetten, and Laura J. Ferris. "Pain as a Social Glue: Shared Pain Increases Cooperation." *Psychological Sciences* 25, no. 11 (2014). 2079–2085.

Bateson, Gregory. "A Theory of Play and Fantasy." In *Steps to an Ecology of Mind,* edited by Gregory Bateson, 175–191. New York: Ballantine, 1972.

Baumard, Nicolas, and Pascal Boyer. "Explaining Moral Religions." *Trends in Cognitive Science* 17, no. 6 (2013). 272–280.

Baumard, Nicolas, Alexandre Hyafil, and Pascal Boyer. "What Changed during the Axial Age: Cognitive Styles or Reward Systems?" *Communicative & Integrative Biology* 8 (2015). www.tandfonline.com/doi/full/10.1080/19420889 .2015.1046657?scroll=top&needAccess=true.

Beall, Todd S. *Josephus' Description of the Essenes.* Cambridge, UK: Cambridge University Press, 2004.

Beauchamp, G., and Owen Maller. "The Development of Flavor Preference in Humans: A Review." In *The Chemical Senses and Nutrition*, edited by Morley R. Kare and Owen Maller, 292–315. New York: Academic Press, 1977.

Bellah, Robert N. *Religion in Human Evolution: From the Paleolithic to the Axial Age.* Cambridge, MA: Harvard University Press, 2011.

Bellah, Robert N., and Hans Joas. *The Axial Age and Its Consequences.* Cambridge, MA: Harvard University Press, 2012.

Berlyne, Daniel. *Aesthetics and Psychology.* New York: Appleton-Century-Crofts, 1971.

Berns, Gregory. *Satisfaction: Sensation Seeking, Novelty and the Science of Finding True Fulfillment.* New York: Henry Holt & Company, 2005.

Berridge, Kent C. "Pleasure of the Brain." *Brain and Cognition* 52, no. 1 (2003). 106–128.

———. "Pleasure, Pain, Desire, and Dread: Hidden Core Processes of Emotion." In *Well-Being: The Foundations of Hedonic Psychology*, edited by D. Kahneman et al., 525–557. New York: Russell Sage Foundation, 1999.

Bettelheim, Bruno. *The Uses of Enchantment: The Meaning and Importance of Fairy Tales.* New York: Vintage Books, 2010.

Bisschop, Peter, and Arlo Griffith. "The Pāśupata Observance (Atharvavedapariśiṣta 40)." *Indo-Iranian Journal* 46, no. 4 (2003). 315–348.

Bland, Earl D. "An Appraisal of Psychological & Religious Perspectives of Self-Control." *Journal of Religion and Health* 47, no. 1 (2008). 4–16.

Bloch, Ariel, and Chana Block. *The Song of Songs: A New Translation.* Berkeley: University of California Press, 1995.

Bloom, Paul. *How Pleasure Works: The New Science of Why We Like What We Like.* New York: W. W. Norton & Company, 2010.

Boccaccini, Gabriele. *Beyond the Essene Hypothesis: The Parting of the Ways between Qumran and the Enochic Judaism.* Grand Rapids, MI: William B. Erdman, 1998.

Bodhi, Bhikkhu. *In the Buddha's Own Words: An Anthology of Discourses from the Pali Canon.* Somerville, MA: Wisdom Publications, 2005.

Bond, H. *Lawrence. Nicholas of Cusa: Selected Spiritual Writings.* New York: Paulist Press, 1997.

Bonnfoy, Yves. *American, African and Old European Mythologies.* Chicago: University of Chicago Press, 1993.

Bosacki, Sandra. *Social Cognition in Middle Childhood and Adolescence: Integrating the Personal, Social and Educational Lives of Young People.* West Sussex: Wiley Blackwell, 2016.

Boy, John D. "Inventing the Axial Age: The Origins and Uses of a Historical Concept." *Theory and Society* 42, no. 3 (2013). 241–259.

Boyer, Pascal. *Religion Explained: The Evolutionary Origins of Religious Thought.* New York: Basic Books, 2007.

Brandes, Stanley. *Skulls to the Living, Bread to the Dead: The Day of the Dead in Mexico and Beyond.* Malden, MA: Blackwell Publishing, 2006.

Brant, D. H., and Lee J. Kavanau. "Unrewarded Exploration and Learning Complex Mazes by Wild and Domestic Mice." *Nature* 204, no. 4955 (1964). 267–269.

Braun, Joachim. *Music in Ancient Israel/Palestine: Archaeological, Written and Comparative Sources.* Grand Rapids, MI: William B. Eerdmans Publishing Co., 2002.

Broshi, Magen. *Hamegillot Hagenuzot, Qumran ve-Hasi'im.* Jerusalem, Israel: Yad Ben Tzvi Publication, 2010.

Brown, Peter. *The Body and Society: Men, Women, and Sexual Renunciation in Early Christianity.* New York: Columbia University Press, 1988.

Bruner, Jerome. *Actual Minds, Possible Worlds.* Cambridge, MA: Harvard University Press, 1986.

Bryant, Edwin F. *Krishna: The Beautiful Legend of God.* London: Penguin, 2003.
Krishna: A Sourcebook. New York: Oxford University Press, 2007.
The Yoga Sutras of Patanjali. New York: North Point Press, 2009.

Bughetti, B. *I Fioretti di San Fancesco.* Roma, Italy: Citta Nuova Editrice, 1999.

van Buitenen, J. A. B. "Ānanda, or All Desires Fulfilled." *History of Religions* 19, no. 1 (1979). 27–36.

Burghardt, Gordon M. *The Genesis of Animal Play: Testing the Limits.* Cambridge, MA: MIT Press, 2005.

Bussanich, John R. *The One and Its Relation to Intellect in Plotinus.* Leiden, the Netherlands: E. J. Brill, 1988.

Butler, Chris. "Riding Transcendental Waves; Surfing and Meditation." www.freebsd.nfo.sk/hinduism/meditacia.htm.

Cabanac, Michel. "Pleasure: The Common Currency." *Journal of Theoretical Biology* 155, no. 2 (1992). 173–200.

Caillois, Roger. *Man, Play and Games.* Translated by Meyer Barush. Urbana, IL: University of Illinois Press, 2001.

Caporael, Linda R. *Developing Scaffolds in Evolution.* Cambridge, MA: MIT Press, 2014.

Carrasco, David. "Sacrifice/Human Sacrifice in Religious Traditions." In *The Oxford Handbook of Religion and Violence,* edited by Mark Juergensmeyer et al., 209–225. New York: Oxford University Press, 2013.

Carroll, John. *Guilt: The Grey Eminence behind Character, History and Culture.* London: Routledge and Kegan Paul, 1985.

Carver, C. S., and M. F. Scheier. "Principles of Self-Regulation: Action and Emotion." In *Handbook of Motivation and Cognition: Foundations of Social Behavior,* edited by E. T. Higgins and R. M. Sorrentino, 3–52. New York: Guilford Press, 1990.
"Self-Regulation of Action and Affect." In *Handbook of Self-Regulation: Research, Theory and Applications,* edited by Kathleen D. Vohs and Roy F. Baumeister, 3–21. 2nd edn. New York: The Guilford Press, 2011.

Casey, Thomas G. "Levinas' Idea of the Infinite and the Priority of the Other." *Gregorianum* 84, no. 2 (2003). 383–417.

Chen, Mark, and John A. Bargh. "Consequences of Automatic Evaluation: Immediate Behavioral Predispositions to Approach or Avoid the Stimulus." *Personality and Social Psychology Bulletin* 25, no. 2 (1999). 215–224.

Ciapalo, Roman T. "Seriousness and Playfulness in Plotinus' Enneads." Master's Thesis, Loyola University Chicago. Paper 2971 (1978). http://ecommons .luc.edu/luc_theses/2971.

Cicero, Marcus Tullius. *On Moral Ends*. Translated by Raphael Woolf. Cambridge, UK: Cambridge University Press, 2001.

Clark, Stephen R. L. "Plotinus: Body and Soul." In *Cambridge Companion to Plotinus*, edited by Lloyd P. Gerson, 275–291. Cambridge, UK: Cambridge University Press, 1999.

Clement of Alexandria. *Christ the Educator*. Translated by Simon P. Wood. New York: Fathers of the Church Publication, 1954.

Clement, Fabrice, Melissa Koenig, and Paul Harris. "The Ontogenesis of Trust." *Mind and Language* 19, no. 4 (2004). 360–379.

Clore, Gerald L., and Aandrew Ortony. "Appraisal Theories: How Cognition Shapes Affect into Emotion." In *Handbook of Emotions*, edited by Michael Lewis, Jeannette M. Haviland-Jones, and Lisa F. Barrett, 628–644. 3rd edn. New York: Guilford Press, 2008.

Coleman, Tracy. "Viraha-Bhakti and Strīdharma – Rereading the Story of Kṛṣṇa and the Gopīs in the Harivaṃśa and the Bhāgavata Purāṇa." *Journal of the American Oriental Society* 130, no. 3 (2010). 385–412.

Colson, Francis H., and George H. Whitaker. *Philo*. Loeb Classical Library. Cambridge, MA: Harvard University Press, 1985, 1988.

Cooper, Joel. *Cognitive Dissonance: 50 Years of a Classic Theory*. Los Angeles: Sage Publishers, 2007.

Corrigan, Kevin. *Reading Plotinus: A Practical Introduction to Neoplatonism*. West Lafayette, IN: Purdue University Press, 2004.

Cosby, James A. *Devil's Music, Holy Rollers and Hillbillies: Haw America Gave Birth to Rock and Roll*. Jefferson, NC: McFarland and Company, 2016.

Costello, Brigid, and Ernst Edmonds. "A Study in Play, Pleasure and Interaction Design." *Proceedings of the 2007 Conference on Designing Pleasurable Products and Interfaces*. Helsinki, Finland, 2007. 76–91.

Cox, Harvey. *The Feast of Fools: A Theological Essay on Festivity and Fantasy*. Cambridge, MA: Harvard University Press, 1969.

Crisp, Roger. "Homeric Ethics." In *The Oxford Handbook of the History of Ethics*, edited by Roger Crisp, 1–20. Oxford: Oxford University Press, 2013.

Csikszentmihalyi, Mihaly. *Flow: The Psychology of Happiness*. New York: Harper Collins, 2008.

D'Angour, Arman. "Plato and Play: Taking Education Seriously in Ancient Greece." *American Journal of Play* 5, no. 3 (2013). 293–307.

Dalai Lama and Howard C. Cutler. *The Art of Happiness: A Handbook for Living*. New York: Riverhead Books, 1998.

Daniel, E. Valentine. *Fluid Signs: Being a Person the Tamil Way*. Berkeley: University of California Press, 1984.

Danielou, Jean. *Philo of Alexandria.* Translated by James G. Colbert. Cambridge, UK: James Clark & Co., 2014.

Darwin, Charles. *The Expression of Emotion in Man and Animals.* New York: Oxford University Press, 1998.

Davidson, Scott, and Diane Perpich. *Totality and Infinity at 50.* Pittsburgh, PA: Duquesne University Press, 2012.

Dewey, John. *Experience and Nature.* LaSalle, IL: Open Court, 1925.

de Young, Mary. "The Devil Goes to Day Care: McMartin and the Making of Moral Panic." *The Journal of American Culture* 20, no. 1 (1997). 19–25.

Dias, Diana, and Maria Jose Sa. "Initiation Rituals in University as Lever for Group Cohesion." *Journal of Further and Higher Education* 38, no. 4 (2014). 447–464.

Dijksterhuis, Ap. "Why We Are Social Animals: The High Road to Imitation as a Social Glue." In *Perspectives on Imitation: From Neuroscience to Social Science* vol. 2, edited by Susan L. Hurley and Nick Chater, 207–220. Cambridge, MA: MIT Press, 2005.

Dimock Jr., Edward C. *Caitanya caritāmṛta of Kavirāja Kṛṣṇadāsa: A Translation and Commentary. Harvard Oriental Series.* Cambridge, MA: Harvard University Press, 1999.

Dissanayake, Ellen. "From Play and Ritualisation to Ritual and Its Arts: Sources of Upper Pleistocene Ritual Practices in Lower Middle Pleistocene Ritualised and Play Behaviours in Ancestral Hominins." In *Ritual, Play and Belief in Evolution and Early Human Societies*, edited by Colin Renfrew et al., 87–100. Cambridge, UK: Cambridge University Press, 2017.

Divine, Donald L. "Note on the Concept of an Axial Turning in Human History." In *Rethinking Civilizational Analysis*, edited by Said Amir Arjomand and Edward A. Tiryakian, 67–70. London: Sage, 2004.

Dodds, E. R. *The Greeks and the Irrational.* Berkeley: University of California Press, 1951.

Donald, Merlin. *A Mind So Rare: The Evolution of Human Consciousness.* New York: W. W. Norton, 2002.

"The Neurobiology of Human Consciousness: An Evolutionary Approach." *Neuropsychologia* 33, no. 9 (1995). 1087–1102.

The Origins of the Human Mind: Three Stages in the Evolution of Culture and Cognition. Cambridge, MA: Harvard University Press, 1991.

Donin, Hayim Halevy. *To Be a Jew.* New York: Basic Books, 2001.

Douglas, Mary. *Natural Symbols: Explorations in Cosmology.* London: Routledge, 2003.

Droogers, Andre, Peter B. Clarke, Grace Davie, Sidney M. Greenfield, and Peter Versteeg. *Playful Religion: Challenges for the Study of Religion.* Delft: The Netherlands: Eburon Delft, 2006.

Dubay, Thomas. *Fire Within: St. Teresa of Avila, St. John of the Cross, and the Gospel – On Prayer.* San Francisco: Ignatius Press, 1989.

Dufour, Richard. *Plotinus: A Bibliography, 1950–2000.* Leiden, the Netherlands: E. J. Brill, 2002.

Dunbabin, Katherine M. D. *The Roman Banquet: Images of Conviviality.* Cambridge, UK: Cambridge University Press, 2003.

Eisenberg, Nancy, Cynthia L. Smith, Adrienne Sadovsky, and Tracy L. Spinard. "Effortful Control: Relations with Emotion Regulation, Adjustment, and Socialization in Childhood." In *Handbook of Self-Regulation: Research, Theory, and Applications*, edited by Kathleen D. Vohs and Roy F. Baumeister, 263–283. 2nd edn. New York: Guilford Press, 2011.

Eisenstadt, Shmuel N. *The Origins and Diversity of the Axial Age Civilizations*. Albany: State University of New York Press, 1986.

Eiser, J. Richard, and Russell H. Fazio. "How Approach and Avoidance Decisions Influence Attitude Formation and Change." In *Handbook of Approach and Avoidance Motivation*, edited by Andrew J. Elliot, 323–342. New York: Psychology Press, 2008.

Eliade, Mircea. *Rites and Symbols of Initiation*. New York: Harper & Row, 1965.

Elkana, Yehudah. "The Emergence of Second-Order Thinking in Classical Greece." In *The Origins and Diversity of the Axial Age Civilizations*, edited by Shmuel N. Eisenstadt, 40–64. Albany: State University of New York Press, 1986.

Elliot, Andrew J. *Handbook of Approach and Avoidance Motivation*. New York: Psychology Press, 2008.

Elliot, Andrew J., and Todd M. Thras. "Approach-Avoidance in Personality: Approach-Avoidance Temperaments and Goals." *Journal of Personality and Social Psychology* 82, no. 5 (2002). 804–818.

Ellsworth, Phoebe C. "Appraisals, Emotions, and Adaptation." In *Evolution and the Social Mind*, edited by Joseph P. Forgas et al., 71–88. New York: Psychology Press, 2007.

Esau, Alvin J. *The Courts and the Colonies: The Litigation of Hutterites Church Disputes*. Vancouver, Canada: University of British Columbia Press, 2004.

Evans-Pritchard, E. E. *Witchcraft, Oracles and Magic among the Azande*. Oxford: Clarendon, 1977.

Fagels, Robert. *The Iliad*. New York: Penguin, 1990.

Feldman, Fred. "Hedonism." In *Encyclopedia of Ethics*, edited by Lawrence C. Becker and Charlotte B. Becker, 662–669. 2nd edn. New York: Routledge, 2001.

Pleasure and the Good Life: Concerning the Nature, Varieties, and Plausibility of Hedonism. New York: Oxford University Press, 2004.

Ferguson, Everett. *Backgrounds of Early Christianity*. Grand Rapids, MI: W. B. Erdmans Publishing, 2003.

Festinger, Leon F. *A Theory of Cognitive Dissonance*. Evanston, IL: Row, Peterson, 1957.

Feynman, Richard P. *The Pleasure of Finding Things Out*. Cambridge, MA: Perseus Books, 1999.

Filliozat, J. "La Doctrine des Brahmanes d'apres Saint Hippolyte." *Revue de L'Histoire des Religions* 130, no. 1 (1945). 59–61.

Finke, Roger, and Rodney Stark. "The New Holy Clubs: Testing Church-to-Sect Propositions." *Sociology of Religion* 62, no. 2 (2001). 175–189.

Finnegan, William. *Barbarian Days: A Surfing Life.* New York: Penguin Books, 2015.

Fisk, Susan T., Daniel T. Gilbert, and Gardner Lindzey. *Handbook of Social Psychology,* vol. 1. Hoboken, NJ: John Wiley and Sons, 2010.

Fivush, Robin, and Catherine A. Haden. *Autobiographical Memory and the Construction of the Narrative Self: Developmental and Cultural Perspectives.* Mahwah, NJ: Lawrence Erlbaum, 2003.

Folk, Harry. "The Purpose of Rigvedic Ritual." In *Inside the Texts,* edited by Michael Witzel, 69–88. Harvard Oriental Series. Cambridge, MA: Harvard University Press, 1997.

Forgas, Joseph P. *Affect in Social Thinking and Behavior.* New York: Psychology Press, 2012.

Forman, Robert. *The Problem of Pure Consciousness: Mysticism and Philosophy.* New York: Oxford University Press, 1990.

Fox, Michael V. *The Song of Songs and the Ancient Egyptian Love Songs.* Madison: University of Wisconsin Press, 1985.

Freeman, Walter. "A Neurobiological Role of Music in Social Bonding." In *The Origins of Music,* edited by Nils L. Wallin, 419–420. Cambridge, MA: MIT Press, 2000.

Fuller, Christopher J. *The Camphor Flame: Popular Hinduism and Society.* Princeton, NJ: Princeton University Press, 2012.

Fuller, Robert C. *The Body of Faith: A Biological History of Religion in America.* Chicago: University of Chicago Press, 2013.

Gable, Philip A., and Eddie Harmon-Jones. "Approach-Motivated Positive Affect." *Psychological Science* 19, no. 5 (2008). 476–482.

Gable, Shelly L., and Elliot T. Berkman. "Making Connections and Avoiding Loneliness: Approach and Avoidance Social Motives and Goals." In *Handbook of Approach and Avoidance Motivation,* edited by Andrew J. Elliot, 203–216. New York: Psychology Press, 2008.

Gaca, Kathy L. *The Making of Fornication: Eros, Ethics, and Political Reform in Greek Philosophy and Early Christianity.* Berkeley: University of California Press, 2003.

Gadamer, Hans-Georg. *Truth and Method.* Translated by Joel Weinsheiner. 2nd edn. London: Continuum, 1989.

Games, Alison. *Witchcraft in Early North America.* Lanham, MD: Rowman & Littlefield Publishers, 2010.

Garfield, Jay. *Wisdom of the Middle Way: Nāgārjuna's Mūlamadhyamikakārikā.* New York: Oxford University Press, 1995.

Garfinkel, Yosef. "Dancing with Masks in the Proto-Historic Near East." In *Ritual, Play and Belief, in Evolutionary and Early Human Societies,* edited by Colin Renfrew et al., 143–169. Cambridge, UK: Cambridge University Press, 2018.

Gawronski, Bertram. "Back to the Future of Dissonance Theory: Cognitive Consistency as Core Motive." *Social Cognition* 30, no. 6 (2012). 652–668.

Geary, David C. *The Origin of Mind: Evolution of Brain, Cognition and General Intelligence*. Washington, DC: American Psychological Association, 2005.

Geljon Albert C., and David T. Runia. *Philo of Alexandria on Cultivation: Introduction, Translation, and Commentary*. Leiden, the Netherlands: E. J. Brill, 2013.

Gerson, Lloyd P. *The Cambridge Companion to Plotinus*. Cambridge, UK: Cambridge University Press, 1996.

"Plotinus." In *Stanford Encyclopedia of Philosophy*. https://plato.stanford.edu/entries/plotinus.

Gervais, Will M. "Perceiving Minds and Gods: How Mind Perception Enables, Constrains, and Is Triggered by Belief in Gods." *Perspectives on Psychological Science* 8, no. 4 (2013). 380–394.

Geyer, Anne L., and Roy F. Baumeister. "Religion, Morality, and Self-Control: Values, Virtues and Vices." In *Handbook of the Psychology of Religion and Spirituality*, edited by Raymond F. Paloutzian and Crystal L. Park, 412–432. New York: Guilford Press, 2005.

Glucklich, Ariel. *Dying for Heaven*. New York: Harper Collins, 2009.

Sacred Pain: Hurting the Body for the Sake of the Soul. New York: Oxford University Press, 2001.

"Virtue and Happiness in the Law Book of Manu." *International Journal of Hindu Studies* 15, no. 1 (2011). 165–190.

Godwyn, Mary. *Jody Hoffer Gittell. Sociology of Organizations: Structures and Relationships*. Los Angeles: Sage Publishers 2012.

Goldman, Robert P. "Rāmaḥ Sahalakṣmaṇaḥ: Psychological and Literary Aspects of the Composite Hero of Vālmīki's *Rāmayāṇa*." *Journal of Indian Philosophy* 8 (1980). 149–189.

Gopnik, Alison, Andrew N. Meltzoff, and Patricia K. Kuhl. *The Scientist in the Crib: What Early Learning Tells Us about the Mind*. New York: William Morrow, 1999.

Gosling, J. C. B., and C. C. W. Taylor. *The Greeks on Pleasure*. Oxford: Clarendon Press, 1982.

Gosso, Yumi, Emma Otta, Maria Morais, Fernando Ribiero, and Vera Dusab. "Play in Hunter-Gatherer Society." In *The Nature of Play: Great Apes and Humans*, edited by Anthony D. Pellegrini and Peter K. Smith, 213–253. New York: Guilford Press, 2005.

Grabbe, Lester L. *Ezra-Nehemiah*. London: Routledge, 1998.

Judaism from Cyrus to Hadrian. Minneapolis, MN: Fortress, 1992.

Gray, Peter. *Free to Learn: Why Unleashing the Instinct to Play Will Make Our Children Happier, More Self-Reliant and Better Students for Life*. New York: Basic Books, 2013.

Green, Arthur. *Tormented Master: A Life of Rabbi Nahman of Bratslav*. Tuscaloosa, AL: University of Alabama Press, 1979.

Greenspan, Stanley, I., and Shanker, Stuart G. *The First Idea: How Symbols, Language and Intelligence Evolved from Our Primate Ancestors to Modern Humans.* Cambridge, MA: Da Capo Press, 2004.

Gregorios, Paulos Mar. *Neoplatonism and Indian Philosophy.* Albany: State University of New York Press, 2001.

Griffin, James L. *Religion That Heals, Religion That Harms: A Guide for Clinical Practice.* New York: Guilford Press, 2010.

Gross, James J., Maya Tamir, and Chi-Yue Chiu. "Business or Pleasure? Utilitarian versus Hedonic Considerations in Emotion Regulation." *Emotion* 7, no. 3 (2007). 546–554.

Gupta, Ravi M., and Kenneth R. Valpey. *The Bhāgavata Purāṇa: Sacred Text and Living Tradition.* New York: Columbia University Press, 2013.

Haberman, David L. "A Selection from the Bhaktirasamritasindhu of Rupa Gosvamin: The Foundational Emotions (Sthayi-Bhavas)." In *Krishna: A Sourcebook,* edited by Edwin F. Bryant and Tony K. Stewart, 409–440. New York: Oxford University Press, 2007.

Haidt, Jonathan. *The Righteous Mind: Why Good People Are Divided by Politics and Religion.* New York: Vintage, 2012.

Hamilton, W. D. "The Evolution of Social Behavior." *Journal of Theoretical Biology* 7, no. 1 (1964). 1–52.

Hanbury-Tenison, Robin. *The Oxford Book of Exploration.* Oxford: Oxford University Press, 2005.

Handelman, Don, and David Shulman. *God Inside Out: Śiva's Game of Dice.* New York: Oxford University Press, 1997.

Handelman, Maxine Segal. *Jewish Every Day: The Complete Handbook for Early Childhood Teachers.* Denver, CO: A. R. E. Publishing, 2000.

Hara, Minoru. "Nakulīśa Pāśupata Darśanam." *Indo-Iranian Journal* 2, no. 1 (1957–1958). 8–32.

"Pāśupata Studies II." *Vienna Journal of South Asia Studies* 38 (1994). 323–335.

Hariharānanda, Swami Āraṇya. *Yoga Philosophy of Patañjali.* Albany: State University of New York Press, 1983.

Harmon-Jones, Eddie, and Judson Mills. "An Introduction to Cognitive Dissonance Theory and an Overview of Current Perspectives on the Theory." *Science Confluence Series.* Washington, DC: American Psychological Association, 1999. 3–21.

Harvey, Susan H., and David G. Hunter. *The Oxford Handbook of Early Christianity.* Oxford: Oxford University Press, 2008.

Hay, David M. "Things Philo Said and Did Not Say about the Therapeutae." *SBL 1992 Seminar Papers.* Atlanta, GA: Scholars Press, 1992. 672–683.

Heesterman, Jan C. "Ritual, Revelation, and the Axial Age." In *The Origins and Diversity of the Axial Age Civilizations,* edited by Shmuel Eisenstadt, 393–406. Albany: State University of New York Press, 1986.

Hefferman, Thomas J. *The Passion of Perpetua and Felicity.* New York: Oxford University Press, 2012.

Helm, Bennett W. "Felt Evaluations: A Theory of Pleasure and Pain." *American Philosophical Quarterly* 39, no. 1 (2002). 13–30.

Hengel, Martin. *Judaism and Hellenism: Studies in Their Encounter in Palestine during the Early Hellenistic Period.* Translated by John Bowden. Eugene, OR: Wipf and Stock Publishers, 1974.

Herren, Michael W. "Classical Exegesis – From Theagenes of Rhegium to Bernard Silvestris." *Florilegium* 30, no. 1 (2013). 59–102.

Herrigel, Eugen. *Zen in the Art of Archery.* New York: Vintage, 1999.

Heschel, Abraham Joshua. *The Shabbat: Its Meaning for Modern Man.* New York: Farrar, Strauss, Giroux, 2005.

Heyes, Cecilia. *Cognitive Gadgets: The Cultural Evolution of Thinking.* Cambridge, MA: Harvard University Press, 2018.

Hick, John. *Evil and the God of Love.* New York: Palgrave Macmillan, 2010.

Higgins, E. Tory. "Beyond Pleasure and Pain." *American Psychologist* 52, no. 12 (1997). 1280–1300.

Hindery, Roderick. "Hindu Ethics in the *Rāmāyana.*" *Journal of Religious Ethics* 4, no. 2 (1976). 287–322.

Hogg, Michael A., and Scott Tindale. *Blackwell Handbook of Social Psychology: Group Processes.* Malden, MA: Blackwell, 2001.

Holdrege, Barbara. *Veda and Torah: Transcending the Textuality of Scripture.* Albany: State University of New York Press, 1996.

Hood, Ralph W., Peter C. Hill, and Bernard Spilka. *The Psychology of Religion: An Empirical Approach.* New York: Guilford Press, 2009.

Hopkins, Thomas J. "The Social Teachings of the Bhāgavata Purāṇa." In *Krishna: Myths, Rites, Attitudes,* edited by Milton B. Singer, 3–22. Chicago: University of Chicago Press, 1971.

Huizinga, Johan. *Homo Ludens: The Play-Element in Culture.* Boston, MA: Beacon Press, 1971.

Hurley, Susan, and Nick Chater. "Introduction." In *Perspectives on Imitation: From Neuroscience to Social Science,* edited by Susan L. Hurley and Nick Chater, 1–52. Cambridge, MA: MIT Press, 2005.

Iannaccone, Laurence R. "Introduction to the Economics of Religion." *The Journal of Economic Literature* 36, no. 3 (1998). 1465–1495.

"Sacrifice and Stigma: Reducing Free-Riding in Cults, Communes, and Other Collectives." *Journal of Political Economy* 100, no. 2 (1992). 271–297.

Ihde, Don. *Hermeneutic Phenomenology: The Philosophy of Paul Ricoeur.* Evanston, IL: Northwestern University Press, 1971.

Inwood, Brad. "Who Do We Think We Are?" In *The Virtuous Life in Greek Ethics,* edited by Burkhard Reis, 230–243. New York: Cambridge University Press, 2006.

James, Wendy, and N. J. Allen. *Marcel Mauss: A Centenary Tribute.* New York: Berghahn Books, 1998.

James, William. *The Varieties of Religious Experience.* New York: Collier Books, 1961.

Writings, 1878–1899. New York: Library of America, 1992.

Jameson, Frederic. *Formations of Pleasure*. London: Routledge and Keagan Paul, 1983.

Jamison, Kay Redfield. *Exuberance: The Passion for Life*. New York: Vintage Books, 2005.

Jamison, Stephanie W., and Joel P. Brereton. *The Rigveda: The Earliest Religious Poetry of India*. New York: Oxford University Press, 2014.

Janowitz, Naomi. *Icons of Power: Ritual Practices in Late Antiquity*. University Park: Pennsylvania State University Press, 2002.

Jaspers, Karl. *The Origins and Goal of History*. Translated by Michael Bullock. London: Routledge and Kegan Paul, 1953.

Jaynes, Julian. *The Origins of Consciousness in the Breakdown of the Bicameral Mind*. Boston: Houghton Mifflin Company, 2000.

Jespers, Frans, Karin van Nieuwkerk, and Paul van der Velde. *Enjoying Religion: Pleasure and Fun in Established and New Religious Movements*. Lanham, MD: Lexington Books, 2018.

Johnson, Benton. "On Church and Sect." *American Sociological Review* 28, no. 4 (1963). 539–549.

Johnson, Cardyn, and Linda Wilbrecht. "Juvenile Mice Show Greater Flexibility in Multiple Choice Reversal Learning Than Adults." *Developmental Cognitive Neuroscience* 1, no. 4 (2011). 540–551.

Jokiranta, Jutta M. "Sectariansm of the Qumran 'Sect:' Sociological Notes." *Revue de Qumran* 20, no. 2 (2001). 223–239.

Joseph, Simon J. *Jesus, The Essenes, and Christian Origins: New Light on Ancient Texts and Communities*. Waco, TX: Baylor University Press, 2018.

Josephus, Flavius. *Jewish Antiquities, Books 18–19*. Translated by L .H. Feldman. Cambridge, MA: Harvard University Press, 1996.

Julian of Norwich. *Revelations of Divine Love*. S.l.: Skyros Publishing 2015.

Kahneman, Daniel. "Objective Happiness." In *Well-Being: The Foundations of Hedonic Psychology*, edited by Daniel Kahneman et al., 3–25. New York: Russell Sage Foundations, 1999.

Kamesar, Adam. *The Cambridge Companion to Philo*. New York: Cambridge University Press, 2009.

Kapferer, Bruce. *Beyond Rationalism: Rethinking Magic, Witchcraft and Sorcery*. New York: Berghahn Books, 2003.

Kaplan, Aryeh, and Chaim Kramer. *The Seven Beggars & Other Kabbalistic Tales of Rebbe Nahman of Breslov*. Woodstock, VT: Breslov Research Institute, 2005.

Katz, Leonard D. "Pleasure." In *Stanford Encyclopedia of Philosophy*. https://plato .stanford.edu/.

Katz, Steven T. *Mysticism and Language*. New York: Oxford University Press, 1992.

Mysticism and Religious Traditions. New York: Oxford University Press, 1983.

Katz, Yossi, and John Lehr. *Inside the Ark: The Hutterites in Canada and the United States*. Regina, Canada: University of Regina Press, 2012.

Kealey, Daniel. "The Theoria of Nature in Plotinus and the Yoga of the Earth Consciousness in Aurobindo." In *Neoplatonism and Indian Philosophy*, edited by Paulos Gregorios, 173–186. Albany: State University of New York Press, 2002.

Keinan, Giora. "Effects of Stress and Tolerance of Ambiguity on Magical Thinking." *Journal of Personality and Social Psychology* 67, no. 1 (1994). 48–55.

Keller, Kirsten M., Kimberly Curry Hall, William Marcellino, and Jacqueline A. Mauro. *Hazing in the U.S. Armed Forces: Recommendations for Hazing Prevention Policy and Practice.* Santa Monica, CA: Rand Corporation, 2015.

Keltner, Dacher, E. J. Horberg, and Christopher Oveis. "Emotion as Moral Intuition." In *Handbook of Affect and Social Cognition*, edited by Joseph Forgas, 161–175. Mahwah, NJ: Lawrence Erlbaum Associates, 2001.

Kirkpatrick, Lee A. *Attachment, Evolution, and the Psychology of Religion.* New York: Guilford Press, 2005.

Knapp, Mark L., Judith A. Hall, and Terrence G. Horgan. *Nonverbal Communication in Human Interaction.* Boston, MA: Wadsworth Publishing, 2007.

Knox, Bernard. "Introduction." In *The Iliad.* Translated by Robert Fagels, 3–64. New York: Penguin, 1990.

Koenig, Melissa A., and Paul L. Harris. "The Role of Social Cognition in Early Trust." *Trends in Cognitive Sciences* 9, no. 10 (2005). 457–459.

Konstan, David. "Of Two Minds: Philo on Cultivation." *The Studia Philonica Annual* 22, no. 1 (2010). 131–138.

Kosambi, Damodar Dharmanand. *An Introduction to the Study of Indian History.* Bombay, India: Popular Prakashan, 1975.

Kraemer, David C. *Jewish Eating and Identity through the Ages.* New York: Taylor & Francis, 2007.

Kramer, Samuel Noah. "The Biblical Song of Songs and the Sumerian Love Songs." *Penn Museum: Expedition* 5, no. 1 (1962). 25.

Krentz, Arthur A. "Play and Education in Plato's Republic." In *Philosophy of Education.* www.bu.edu/wcp/Papers/Educ/EducKren.htm.

Kulke, Hermann. "The Historical Background of India's Axial Age." In *The Origins and Diversity of the Axial Age Civilizations*, edited by S. Eisenstadt, 374–392. Albany: State University of New York Press, 1986.

Lacan, Jacques. *Ecrits: A Selection.* Translated by Bruce Fink. New York: W. W. Norton & Co., 2002.

Landman, Eva. *A Kindergarden Manual for Jewish Religious Schools.* Cincinnati, OH: Union of American Hebrew Congregations, 1918.

Langenthal, Edna. "Welcoming the Other: Hospitality, Subjectivity and Otherness in the Thought of Emmanuel Levinas and the Biblical Story of the Hospitality of Abraham." In *Levinas Faces Biblical Figures*, edited by Yael Lin, 35–60. Lanham, MD: Lexington Books, 2014.

Larsen, Gerald James. *Classical Samkhya: An Interpretation of Its History and Meaning.* Delhi, India: Motilal Banarsidass, 1998.

Larsen, Randy J., and Zvjezdana Priznic. "Affect Regulation." In *Handbook of Self-Regulation: Research, Theory, and Applications*, edited by Kathleen D. Vohs and Roy F. Baumeister, 40–61. 1st edn. New York: Guilford Press, 2004.

Le Billon, Karen. *French Kids Eat Everything*. New York: Little, Brown Book Group, 2012.

Lefeber, Rosalind. *The Rāmāyaṇa of Vālmīki: An Epic of Ancient India, Kiṣkindhākāṇḍa*. Princeton, NJ: Princeton University Press, 1994.

Levinas, Emanuel. *Totality and Infinity: An Essay on Exteriority*. Translated by Alphanso Lingis. Pittsburgh, PA: Duquesne University Press, 2004.

Levy, Carlos. "Philo's Ethics." In *The Cambridge Companion to Philo*, edited by Adam Kamesar, 146–174. New York: Cambridge University Press, 2010.

Lewis, C. S. *Surprised by Joy: The Shape of My Early Life*. New York: Harper One, 2017.

Lewis, Kerrie P. "Social Play in the Great Apes." In *The Nature of Play: Great Apes and Humans*, edited by Anthony D. Pellegrini and Peter K. Smith, 27–53. New York: Guilford Press, 2005.

Lieber, David L. *Etz Hayim: Torah and Commentary*. New York: Rabbinical Assembly, 2001.

Liebes, Yehudah. *Studies in Jewish Myth and Messianism*. Albany: State University of New York Press, 1993.

Lifton, Robert. *Thought Reform and the Psychology of Totalism*. New York: W. W. Norton, 1963.

Lincoln, Bruce. "Mythic Narrative and Cultural Diversity in American Society." In *Myth and Method*, edited by Laurie Patton and Wendy Doniger, 163–176. Charlottesville: University of Virginia Press, 1996.

Theorizing Myth: Narrative, Ideology, and Scholarship. Chicago: University of Chicago Press, 1999.

Lissarrague, Francois, and Andrew Szegdy-Maszk. *The Aesthetics of the Greek Banquet: Images of Wine and Ritual*. Princeton, NJ: Princeton University Press, 1990.

Luther, Martin. *The Complete Sermons of Martin Luther, Volume 1*. Translated by John Nicholas Lenker. DelmarvaPublications.com. 2014.

MacKenna, Stephen. *Plotinus: The Enneads*. London: Penguin, 1991.

Mann, Thomas. *Death in Venice*. Translated by Stanley Appelbaum. New York: Dover Publications, 1995.

Marchi, Regina M. *Day of the Dead: The Migration and Transformation of a Cultural Phenomenon*. New Brunswick, NJ: Rutgers University Press, 2009.

Marcus, George E., and Michael M. J. Fischer. *Anthropology as Cultural Critique: An Experimental Moment in the Human Sciences*. Chicago: University of Chicago Press, 2014.

Marion, Jean-Luc. "The Intentionality of Love." In *Prolegomena to Charity*. Translated by Stephen D. Lewis. New York: Fordham University Press, 2002.

Mark, Zvi. *Mysticism and Madness: The Religious Thought of Rabbi Nahman of Bratslav*. New York: Continuum, 2009.

The Revealed and Hidden Writings of Rabbi Nahman of Bratslav. Berlin, Germany: Walter de Gruyter, 2015.

Marques, Jose M., Dominic Abrams, and Rui G. Serodio. "Being Better by Being Right: Subjective Groups Dynamics and Derogation of In-Group Deviants When Generic Norms are Undermined." In *Small Groups*, edited by John M. Levine, and Richard Moreland, 157–176. New York: Routledge, 2006.

Marriott, McKim. "Holi: The Feast of Love." In *Krishna: Myths, Rites and Attitudes*, edited by Milton B. Singer, 200–212. Chicago: University of Chicago Press, 1966.

Martin, Joseph D., Review in *Acta Biotheoretica* 62, no. 4 (2014): 531–535.

Mason, Elinor. "The Nature of Pleasure: A Critique of Feldman." *Utilitas* 19, no. 3 (2007). 379–387.

Mauss, Marcel. *The Gift: The Form and Reason for Exchange in Archaic Societies.* London: Routledge, 2002.

Mayhew, Robert. *Prodicus the Sophist: Texts, Translations, and Commentary.* New York: Oxford University Press, 2011.

McCabe, Lisa, Marisol Cunnington, and Jeanne Brooks-Gunn. "The Development of Self-Regulation in Young Children: Individual Characteristics and Environmental Contexts." In *Handbook of Self-Regulation: Research, Theory and Applications*, edited by Kathleen D. Vohs and Roy F. Baumeister, 340–356. 1st edn. New York: Guilford Press, 2004.

McCullough, Michael E., and Brian L. B. Willoughby. "Religion, Self-Control, and Self-Regulation: Associations, Explanations, and Implications." *Psychological Bulletin* 135, no. 1 (2009). 69–93.

McCutcheon, Russell T. "Introduction." In *Religious Experience: A Reader*, edited by Craig Martin and Russell T. McCutcheon, 1–18. Sheffield: Equinox Publishing, 2012.

McGinn, Bernard. "The Language of Inner Experience." *Spiritus: A Journal of Christian Spirituality* 1, no. 2 (2001). 156–171.

McIntyre, Alasdair. *Dependent Rational Animals: Why Human Beings Need the Virtues.* Peru, IL: Carus Press, 2001.

— *After Virtue.* London: Bloomsbury, 2013.

Meadows, Sara. *Parenting Behavior and Children's Cognitive Development.* East Sussex: Psychology Press, 1996.

Mehrabian, Albert. *Nonverbal Communication.* New York: Routledge 2017.

Melzack, Ronald. "The McGill Pain Questionnaire: Major Properties and Scoring Methods." *Pain* 1, no. 3 (1975). 277–299.

Merleau-Ponty, Maurice. *Phenomenology of Perception.* Translated by Colin Smith. London: Routledge, 2003.

Miller, David L. *Gods and Games: Toward a Theology of Play.* New York: The World Publishing, 1970.

Miller, Vincent J. *Consuming Religion: Christian Faith and Practice in Consumer America.* New York: Bloomsbury Academic, 2005.

Millon, Theodore, and Melvin J. Lerner. *Handbook of Psychology, Personality and Social Psychology.* Hoboken, NJ: Wiley and Sons, 2003.

Mintz, Sidney W. *Sweetness and Power: The Place of Sugar in Modern History.* New York: Penguin, 1986.

Mischel, Walter. *The Marshmallow Test: Why Self-Control Is the Engine of Success.* New York: Little, Brown and Company, 2014.

Mischel, Walter, and E. B. Ebbesen. "Attention in Delay of Gratification." *Journal of Personality and Social Psychology* 16, no. 2 (1970). 329–337.

Mischel, Walter, and Ozlem Ayduk. "Willpower in a Cognitive-Affective Processing System: The Dynamics of Delay of Gratification." In *Handbook of Self-Regulation: Research, Theory and Applications*, edited by Kathleen D. Vohs and Roy F. Baumeister, 83–105. 2nd edn. New York: Guilford Press, 2011.

Momigliano, Arnaldo. *Alien Wisdom: The Limits of Hellenization.* Cambridge, UK: Cambridge University Press, 1975.

Morreal, John. "Enjoying Negative Emotions in Fiction." *Philosophy and Literature* 9, no. 1 (1985). 95–103.

Mortley, Raoul. *Plotinus, Self and the World.* Cambridge UK: Cambridge University Press, 2013.

Most, Glen W. *Hesiod, Theogony, Work and Days, Testimonia.* Cambridge, MA: Harvard University Press, 2006.

Mullins, Daniel A., Harvey Whitehouse, and Quentin D. Atkinson. "The Role of Writing and Recordkeeping in the Cultural Evolution of Human Cooperation." *Journal of Economic Behavior & Organization* 90, no. 1 (2013). 141–151.

Murray, Joanne, Anna Theakston, and Anna Wells. "Can the Attention Training Technique Turn One Marshmallow into Two? Improving Children's Ability to Delay Gratification." *Behavior Research and Therapy* 77, no. 1 (2016). 34–39.

Nagel, Thomas. "What Is It Like to Be a Bat?" *The Philosophical Review* 83, no. 4 (1974). 435–450.

Nahman of Bratslav. *The Lost Princess & Other Kabbalistic Tales of Rebbe Nahman of Bratslav.* Woodstock, VT: Jewish Lights Publications, 2005.

Nahman of Brastlav. *Likutei Moharan.* www.sefaria.org/Likutei_Moharan?lang=bi.

Nahman of Bratslav. *Likutey Moharan.* Edited by Chaim Kramer. Jerusalem, Israel: Breslov Research Institute, 1993.

Likutey Moharan ha-Menukad. Jerusalem, Israel: Moharanat Institute, 1994.

Nanamoli, Bhikkhu, and Bhikkhu Bodhi. *The Middle Length Discourses of the Buddha: A Translation of Majjhima Nikaya.* Somerville, MA: Wisdom Publications, 2015.

Narayanan, Vasudha. "Tamil Nadu: The Poetry of the Alvars." In *Krishna: A Sourcebook*, edited by Edwin F. Bryant, 187–204. New York: Oxford University Press, 2007.

Nencini, Paolo. "Psychobiology of Drug-Induced Religious Experience: From the Brain 'Locus of Religion' to Cognitive Unbinding." *Substance Use and Misuse* 45, no. 13 (2010). 2130–2151.

Newberg, A., and E. d'Aquili. *Why God Won't Go Away.* New York: Ballantine, 2001.

Niehoff, Maren R. "The Symposium of Philo's Therapeutae: Displaying Jewish Identity in an Increasingly Roman World." *Greek, Roman, Byzantine Studies* 50, no. 1 (2010). 95–116.

van Nieuwenhove, Rik, S. J. Robert Faesen, and Helen Rolfson. *Late Medieval Mysticism of the Low Countries*. New York: Paulist Press, 2008.

Norenzayan, Ara. *Big Gods: How Religion Transformed Cooperation and Conflict*. Princeton, NJ: Princeton University Press, 2013.

Notenzayan, Ara, Azim F. Shariff, Will M. Gervais, Aiyana K. Willard, Rita A. McNamara, Edward Slingerland, and Joseph Henrich. "The Cultural Evolution of Prosocial Religions." *Behavioral and Brain Sciences* 39, no. 1 (2016). 1–65.

Nowak, Martin A. *Super-Cooperators: Evolution, Altruism and Human Behavior, or Why We Need Each Other to Succeed*. New York: Free Press, 2011.

Nussbaum, Martha. *The Fragility of Goodness: Luck and Ethics in Greek Tragedy and Philosophy*. New York: Cambridge University Press, 2001.

Obeyesekere, Gananath. *Karma and Rebirth: A Cross Cultural Study*. Delhi, India: Motilal Banarsidass, 2006.

O'Conner Walshe, M. *Meister Eckhart: Tractates and Sermons*. London: Watkins, 1978.

O'Flaherty, Wendy Doniger. *The Origins of Evil in Hindu Mythology*. Berkeley: University of California Press, 1976.

Olivelle, Patrick. *Upaniṣads*. New York: Oxford University Press, 1996.
  Ascetics and Brahmins: Studies in Ideologies and Institutions. London: Anthem Press, 2011.

Otto, Rudolf. *The Idea of the Holy: An Inquiry into the Non-Rational Factor in the Idea of the Divine and Its Relation to the Rational*. Translated by John W. Harvey. London: Oxford University Press, 1958.

Oved, Yaacov. *The Witness of the Brothers: A History of the Bruderhof*. New Brunswick, Canada: Transaction Publishers, 1996.

Panksepp, Jaak, and Joseph Moskal. "Dopamine and SEEKING: Subcortical 'Reward' Systems and Appetitive Urges." In *Handbook of Approach and Avoidance Motivation*, edited by Andrew J. Elliot, 67–88. New York: Psychology Press, 2008.

Parpola, Asko. "Human Sacrifice in India in Vedic Times and Before." In *The Strange World of Sacrifice*, edited by Jan N. Bremmer, 157–178. Leuven, the Netherlands: Peeters, 2007.

Parry, Jonathan P. *Death in Banaras*. Cambridge, UK: Cambridge University Press, 1994.

Pashupatasutram with the Commentary of Bhagavatpad Shri Kaundinya. Varanasi, India: Acharya Krishnananda Sagar, 1987.

Pāśupata Sūtram with Pañchārtha-Bhāṣya of Kauṇḍinya, edited by Haripada Chakraborti. Calcutta, India: Academic Publishers, 1970.

Patel, Aniruddh D. *Music, Language and the Brain*. New York: Oxford University Press, 2008.

Patterson, Lindsey, and Robert Biswas-Diener. "Consuming Happiness." In *The Good Life in a Technological Age*, edited by Philip Brey et al., 147–156. New York: Routledge, 2012.

Patton, Laurie, and Wendy Doniger. *Myth and Method.* Charlottesville: University of Virginia Press, 1996.

Pellauer, David, and Bernard Dauenhauer. "Paul Ricoeur." In *The Stanford Encyclopedia of Philosophy.* https://plato.stanford.edu/archives/win2016/entries/ricoeur/.

Pellegrini, Anthony D., and Peter K. Smith. *The Nature of Play: Great Apes and Humans.* New York: Guilford Press, 2005.

"Play in Great Apes and Humans." In *The Nature of Play: Great Apes and Humans,* edited by Anthony D. Pellegrini and Peter K. Smith, 3–12. New York: Guilford Press, 2005.

Pennington, Donald C. *The Social Psychology of Behavior in Small Groups.* East Sussex: Psychology Press, 2002.

Piaget, Jean. *The Construction of Reality in the Child.* Oxon: Routledge and Kegan Paul, 2002.

Play, Dreams, and Imitation in Childhood. London: Routledge, 1999.

The Psychology of the Child. New York: Basic Books, 2000.

Pinker, Steven. *How the Mind Works.* New York: Norton, 1997.

Pliny, The Elder. *Natural History.* Translated by John Healey. New York: Penguin, 1991.

Proudfoot, Wayne. *Religious Experience.* Berkeley: University of California Press, 1985.

Proudfoot, Wayne, and Phillip Shaner. "Attribution Theory and the Psychology of Religion." *Journal of the Scientific Study of Religion* 4, no. 4 (1975). 317–330.

Qimron, Elisha. *Megilot Midvar Yehudah: Hahiburim Ha'ivriim.* Jerusalem, Israel: Yad Itzhak Ben Tzvi, 2010.

Rahner, Hugo. *Man at Play.* Translated by Brian Bettershaw and Edward Quinn. New York: Herder and Herder, 1967.

Ramachandran, V. S., and S. Blakelee. *Phantoms in the Brain.* New York: William Morrow, 1999.

Ramelli, Ilaria. *Hierocles the Stoic: Elements of Ethics, Fragments, and Excerpts.* Atlanta, GA: Society of Biblical Literature, 2009.

Read, Stephen J., and Lynn Miller. *Connectionist Models of Social Reasoning and Social Behavior.* New York: Routledge, 1998.

Redfield, James M. *Nature and Culture in the Iliad: The Tragedy of Hector.* Durham, NC: Duke University Press, 1994.

Reisenzein, Rainer. "Pleasure-Arousal and the Intensity of Emotions." *Journal of Personality and Social Psychobiology* 67, no. 3 (1994). 525–539.

Renfrew, Colin. "Introduction: Play as the Precursor of Ritual in Early Human Societies." In *Ritual, Play, and Belief in Evolution and Early Human Societies,* edited by Colin Renfrew et al., 9–2. Cambridge, UK: Cambridge University Press, 2017.

Renfrew, Colin, Lain Morley, and Michael Boyd. *Ritual, Play, and Belief in Evolution and Early Human Societies.* Cambridge, UK: Cambridge University Press, 2017.

Richerson, Peter J., and Robert Boyd. *Not by Genes Alone: How Culture Transformed Human Evolution.* Chicago: University of Chicago Press, 2005.

Ricoeur, Paul. *The Conflict of Interpretations: Essays in Hermeneutics.* London: Continuum Press, 2005.

    Fallible Man. New York: Fordham University Press, 1986.

    Philosophical Anthropology. Cambridge, UK: Polity, 2013.

van Riel, Gerd. *Pleasure and the Good Life: Plato, Aristotle and the Neoplatonists.* Leiden, the Netherlands: E. J. Brill, 2000.

Robinson, Paschal. *The Writings of St. Francis of Assisi.* New York: Magisterium Press, 2015.

Roland, Alan. *In Search of Self in India and Japan: Toward A Cross-Cultural Psychology.* Princeton, NJ: Princeton University Press, 1989.

Rosenzweig, Franz. *The Star of Redemption.* Translated by Barbara E. Galli. Madison: University of Wisconsin Press, 2005.

Rossoff, Barbara L. "Practical Application of Child Development Theory in Our Classrooms: Overview of Developmental Theories and Moral Development." In *The Jewish Educational Leader's Handbook*, edited by Robert E. Tornberg, 223–236. Denver, CO: A. R. E. Publishing, 1998.

Rozin, Paul. "Preadaptation and the Puzzles and Properties of Pleasure." In *Wellbeing: The Foundations of Hedonic Psychology*, edited by Daniel Kahneman et al., 109–133. New York: Russell Sage Foundation, 1999.

    "Toward a Psychology of Food and Eating: From Motivation to Module to Marker, Morality, Meaning and Metaphor." *Current Directions in Psychological Science* 5, no. 1 (1996). 18–24.

Rozin, Paul, and Deborah Schiller. "The Nature and Acquisition of a Preference for Chili Pepper by Humans." *Motivation and Emotion* 4, no. 1 (1980). 77–101.

Rubin, Kenneth, Robert Coplan, Nathan Fox, and Susan Calkins. "Emotionality, Emotion Regulation, and Preschoolers' Social Adaptation." *Development and Psychopathology* 7, no. 1 (1995). 49–62.

Ruether, Rosemary Radford. *Goddess and the Divine Feminine.* Berkeley: University of California Press, 2005.

Ruff, Wilfried. "Entwicklung religioser Glaubensfahigkeit." *Forum der Psychoanalyse: Zeitschrift fur Klinische Theorie & Praxis* 21, no. 3 (2005). 293–307.

Runia, David T. *Philo in Early Christian Literature: A Survey.* Van Gorcum Assen, the Netherlands: Fortress Press, 1993.

Runia, David T., and Gregory E. Sterling. *Studia Philonica Annual XXVI.* Atlanta, GA: Society of Biblical Literature, 2014.

Russell, James A. "Emotion, Core Affect and Psychological Construction." *Cognition and Emotion* 23, no. 7 (2009). 1259–1283.

Russell, Jeffrey Burton. "Witchcraft." In *Encyclopedia of Religion*, edited by Mircea Eliade, 415–423. New York: Macmillan, 1987.

Ryle, Gilbert. *Dilemmas: The Tarner Lectures.* Cambridge, UK: Cambridge University Press, 1954.

Saint Augustine. *The Confessions.* Translated by Philip Burton. New York: Alfred A. Knopf, 2001.

Sahlins, Marshall. "The Sadness of Sweetness: The Native Anthropology of Western Cosmology." *Current Anthropology* 37, no. 3 (1996). 395–428.

Saltz, E., and J. Brodie. "Pretend-Play Training in Childhood: A Review and Critique." *Contributions to Human Development* 6, no. 1 (1982). 97–113.

Saltz, E., D. Dixon, and J. Johnson. "Training Disadvantaged Preschoolers on Various Fantasy Activities: Effects on Cognitive Functioning and Impulse Control." *Child Development* 48, no. 2 (1977). 367–380.

Sax, William Sturman. *The Gods at Play: Lila in South Asia.* New York: Oxford University Press, 1995.

Schafer, Roy. "Taking/Including Pleasure in the Experienced Self." *Psychoanalytic Psychology* 23, no. 4 (2006). 609–618.

Schemichel, Brandon J., and Roy F. Baumeister. "Self-Regulatory Strength." In *Handbook of Self-Regulation: Research, Theory and Applications*, edited by Kathleen D. Vohs and Roy F. Baumeister, 84–98. 1st edn. New York: Guilford Press, 2004.

Schiffman, Lawrence H. *From Text to Tradition: A History of Second Temple and Rabbinic Judaism.* Hoboken, NJ: Ktav Publishing House, 1991.

Schleicher, Marianne. *Intertextuality in the Tales of Rabbi Nahman of Bratslav: A Close Reading of Sippurey Ma'asiyot.* Leiden, the Netherlands: E. J. Brill, 2007.

Schofield, Allison. *From Qumran to the Yaḥad: A New Paradigm of Textual Development for the Community Rule.* Leiden, the Netherlands: E. J. Brill, 2009.

Scholem, Gershom. *On the Kabbalah and Its Symbolism.* New York: Random House, 1996.

Scholer, Abigail A., and E. Tory Higgins. "Distinguishing Levels of Approach and Avoidance: An Analysis Using Regulatory Focus Theory." In *Handbook of Approach and Avoidance Motivation*, edited by Andrew J. Elliot, 489–504. New York: Psychology Press, 2008.

Schulkin, Jay. *Adaptation and Well-Being: Social Allostasis.* New York: Cambridge University Press, 2011.

Schwartz, Daniel R. "Philo, His Family, and His Times." In *The Cambridge Companion to Philo*, edited by Adam Kamesar, 9–31. New York: Cambridge University Press, 2009.

Schweig, Graham M. *Dance of Divine Love: The Rāsa Līlā from the Bhāgavata Purāṇa.* Princeton, NJ: Princeton University Press, 2005.

Scourfield, Jonathan, Sophie Gilliat-Ray, Asma Khan, and Sameh Otri. *Muslim Childhood: Religious Nurture in a European Context.* Oxford: Oxford University Press, 2013.

Searle, John. *The Construction of Social Reality.* New York: Simon and Schuster, 2010.

Segvic, Heda. *From Protagoras to Aristotle: Essays in Ancient Moral Philosophy.* Princeton, NJ: Princeton University Press, 2008.

Shankar, Jishu. "From Liminal to Social in the Modern Age." In *Lines in the Water: Religious Boundaries in South Asia*, edited by Eliza Kent and Tazim Kassam, 330–355. Syracuse, NY: Syracuse University Press, 2013.

Sherkat, Darren E. "Investigating the Sect-Church-Sect Cycle: Cohort-Specific Attendance Differences across African American Denominations." *Journal of the Scientific Study of Religion* 40, no. 2 (2001). 221–234.

Shoda, Yuichi, and Walter Mischel. "Personality as a Stable Cognitive-Affective Activation Network." In *Connectionist Models of Social Reasoning and Social Behavior*, edited by Stephen J. Read and Lynn C. Miller, 175–208. New York: Routledge, 1998.

Shulman, David. *The Hungry God: Hindu Tales of Filicide and Devotion*. Chicago: University of Chicago Press, 1993.

Siddur Sim Shalom for Shabbat and Festivals. New York: The Rabbinical Assembly, 1998.

Singer, Jerome. "Imaginative Play in Childhood: Precursor of Subjunctive Thoughts, Daydreaming, and Adult Pretending Games." In *The Future of Play Theory: A Multidisciplinary Inquiry into the Contributions of Brian Sutton Smith*, edited by Anthony D. Pellegrini, 187–220. Albany: State University of New York Press, 1995.

Singh, Gary. "The Joy of Exploration and Discovery." *IEEE Computer Graphics and Applications* 33, no. 1 (2013). 4–5.

Sinnige, Th. G. *Six Lectures on Plotinus and Gnosticism*. Dordrecht, the Netherlands: Springer, 1999.

Slingerland, Edward, Joseph Henrich, and Ara Norenzayan. "The Evolution of Prosocial Religions." In *Cultural Evolution: Society Technology, Language and Religion*, edited by Peter J. Richerson and Morten H. Christiansen, 335–348. Cambridge, MA: MIT Press, 2013.

Smith, Craig, Bieke David, and Leslie Kirby. "Emotion-Eliciting Appraisals of Social Situations." In *Handbook of Affect and Social Cognition*, edited by Joseph P. Forgas, 85–102. Mahwah, NJ: Lawrence Erlbaum, 2001.

Smith, Frederick M. *The Self Possessed: Deity and Spirit Possession in South Asia, Literature and Civilization*. New York: Columbia University Press, 2006.

Smith, Jonathan Z. *Imagining Religion: From Babylon to Jonestown*. Chicago: University of Chicago Press, 1982.

    Map Is Not Territory: Studies in the History of Religions. Chicago: University of Chicago Press, 1978.

Smith, Peter K. "Social and Pretend Play in Children." In *The Nature of Play: Great Apes and Humans*, edited by Anthony D. Pellegrini and Peter K. Smith, 173–209. New York: The Guilford Press, 2005.

Snaith, R. P., M. Hamilton, S. Morley, and A. Humayan. "A Scale for the Assessment of Hedonic Tone the Snaith-Hamilton Pleasure Scale." *The British Journal of Psychiatry* 167, no. 1 (1995). 99–103.

Solomon, R. L. "The Opponent-Process Theory of Acquired Motivation: The Costs of Pleasure and the Benefits of Pain." *American Psychologist* 35, no. 8 (1980). 691–712.

Sosis, Richard. "The Adaptive Value of Religious Ritual: Rituals Promote Group Cohesion by Requiring Members to Engage in Behavior That Is Too Costly to Fake." *American Scientist* 92, no. 1 (2004). 166–172.

Sosis, Richard, and Candace Alcorta. "Signaling, Solidarity and the Sacred: The Evolution of Religious Behavior." *Evolutionary Anthropology* 12, no. 6 (2003). 264–274.

Spalinger, Anthony, and Jeremy Armstrong. *Rituals of Triumph in the Mediterranean World*. Leiden, the Netherlands: E. J. Brill, 2014.

Spitz, Ellen Handler. "Reflections on Psychoanalysis and Aesthetic Pleasure: Looking and Longing." In *Pleasure beyond the Pleasure Principle*, edited by Robert A. Glick and Stanley Bone, 221–238. New Haven, CT: Yale University Press, 1990.

Stark, Rodney, and Roger Fink. *Acts of Faith: Explaining the Human Side of Religion*. Berkeley: University of California Press, 2000.

Stark, Rodney, and William S. Bainbridge. "Of Churches, Sects and Cults: Preliminary Concepts for a Theory of Religious Movements." *Journal for the Scientific Study of Religion* 18, no. 1 (1979). 117–131.

Sternberg, Robert J. *Why Smart People Can Be So Stupid*. New Haven, CT: Yale University Press, 2002.

Stokes, Martin. *Ethnicity, Identity and Music: The Musical Construction of Place*. New York: Bloomsbury Academic, 1997.

Strathern, Marylin. *The Gender of the Gift: The Problem with Women and Problems with Society in Melanesia*. Berkeley: University of California Press, 1988.

Subbotsky, Eugene. *Magic and the Mind: Mechanisms, Functions, and Development of Magical Thinking and Behavior*. New York: Oxford University Press, 2010.

"The Permanence of Mental Objects: Testing Magical Thinking on Perceived and Imaginary Realities." *Developmental Psychology* 41, no. 2 (2005). 301–318.

Susskind, Patrick. *Perfume: The Story of a Murderer*. Translated by John E. Woods. New York: Vintage International, 2001.

Tambiah, Stanley J. "The Form and Meaning of Magical Acts: A Point of View." *HAU: Journal of Ethnographic Theory* 7, no. 3 (2017). 451–473.

Tan, Chade-Meng. *Search Inside Yourself: The Unexpected Path to Achieving Success, Happiness (and World Peace)*. San Francisco: HarperOne, 2012.

Taves, Ann. "Ascription, Attribution, and Cognition in the Study of Experiences Deemed Religious." *Religion* 38, no. 2 (2008). 125–140.

Fits, Trances and Visions: Experiencing Religion and Explaining Experience from Wesley to James. Princeton, NJ: Princeton University Press, 1999.

Taylor, Charles. *Sources of the Self: The Making of the Modern Identity*. Cambridge, UK: Cambridge University Press, 2006.

Taylor, Joan E., and Philip R. Davies. "The So-Called Therapeutae of De Vita Contemplativa: Indentity and Character." *Harvard Theological Review* 91, no. 1 (1998). 3–24.

Teresa of Avila. *Interior Castle*. Jersey City, NJ: First Start Publishing eBook, 2012.

Termini, Cristina. "Philo's Thought within the Context of Middle Judaism." In *The Cambridge Companion to Philo*, edited by Adam Kamesar, 95–123. New York: Cambridge University Press, 2009.

Thapar, Romila. *Ancient Indian Social History: Some Interpretations*. New Delhi, India: Orient Langman, 1978.
    Early India: From the Origins to AD 1300. Berkeley: University of California Press, 2004.
Thompson, George. "Ahaṃkāra and Ātmastuti: Self Assertion and Impersonation in the *Ṛgveda*." *History of Religions* 37, no. 1 (1997). 141–171.
Tillich, Paul. *Systematic Theology*. Chicago: University of Chicago Press, 1951.
Tomasello, Michael, Ann Cale Kruger, and Hilary Horn Ratner. "Cultural Learning." *Behavioral and Brain Science* 16, no. 3 (1993). 495–511.
Tremlin, Todd. *Minds and Gods: The Cognitive Foundations of Religion*. New York: Oxford University Press, 2006.
Trivers, R. L. "The Evolution of Reciprocal Altruism." *Quarterly Review of Biology* 46, no. 1 (1971). 35–57.
Troeltsch, Ernst. *The Social Teachings of the Christian Churches*. Translated by O. Wyon. New York: Macmillan, 1931.
Turner, Jonathan H. *On the Origins of Human Emotions: A Sociological Inquiry into the Evolution of Human Affect*. Stanford, CA: Stanford University Press, 2000.
Turner, Victor. *The Forest of Symbols: Aspects of Ndembu Ritual*. Ithaca, NY: Cornell University Press, 1967.
Uzdavinys, Algis. *The Heart of Plotinus: The Essential Enneads*. Bloomington, IN: World Wisdom, 2009.
Van Troy, J., and J. Von Troy. "Ayatana in the Pāśupata Tradition." *Proceedings of the Indian History Congress* 33, no. 1 (1971). 164–179.
Vemsani, Lavanya. *Krishna in History, Thought, and Culture: An Encyclopedia of the Hindu Lord*. Santa Barbara, CA: ABC-CLIO, 2016.
Vermes, Geza. *The Dead Sea Scrolls in English*. London: Penguin, 1996.
Vogel, Corenelia J. "On the Neoplatonic Character of Platonism and the Platonic Character of Neoplatonism." *Mind* 62, no. 1 (1953). 43–64.
Volf, Miroslav. *Work in the Spirit: Toward a Theology of Work*. New York: Oxford University Press, 1991.
Vygotsky, L. S. *Mind in Society: The Development of Higher Psychological Processes*. Cambridge, MA: Harvard University Press, 1980.
Vyse, Stuart A. *Believing in Magic: The Psychology of Superstition*. New York: Oxford University Press, 2014.
Wallin, Nils. *Biomusicology: Neurophysiological, Neuropsychological and Evolutionary Perspectives on the Origins and Purpose of Music*. York: Pendragon Press, 1991.
Wallin, Nils, B. Merker, and S. Brown. *The Origins of Music*. Cambridge, MA: MIT Press, 2000.
Walters, Barbara R. "Church-Sect Dynamics and the Feast of Corpus Christi." *Sociology of Religion* 65, no. 3 (2004). 285–301.
Warner, Marina. *From the Beast to the Blonde: On Fairy Tales and Their Tellers*. New York: Farrar, Straus and Giroux, 1995.

Weber, Max. *Ancient Judaism*. Translated by Hans Gerth and Dan Martindale. New York: Free Press, 1952.

—. *Essays in Sociology*. Translated by Hans Gerth and C. Wright Mills. Oxon: Routledge, 2007.

White, David Gordon. *Myths of the Dog-Man*. Chicago: University of Chicago Press, 1991.

Whitehouse, Harvey. "Rites of Terror: Emotions, Metaphor and Meaning in Melanesian Initiation Cults." *Journal of the Royal Anthropological Society* 2, no. 4 (1996). 703–715.

Whitehouse, Harvey, and Jonathan A. Lanman. "The Ties That Bind Us: Ritual, Fusion, and Identification." *Current Anthropology* 55, no. 6 (2014). 674–695.

Wilson, David Sloan. *Darwin's Cathedral: Evolution, Religion and the Nature of Society*. Chicago: University of Chicago Press, 2002.

Wilson, Donna F. *Ransom, Revenge and Heroic Identity in the Iliad*. New York: Cambridge University Press, 2002.

Winkielman, Piotr, and John Cacioppo. "A Social Neuroscience Perspective on Affective Influences on Social Cognition and Behavior." In *Handbook of Affect and Social Cognition*, edited by Joseph P. Forgas, 41–64. Mahwah, NJ: Lawrence Erlbaum, 2001.

Winnicott, D. W. *Playing and Reality*. London: Tavistock, 1971.

Winston, David. *Philo of Alexandria: The Contemplative Life, the Giants and Selections*. New York: Paulist Press, 1981.

Wisking-Elper, Ora. *Tradition and Fantasy in the Tales of Reb Nahman of Bratslav*. Albany: State University of New York Press, 1998.

Witzel, Michael. *The Origins of the World's Mythologies*. New York: Oxford University Press, 2012.

Wolfsdorf, David. *Pleasure in Ancient Greek Philosophy*. Cambridge, UK: Cambridge University Press, 2013.

Woolley, Jacqueline D. "The Development of Beliefs about Direct Mental-Physical Causality in Imagination, Magic, and Religion." In *Imagining the Impossible: Magical, Scientific and Religious Thinking in Children*, edited by Karl S. Rosengren, et al., 99–129. Cambridge, UK: Cambridge University Press, 2000.

Woolley, Jacqueline D., Katrina E. Phelps, Debra L. Davis, and Dorothy J. Mandell. "Where Theories of Mind Meet Magic: The Development of Children's Beliefs about Wishing." *Child Development* 70, no. 3 (1999). 571–587.

Yhap, Jennifer. *Plotinus on the Soul: A Study in the Metaphysics of Knowledge*. Selingrove, PA: Susquehanna University Press, 2003.

Yonge, C. D. *The Works of Philo: Complete and Unabridged*. Peabody, MA: Hendrikson Publishers, 1993.

Yount, David J. *Plato and Plotinus on Mysticism, Epistemology and Ethics*. London: Bloomsbury, 2017.

   Plotinus the Platonist: A Comparative Account of Plato and Plotinus' Metaphysics.
      London: Bloomsbury, 2014.
Zablocki, Benjamin. *The Joyful Community.* Chicago: University of Chicago
      Press, 1980.
Zaehner, R. C. *The Bhagavad-Gita: With a Commentary Based on the Original
      Sources.* London: Oxford University Press, 1976.
Zatorre, Robert J., and Valorie N. Salimpoore. "From Perception to Pleasure:
      Music and Its Neural Substrate." *Proceedings of the National Academy of
      Sciences* 110, no. 2 (2013). 225–241.
Zilioli, Ugo. *The Cyrenaics.* New York: Routledge, 2012.
Zimmermann, Nigel. *Facing the Other: John Paul II, Levinas, and the Body.*
      Eugene, OR: Cascade Books, 2015.

Index